Soul on Fire

Soul on Fire

Martin Luther King Jr. and the Psychology of Nonviolence

NASSIR GHAEMI

OXFORD
UNIVERSITY PRESS

OXFORD
UNIVERSITY PRESS

Oxford University Press is a department of the University of Oxford.
It furthers the University's objective of excellence in research, scholarship,
and education by publishing worldwide. Oxford is a registered trade mark of
Oxford University Press in the UK and in certain other countries.

Published in the United States of America by Oxford University Press
198 Madison Avenue, New York, NY 10016, United States of America.

Library of Congress Cataloging-in-Publication Data
Names: Ghaemi, Nassir, author.
Title: Soul on fire: Martin Luther King Jr and the psychology of
nonviolence / Nassir Ghaemi.
Description: New York : Oxford University Press, 2026. |
Includes bibliographical references and index.
Identifiers: LCCN 2025035519 (print) | LCCN 2025035520 (ebook) |
ISBN 9780197657584 (paperback) | ISBN 9780197657607 (epub) |
ISBN 9780197657614 | ISBN 9780197657591
Subjects: LCSH: King, Martin Luther, Jr., 1929-1968 | African
Americans—Civil rights | Civil rights workers—United States—Biography
Classification: LCC E185.97.K5 G62 2026 (print) | LCC E185.97.K5 (ebook) |
DDC 323/.092 [B]—dc23/eng/20260121
LC record available at https://lccn.loc.gov/2025035519
LC ebook record available at https://lccn.loc.gov/2025035520

DOI: 10.1093/9780197657614.001.0001

The manufacturer's authorized representative in the EU for product safety is
Oxford University Press España S.A. of Parque Empresarial San Fernando de Henares,
Avenida de Castilla, 2 – 28830 Madrid (www.oup.es/en or product.safety@oup.com).
OUP España S.A. also acts as importer into Spain of products made by the manufacturer.

To my father, Kamal Ghaemi, for the world I inherited.

For my children, Valentine and Zane Ghaemi, with hope for the world to come.

The salvation of our world lies in the hands of the creatively maladjusted.
—Martin Luther King Jr.

CONTENTS

A PERSONAL TIMELINE

1929: Born Michael King Jr. in Atlanta, Georgia.

1932: His father officially obtains a birth certificate for himself and his son as Martin Luther King Sr. and Martin Luther King Jr., respectively. His family called him "ML," and his friends called him "Mike."

1941: Twice jumps out of a second story window in his boyhood Atlanta home, the first time when his grandmother was knocked unconscious and the second time when she died.

1944–1948: Enters Morehouse College at age 15 years, gets mostly B's and C's, obtains a Bachelor of Arts degree in sociology, and graduates with lukewarm recommendations.

1948–1951: Obtains Bachelor of Divinity degree from Crozer Theological Seminary in Chester, Pennsylvania, near Philadelphia; graduates at the top of his class; is elected student president; receives a scholarship for PhD studies.

1951–1954: Studies for PhD in philosophical theology at Boston University; meets Coretta Scott; begins to preach regularly in Boston and elsewhere.

1954–1955: Gets first full-time job as pastor of Dexter Avenue Baptist Church in Montgomery, Alabama, his only period of full-time ministerial activity. First child is born.

June 1955: PhD is awarded from Boston University.

1955–1957: Montgomery bus boycott makes him an international figure. He is on the cover of *TIME* magazine at age 28 years.

September 1958: Stabbed at a book signing in New York City.

1960–1961: Sit-ins, Freedom Rides.

1963: Birmingham movement, followed by March on Washington.

1964: Civil Rights Act is passed. *TIME* magazine names him Man of the Year; wins Nobel Prize. He is one of the top 10 most admired Americans in a Gallup poll.

1965: Selma movement. King is hospitalized with probable depression. Voting Rights Act is passed later that year.

June 1966: The Meredith march in Mississippi ends in schism with younger activists.

April 4, 1967: Exactly one year before his assassination, he publicly denounces the Vietnam War. One week later, he is hospitalized in Atlanta with probable depression.

1967–1968: Poor People's Campaign; plans another march on Washington, with an occupation of the city until the government changes its policies. He is severely depressed. His personal physician, Dr. Arthur Logan, recommends psychiatric evaluation.

April 4, 1968: Assassinated. He has a 75% disapproval rating in a Gallup poll.

1977: Receives posthumous Presidential Medal of Freedom from President Jimmy Carter.

1999: He is second to Mother Theresa in a U.S.-based Gallup poll of most admired persons of the 20th century.

PART I

MLK FROM THE INSIDE

1

Maladjusted

On a sunny day in June 1961, Martin Luther King Jr. made one of his least famous but most interesting speeches. The occasion was the commencement exercise at Lincoln University, a tiny historically Black college in southern Pennsylvania. King's "I Have a Dream" speech was two years away. Now, he gave a less polished oration.

He told the college graduates that they would only become worthy American adults if they rejected what their superiors and peers thought they should do. They needed to embrace a willingness to be an outsider, the other, different—in short, "maladjusted." This would help them realize the American dream.

"For in a real sense," King said, "America is essentially a dream, a dream as yet unfulfilled." It would only become real if Blacks were treated as equally as Whites, the poor as well as the rich, and if other nations were treated by America as justly as we wished to treat our own citizens.

The first problem—racism—had been the focus of King's struggle until then; the second and third problems—poverty and militarism—would represent King's final battles in the last years of his life.

King called for empathy:

> We are caught in an inescapable network of mutuality; tied in a single garment of destiny. . . . Strangely enough, I can never be what I ought to be until you are what you ought to be. You can never be what you ought to be until I am what I ought to be. This is the way the world is made.

His empathy was radical, and he knew it was difficult to achieve. It is difficult to imagine caring for people you hate, to understand that your future is bound up in theirs, he said.

At the end of his speech, King spelled out a rejection of conformism and normalcy: "But I say to you, there are certain things within our social order to which I am proud to be maladjusted and to which I call upon all men of good

Soul on Fire. Nassir Ghaemi, Oxford University Press. © Oxford University Press 2026.
DOI: 10.1093/9780197657614.003.0002

will to be maladjusted." Being normal meant accepting what existed without asking if it was right—segregation and discrimination, religious bigotry, militarism. Our greatest leaders, King insisted, weren't normal: "The salvation of our world lies in the hands of the maladjusted. So let us be maladjusted . . . as maladjusted as Abraham Lincoln . . . as maladjusted as Jesus of Nazareth." And trying out his most famous words, he heralded maladjustment as the foundation of a free, just, and inclusive society:

> I believe that it is through such maladjustment that we will be able to emerge from the bleak and desolate midnight of man's inhumanity to man into the bright and glittering daybreak of freedom and justice. That will be the day when all of God's children, Black men and White men, Jews and Gentiles, Catholics and Protestants, will be able to join hands and sing in the words of the old Negro spiritual, "Free at last! Free at last! Thank God almighty, we are free at last!"

* * *

When King spoke of maladjustment, he was referring to a psychological state of mind. But he realized that it might also entail a psychiatric condition. The concept of "adjustment," he noted, was a psychiatric measure of mental health: "Modern psychology and psychiatry has a word that is used probably more than any other word in psychology. This word is 'adjusted.' It is the ringing cry of child psychiatry." In the many versions of his speeches involving maladjustment (dating back to as early as 1958), he frequently would state the following:

> Certainly we all want to avoid the maladjusted life. In order to have real adjustment within our personalities, we all want the well-adjusted life to avoid neurotic and schizophrenic personalities. But I say to you my friends, that there are certain things in the world to which I am proud to be maladjusted, and to which I hope all men of good-will will be maladjusted until the good society is realized.

In other words, despite the risk of getting neurotic (and even psychotic, which is what King meant by the word "schizophrenic"), King believed we should reject the notion of mental health as conformism to our world's norms.

In fact, he once said that "the sin of the South is the sin of conformism."[1] He estimated that only approximately five percent of White Southerners were active proponents or opponents of segregation. The rest just went along. This message was the central theme also of his "Letter From Birmingham Jail," which is aimed at White moderates who say they oppose segregation but won't do what is needed to end it.

Perhaps his most detailed expression of the concept came in the only speech he ever gave to an audience of professionals in mental health.

* * *

Approximately half a year before his death, in September 1967, he was the guest speaker at the annual convention of the American Psychological Association in Washington, DC. His speech title was dry—"The Role of the Behavioral Scientist in the Civil Rights Movement"—but the content was classic King, challenging and stirring.[2]

The conference hall was full of approximately 5,000 psychologists, and King's gaze fell above the crowd. "White America has an appalling lack of knowledge concerning Negro life," he began. He went on to describe urban race riots, the Vietnam War, and the poverty of Northern ghettoes. He defended nonviolent political demonstrations as the best middle ground between aggressive direct action and passive acceptance of racism, militarism, and unrestrained capitalism.

To the surprise of many of his followers, this triad of all-embracing injustices had become his new political theme. The speech had been long; he had prepared the ending with a topic he sometimes used in church sermons, from Romans 12.1–2: "Be not conformed to this world, but be transformed by the renewing of your minds." He was ready to bring his main point home. "Thus, it may well be that our world is in dire need of a new organization," he said, pausing for emphasis: "The International Association for the Advancement of Creative Maladjustment."

He looked around at the audience of mostly White faces, knowing that the psychologists in front of him believed that "adjustment" meant mental health. Many times before he had preached about "creative maladjustment"; now he intended to teach mental health professionals why mental health wasn't always beneficial.

He went on:

> Men and women should be as maladjusted . . . as Abraham Lincoln, who . . . came to see that this nation could not survive half slave and half free; or as maladjusted as Thomas Jefferson, who in the midst of an age amazingly adjusted to slavery, could [say] . . . "that all men are created equal."

King's message was that maladjustment to an unjust world may make you unhappy, but it makes the world better: "And through such creative maladjustment, we may be able to emerge from the bleak and desolate midnight of man's inhumanity to man, into the bright and glittering daybreak of freedom and justice."

He could have stopped with this inspiring ending, but he chose instead to end with a quiet, almost wistful, confession that times were difficult for him: "I have not lost hope. I must confess that these have been very difficult days for me personally. And these have been difficult days for every civil rights leader, for every lover of justice and peace."[3]

He stepped down from the podium.

The psychologists applauded politely, but they likely didn't understand him.[4]

* * *

King didn't give this speech to just psychologists. He gave it frequently. He spoke about this issue in public and in private. He often used the phrase "a creative minority." "The hope of the world is in a creative minority."[5] The majority of people are quiet conformists; they are not bad people individually, but they conform to evil. Only a minority that refuses to conform to what is bad can improve the world.

If you opposed racism in the South at a time when most White Southerners were racist, you would have been maladjusted to the norm of your environment. Years later, Andrew Young, King's close aide and later Mayor of Atlanta, alluded to the fact that King himself was aware of this dilemma:

> "Martin said: You know, you almost have to be clinically insane to do what we're doing; and you have to respect that insanity as a blessing."[6]

We can look back on it now and say that King was sane, and White America was insane. Or we could look at those terms more scientifically and less pejoratively. King's personal psychology is consistent with his political philosophy. He knew that the psychology of militant nonviolence involves being psychologically maladjusted.

There was something abnormal, in a good way, about those who committed themselves to the civil rights movement. It is easy to forget in retrospect that many of us today who value the movement would not have been the kind of persons who would give up everything in their lives to take the risks that the movement demanded. As Bernard Lafayette, another King aide, stated,

> We threw our bodies in the movement. We threw our minds, our souls. Everything we had. We gave no thought to what we would eat or where we would sleep, what we would wear, and all those material things became . . . not significant at all.[7]

King didn't invent the idea of the importance of maladjustment. It was part of the liberal Christian homiletic tradition, and King's sermons on the topic were influenced most directly by his favorite modern liberal White Christian preacher, Harry Emerson Fosdick.[8]

King saw that Fosdick's insights explained a lot about his own experiences, and the key role of maladjustment in recognizing and acting on truth became a central idea in King's life.

* * *

King wasn't the only civil right leader to ponder this paradox of maladjustment, about how the world resists those who improve it.

Joseph Lowery was with King from the Montgomery days. Lowery was a founding member of the Southern Christian Leadership Conference back then, and in the 1980s he was its president. He spoke at Coretta Scott King's funeral in 2006 and was the only speaker directly to criticize President George Bush's war efforts in the presence of the sitting president and three other former presidents. He gave the invocation at the inauguration of Barack Obama three years later.

Lower later came to the same conclusion as King, expressed in a more modern formulation. In a 2009 speech at Duke University, Lowery described how one has to be off in some way, psychologically, to take the risks the movement leaders took. He said he often thought King must be crazy to keep marching, with Ku Klux Klan members sitting in bushes, easily able to kill him. But, Lowery said, "Crazy is just like my cholesterol. There's good crazy and then there's bad crazy." To achieve social change, "you have to be a little crazy. All the leaders of the movement were a little crazy. Including Martin." Don't be afraid, he urged: "God always protects good crazy."

Good cholesterol. And bad cholesterol.

Good crazy. And bad crazy.

Lowery translated King's maladjustment into simpler language. And Lowery repeated this theme, like King, in dozens of speeches and sermons. Even Barack Obama heard Lowery's notion and connected with it. In giving Lowery the Presidential Medal of Freedom in 2009, Obama quoted Lowery: "There's good crazy and there's bad crazy—and sometimes you need a little bit of that good crazy to make the world a better place."

These are not random, throwaway comments, made once at a dinner table and then dismissed. They're serious observations, nurtured over a century of struggle.

But is it just a metaphor? Being "crazy" shouldn't be interpreted literally, many will say.

Or maybe it should.

Notes

1. James Baldwin, "The Highroad to Destiny," in *Martin Luther King Jr.: A Profile*, ed. C. Eric Lincoln (New York: Hill & Wang, 1984 [1970]), p. 106.
2. https://www.apa.org/news/press/releases/2007/08/mlk-anniversary.
3. https://www.gilderlehrman.org/collection/glc0964122.
4. A summary of King's speech published by the American Psychological Association on its 50th anniversary in 2017 does not mention the word "maladjustment" or King's critique of the concept of adjustment. https://www.apa.org/news/press/releases/2007/08/mlk-anniversary.
5. Gurdon Brewster, *No Turning Back: My Summer With Daddy King* (Maryknoll, NY: Orbis Books, 2007), p. 210.
6. A conversation with Andrew Young, National Portrait Gallery, May 17, 2011; at 37 minutes, 13 seconds to 37 minutes, 25 seconds. https://www.youtube.com/watch?v=TZR7r3ROzJ0.
7. Civil Rights History Project, interviews by Prof. James Findlay, 2002–2003, transcript 4, p. 47, https://www.loc.gov/folklife/civilrights/survey/view_collection.php?coll_id=949.
8. Fosdick was the famed minister for the most liberal Protestant church in New York City, Riverside Church, and he had become famous partly through his radio sermons. Fosdick's sermons are full of psychological attention and nuance, partly because he was active as a pastoral counselor. Keith Miller demonstrates the connections: Keith D. Miller, *Voice of Deliverance* (Athens: University of Georgia Press, 1998), pp. 106, 164–165.

2

War on Sleep

In September 1958, a young 29-year-old Martin Luther King Jr. was in New York City attending a book signing for his first book, *Stride Toward Freedom,* in a Harlem department store.

A Black woman approached. "So you are Martin Luther King?" she asked.

She looked like any other middle-class, middle-aged Black woman, carrying a handbag.

King eyed her calmly.

"Yes," he replied.

"I've always wanted to meet you," she answered.

Then she took her hand out of her bag, pulled out a seven-inch Japanese letter opener, and plunged it straight into King's chest.

King sat there, stunned.

After the initial shock, a few bystanders shrieked, as someone grabbed Mrs. Izola Ware Curry. She was taken away and found to be psychotic; she would be psychiatrically hospitalized.

A woman rushed forward to King and put her hands on the protruding knife handle. She was about to pull it out when a man stopped her.

"Don't!" he yelled.

There was no blood; King was breathing normally.

King was rushed to Harlem Hospital. Dr. Aubre de Lambert Maynard, a surgeon from Guyana who had been the first Black intern at the hospital, had done his morning rounds for that day and had just finished watching a Bridget Bardot movie at home. He was paged to come to the hospital, where he found police, a large crowd, and, on the operating floor, Governor Averill Harriman. "Where have you been?" asked the governor. Dr. Maynard went into the operating room and found King lying down, with a blade handle sticking out of his chest. He was awake and silent, with his eyes closed. The doctor whispered into his patient's ears: "Don't worry; you'll be alright."[1]

Soul on Fire. Nassir Ghaemi, Oxford University Press. © Oxford University Press 2026.
DOI: 10.1093/9780197657614.003.0003

Dr. Maynard took his time to examine the area where the knife was located, to clean the skin, and then to operate around the knife so as to bring it out safely—the most famous operation for a doctor who would become chief of surgery and live to age 97 years. Once he began operating inside King's chest, he saw that the knife was near King's aorta. Had the woman in the store moved it inward at all as she tried to remove it, or had King as much as sneezed, he would have bled to death immediately. While in the hospital, King received a letter from a White girl in New York. It made so much of an impression that he recounted it more than a decade later, the night before his assassination, in his final speech. The girl said she had read about the near-fatal wound and the risk of even sneezing. She wanted to let him know that she was glad he had survived and, she wrote, "I'm glad you didn't sneeze."

By 1959, King had succeeded, in a brief span of five years since his graduation from Boston University, in achieving far more than most men of equal age, and more than he himself had dared imagine.

He had become a national and international political leader. He had led Southern Blacks in the first major practical success against segregation. He was running a large and prestigious church in the capital of Alabama. And he was a founder of a new civil rights group, the Southern Christian Leadership Conference (SCLC), with extensive influence throughout the South.

He had a loving wife, cute little children, the support of his father and mother in nearby Atlanta, and apparently an active sexual life outside his marriage.

And yet, with all these achievements and pleasures, King became depressed.

The first inklings of King's lifelong struggle with episodic depression, as will be described, can be seen in a 12-year-old boy's two jumps from a second-story window. Depressive symptoms weren't seen by his peers in college or during his Boston years, but after his experience in Montgomery, Alabama, King's buoyant moods began to be replaced by periods of despondency until, by 1959, he couldn't take it any longer.

After the success of the bus boycott, and his national lionization, and as plans began to be laid for expanding the Montgomery approach to the rest of the South (through the SCLC), King found that he was increasingly used up emotionally. He couldn't keep going—running his church, starting up a new desegregation movement, traveling around the country to spread the word and raise funds, becoming a new father to a growing family. He decided to leave Montgomery and return to Atlanta, where, under his father's wings, he would do what his father wanted all along—co-pastor at Ebenezer Baptist Church—while putting most of his efforts into the SCLC.

He made his reasons clear in his last public talk in Montgomery after formally handing leadership of the Montgomery Improvement Association to his friend Ralph Abernathy:

> For almost four years now I have been faced with the responsibility of trying to do as one man what five or six people ought to be doing. . . . I found myself in a position which I could not get out of. . . . What I have been doing is giving, giving, giving, and not stopping to retreat and meditate like I should—to come back. If the situation is not changed, I will be a physical and psychological wreck. I have to reorganize my personality and reorient my life.

If King thought that leaving Montgomery would reduce his desperation, he would only be partly correct. It's easy to attribute King's depression to the stresses of his life experience, which were great indeed, but such an explanation couldn't explain the repeated nature of his depressive states, their brief nature (usually days to weeks), and the constant contrast to his usual energetic, humorous, happy personality.

In 1960, he formally resigned from Dexter Avenue Baptist Church in Montgomery and returned to Atlanta, as his father had always wanted, to be co-pastor at Ebenezer Baptist Church. He had come home, and although he would always technically serve with his father in his home church, his real work was nationwide, indeed worldwide, through SCLC.[2]

The core years of King Jr.'s life are the most well-known. Those were the years of his national leadership in the civil rights movement. He led the SCLC from Atlanta; participated in sit-ins; was arrested; and led mass movements in Albany, Georgia, and Birmingham and Selma, Alabama, leading to the Civil Rights Bill of 1964 and the Voting Rights Bill of 1965. He allied first with John Kennedy and then with Lyndon Johnson. He became the conscience of the nation; won the Nobel Peace Prize in 1964; became a target of the Federal Bureau of Investigation that same year; and moved north in 1966 to Chicago and Cleveland, trying to expand the civil rights movement from fighting segregation in the South to opposing discrimination in the North. He moved toward expanding the political power of Blacks and expanded to international affairs, becoming a vocal opponent of the Vietnam War in 1967, thereby losing the support of Lyndon Johnson and many White liberals. By 1968, King felt increasingly more isolated, and he became increasingly more depressed.

But the years before King's public life are just as important—the years as a child and a young man, going to college and graduate school, starting a family, and beginning his first job as a minister. Those early years inform the man behind the leader of the later years.

And in most of those years, King was anything but depressed. In fact, he was mostly the opposite.

Most of the time, for most of his life, King was a juggernaut with an incredible amount of energy. Said Bernard Lafayette,

> Oh, my God, that was one of the hallmarks of Martin Luther King. I tried to catch Dr. King asleep. Once in New York, we stayed together in a hotel in one of those extended rooms. I slept on a couch, and I was young, in my 20s; I was determined to catch Martin Luther King asleep. And I fell asleep and when I woke up, he was already awake, standing up, fully dressed, looking out the window.

King had so much energy, Lafayette said, that on King's many travels, his SCLC staff would not only send Bernard Lee, another young twenty-something aide, but also always prepare a second aide to replace Lee, who would typically become too exhausted in the middle of a trip to continue. Lee would then fly back to Atlanta and a second aide would go out to continue traveling with King. "It was nothing for him to give five speeches a day," Lafayette said. King needed little sleep and wasn't tired: "If he got 4½ hours sleep, that was the max. He really had tremendous energy."

King himself described a schedule by the mid-1960s of 20 hours daily of events or activities, leaving only 4 hours for sleep. He described traveling 2 or 3 weeks at a time away from home, and on average being home in Atlanta only two days or less per week.[3]

Lafayette is not the only person to make these observations. "He was high energy," his Boston University friend Rev. Michael Haynes later recalled. "Always talking, always asking questions, always observing."[4] King was a chronic insomniac, rarely going to be bed before 1 or 2 a.m. and usually up before 7 a.m.; yet he wasn't tired. His physically energy level was legendary: "He had so much energy," his friend from high school and later civil rights ally, Dr. William Anderson, related decades later:

> We would have a mass meeting at night lasting until midnight, and then we'd have a strategy meeting for the next day until 1–2 in the morning; and then at 8 a.m. we would meet in a church to begin that day's activities; then we'd march at noon and throughout the afternoon; and then have another mass meeting at night. And we'd do it over and over again for weeks. He never tired.

This observation was confirmed by Vincent Harding, who told me, "He had an amazing amount of energy for the situation he was in. He loved to play sports like basketball, despite being short." In his memoir, Dr. Abernathy writes, "Martin never took catnaps and never ran out of gas."[5] Abernathy describes how King would stay awake late into the night, often with women, and then get working early in the morning at his political activities, without being tired. Journalist David Halberstam traveled with King for a week in 1967 and noted in a contemporary article that King slept approximately 4 hours nightly but had a high amount of energy.[6] His 1964 biographer, Lerone Bennett, also noted that he averaged 4 hours of sleep nightly.[7] Marian Logan described how King would come to her suite when they traveled together, typically at approximately 2 or 3 a.m., and pretend he came to say goodnight. She knew he wanted to banter into the wee hours of the morning, and she'd invite him into her room. Her husband, King's personal physician Dr. Arthur Logan, would give King sleeping pills, to little effect. He would stay awake all night, until 7 a.m., and then "he would maybe sleep for an hour or so, and then get up. I've never in my life seen [such a] man, so brilliant when it came to thinking on his feet, out of a dead sleep."[8] It could have been brilliance, it could have been mania, or it could have been both.

Andrew Young called it a "war on sleep." He describes 1968, the year of King's deep depression, as also a year of "hyper" overactivity; the psychiatric term could be a "mixed state" in which manic and depressive symptoms happen simultaneously. This type of mood state is the most common kind, in fact, rather than pure depression or pure mania (see Appendix 1). In 1980, Young recalled King's last year:

> Martin was keeping a hell of a pace. He was speaking a lot. He was preaching every Sunday at church. He hadn't been on a vacation. He was staying up late at night arguing all the time, and he just wanted to talk. He didn't want to sleep. We used to say he not only had a war on poverty, he had a war on sleep, cause he'd want to stay up and talk until 3, 4 morning, and then he'd go to sleep and be back up at 7. He was just in an extremely hyper social period. I remember talking with I guess it was Stan Levison and Coretta about Martin's health and saying to him and to them that Hey, when we started this movement none of us figured we would live very long. We conducted ourselves like every day was the last, but now it looks like we're gonna be around for a while, and so, we better start taking care of our health. We've got to find a way for Martin to get a bit more rest and pace himself, otherwise he's going to burn himself out physically. And that was just a few months before he was killed.[9]

His high energy level was reflected in his activity level. He always stayed up late and woke early. In his seminary days, he often played pool with his buddy Walter McCall until 3 a.m. Before becoming a famous national leader who was much in demand for talks and for whom fundraising-related travel became a necessity, King in his early to mid-20s was always on the move. Even in his first year as a minister in Montgomery, before he really "got busy" with the bus boycott, he had a heavy schedule.

He would wake up at 5:30 a.m. to work for 3 hours on his PhD dissertation, then he would go to his church for his daytime work activities, then return for another few hours at night to work on his dissertation, usually going to bed after midnight. In that one year (1954–1955), as he described in his year-end report to his church, he had made two trips to Boston for his dissertation, attended 10 conclaves of the National Baptist Convention, given 46 sermons in his own church, performed 20 more in other churches or colleges, and read 26 books and 102 magazines. He made 87 pastoral visits, 49 visits to sick parishioners, conducted 12 baptisms, and officiated at five marriages and five funerals. All this happened on top of the birth of his first child, relocation to a new home, and starting his first year of marriage. Just a year later, in 1956–1957, during the bus boycott, in addition to all his boycott activities and his pastorly duties at Dexter Avenue Baptist Church, he gave approximately 50 out-of-state sermons or talks. In 1961, he traveled to give no fewer than 65 talks in a year (not counting his Sunday sermons at Dexter). Although many trips no doubt were necessary for SCLC fundraising,[10] many seemed remote and not absolutely necessary (e.g., the Knife and Fork Club of Sioux Falls, South Dakota; Monterey Peninsula College in California; or Mankato College in Minnesota) but, rather, driven by King's internal drive to move about.[11] In a 1966 letter to Delta Air Lines, in which he complained about rude treatment to him and to SCLC staff, King noted that he flew more than 300,000 miles yearly, with SCLC spending more than $125,000 on staff travel. King reported having a "Half-Million Miler card" with both United and Eastern Airlines.[12]

Journalist David Halberstam, traveling with King in 1967, was struck by King's headlong itinerary: "Most of King's life is spent going to airports, and it is the only time to talk to him."[13] Traveling with King, he concluded, was like being on a perpetual presidential campaign, one stop after another:

> He has been through it all, there has been too much exposure, the questions have all been asked before; the reporters all look alike, as do the endless succession of airport press conferences. . . . Always those dark, interchangeable suits; the serious shirt and responsible tie.[14]

* * *

King's personality was charismatic, attractive to men and women, an intense appeal that he used for social good but which caused some personal pain.

Before he became Martin Luther King Jr., he was just Mike, a sensitive boy, in stark contrast to the other King boy, his rambunctious and reckless younger brother, A.D. One day, when Mike was approximately 12 years old, A.D. slid down a banister in the King household in Atlanta, slamming into his grandmother, Jennie Williams. She fell to the ground, briefly losing consciousness. Mike, who was very close to his maternal grandmother, ran to a second-floor window and jumped out. The distance jumped appears to have been approximately 12 feet.[15] Mike's mother feared both were dead, but they woke up within minutes of each other.

Six months later, after Mike had snuck away from home to watch a parade, Jennie Williams died suddenly from a heart attack. Someone found Mike and gave him the sad news. Wracked with guilt that he was enjoying himself at a parade while his beloved grandmother died, King ran home crying. When he saw the body, he rushed up to the second floor window and jumped again. He was briefly unconscious once more but woke up only with bruises. For days and weeks, Mike was inconsolable as his father and mother tried to explain to him the ways of God and the facts of mortality.

Those leaps from the second floor of his boyhood home, little mentioned in recent years, might be an essential window into the man.

The preadolescent jumps were well-known to King's aides and friends. The facts are well-established in multiple sources from the 1950s and 1960s.[16] His chosen biographer, Lawrence Reddick, a historian from Montgomery and the only person to travel with King and Coretta for a month throughout India in 1958, specifically called those events suicide attempts: "Twice he seems to have attempted suicide," Reddick wrote in the first biography of King, "each time because of his grandmother."[17] This biography was written and published in 1959, with King's approval and assistance.

It is worth noting that statistically, approximately 90% of children who try to harm themselves have depressive episodes at the time. The mainstream psychiatric approach to understanding suicidality is consistent with viewing these two jumps as suicide attempts, as opposed to trying to write them off as something else.[18] The best historical evidence also supports this view.[19]

In his 1980 memoir, King Sr. describes a boy who was very sad at least for some time: "He cried off and on for several days afterward, and was unable to sleep at night." These symptoms can be part of normal mourning; they also serve as the early warning signs of struggles with depression. King Sr. didn't mention that his son had jumped out of those windows. In later autobiographical essays, King Jr. himself omitted any mention of his childhood jumps.

King Jr. was born Michael King, as was his father, but the reasons for the name change, which happened when the younger King was approximately 5 years old, are complex. At that time, there were no written birth certificates, and his mother and father had disagreed on his name. King Sr. would later write, "Mama insisted that she'd named me Michael, after the archangel, and Papa was just as adamant about saying that I was Martin Luther, after two of his brothers."[20] But Mike is the name that took and that he kept until having his own son years later.

In 1933, Mike Jr.'s paternal grandfather died, and as he became more ill, he asked his son, Mike King Sr, to officially change his name to Martin Luther. King Sr. was about to go on his first voyage abroad to an international Baptist convention in Germany. For reasons at once prosaic (he needed a passport but didn't have a birth certificate) and personal (his father's wishes), Daddy King changed his own name, and that of his son, without consulting the boy. This version is, at least, the story that King Sr. would publish later, although the exact story is not entirely clear.

In later years, a divide could be seen: Those who knew King as an adult, as a civil rights leader, from the mid-1950s onward, called him Martin. Family who knew the young man and the child called him M.L. His friends and peers from that era called him Mike or M.L. His closest friend, Ralph David Abernathy, later remarked: "I called him Michael in private, and he called me David. Michael was his real name."[21]

As an adult, King had a healthy sense of self-esteem, and he was even viewed as somewhat arrogant in his young adulthood.[22] As he entered graduate school and into his later years, however, he exuded a humility and empathy for others that made his own self-confidence unabrasive. Clarence Jones would recall later, "Though Humility with other persons with charisma may be rare, humility was one of THE defining traits of this great man [capitalization in original]."[23] Dr. William Anderson captures his highly sociable temperament:

> He was very even-tempered; I never at any time heard him speak in anger, never heard him yell at anyone, never heard him use profanity. He would enjoy a good joke, sometimes off-color. He could mix with the common man, and make them feel comfortable with him. I have a couple of pictures of him in a pool hall; my office in Albany was above a pool hall and liquor store. When he came to visit, he would stop to shoot a little pool with the boys. He never put himself above the people; they identified with him: He's one of us. He has all these degrees, is highly respected, and yet will come down here and shoot a game of pool. He was the same in all environments.[24]

King wasn't charismatic in a flashy way. As his later close political advisor, Stanley Levison, would recall,

> The personal impression that never leaves me about him was that in personal discussion he didn't seem to be . . . a mass leader. There was nothing flamboyant, nothing even charismatic about him as he sat in an ordinary discussion. He . . . looked like a typical scholarly kind of person—very thoughtful, quiet, and shy—very shy.[25]

The aide who was perhaps closest to him throughout the 1960s, who traveled with him everywhere, was Bernard Lee. He identified humility as "a benchmark of Martin Luther King" and stated that what was special was that his humility "increased as his stature grew . . . it just mushroomed. . . . He became humble, a far more humble person."[26]

His humility was tied to his empathy, which was noted by children who knew him. He always respected and showed interest in them. Susannah Heschel, the daughter of Rabbi Abraham Joshua Heschel, recalls decades later that she was a teenager, and met King just before he spoke to a large rabbinical assembly in March 1968, only approximately 10 days before his death.[27] He took her aside and asked questions about her life, showing sincere interest in who she was.[28] Wilhelmina Harris was a young girl in Montgomery who experienced King as having "a very keen and strong, very sharp, sensibility to suffer with people. . . . He'd express it not only with words, but from the heart. It would penetrate everyone."[29]

Although numerous friends, such as Michael Haynes from his Boston years and Bernard Lee from his last years, saw King as very humble, not all observers drew the same conclusion. Journalist David Halberstam, traveling with King in 1967, thought otherwise:

> King is a frustrating man. Ten years ago *Time* found him humble, but few would find him that way today, though the average reporter coming into contact with him is not exactly sure why; he suspects King's vanity. One senses that he is a shy and sensitive man thrown into a prominence which he did not seek but which he has come to accept, rather likes, and intends to perpetuate. Colleagues find him occasionally pretentious; and the student leaders have often called him De Lawd, a title both mocking, and at the same time a sign of respect.[30]

The Student Nonviolent Coordinating Committee activists, beginning with those who came to respect him greatly and work closely with him, sensed something; maybe arrogance isn't the right word, but humility isn't either. Concluded Halberstam,

> He has finally come to believe his myth, just as the people in the Pentagon believe theirs and the man in the White House believes his; he sticks to the morality of his life and of his decisions, until there becomes something of a mystic quality to him.[31]

King also was a very talkative person, even since childhood.[32] It was said that in later life, it would take King an hour to walk two blocks because he would stop to chat with many people along the way. "He was always asking questions about you, very curious, constantly thinking and talking," said Rev. Michael Haynes.[33]

King's sense of humor was legendary in his circle.[34] Tom Houck was his driver and spent much personal time with King in the last years of his life. Houck says, "Dr. King was gregarious, funny, humorous. . . . He was the consummate prankster, jokester."[35] When asked to describe him as a person, the socialist Michael Harrington's first response was that

> he was, among other things that people might not imagine, a very funny man. I remember one time . . . going to his house in Atlanta . . . and it was a lot of fun, a lot of joking, a lot of kidding around . . . by Dr. King in terms of . . . [Ralph] Abernathy's driving. . . . [He was] a very, a very funny man with a very deep laugh."[36]

His humor often involved long stories; said one long-time friend, "He liked to tell jokes but . . . it took him so long to get to the punch line, you forgot the joke."[37] But more often he used humor in a lengthy way to lighten the mood.

One example is after the March on Washington, DC, when King and his entourage were staying at the Willard Hotel. Ralph Abernathy was complaining that he hadn't received a speaking role at the march. Andrew Young later recalls how King teased Abernathy:

> Martin responded with: "Ralph, you had to be the head of an organization to speak. What we have to do is find you an organization that you can be the head of, so that on the next march, you can have the right to speak." And everybody present agreed that that the one organization that Ralph was unquestionably the president of was the "National Association for the Advancement of Eating Chicken." Martin waxed eloquently, saying, "No one can challenge your preeminence, you have no competition." And they all cracked on Ralph for about an hour.[38]

Michael Harrington, author of a best-selling 1962 book on poverty, *The Other America*,[39] was the recipient of a one-liner that Harrington forever remembered as the best compliment of his life. In 1967, when King and his advisors, including Harrington, were planning the Poor People's Campaign, King asked Harrington to write the first draft of the manifesto for the campaign. Harrington hesitated, asking King if he really wanted a White man to be the author of the main draft of his effort. King smiled and stated, "Why, Mike, we never knew we were poor until we read your book!"[40]

Ralph Abernathy describes how King was an incredible mimic and would routinely get his friends and staff to laugh uproariously as he imitated others:

> Martin was fun-loving, and when he was offstage you could usually find him telling a joke or teasing somebody. He had a perfect sense of timing and he instinctively knew what was funny. Some people have that gift and some people don't. He had it. I'm convinced that if he had wanted to be a stand-up comic he could have been almost as famous in that role.[41]

Dr. William Anderson, King's friend since adolescence, still remembered multiple King jokes four decades later, including the following:

> One Sunday, a preacher was not well prepared for his sermon. "If the Lord can be with you, who can be against you." He had memorized that part of the sermon, but he needed to read the rest. As he stood at the pulpit, he began: "If the Lord can be with you, who can be against you. . . ." Just then, a gust of wind blew the pages over, and he lost his place. So he kept repeating: "If the Lord can be with you, who can be against you . . ." as he searched frantically for his place. "If the Lord can be with you, who can be against you. . . ." "If the Lord can be with you, who can be against you. . . ." Finally, one of the old sisters in the audience yelled: "The colored folks, boy, that's who! Now go ahead and preach the sermon!"[42]

Notes

1. https://www.nytimes.com/1996/01/14/nyregion/neighborhood-report-harlem-reminiscing-with-dr-aubrey-maynard-on-saving-dr-king.html.
2. The next phase of the struggle had two goals: expand direct action movements in targeted Southern cities and assist the growing student movement in its efforts to desegregate buses through the Freedom Rides. The cream of Rev. James Lawson's Student Nonviolent Coordinating Committee (SNCC) protégés—James Bevel, Andrew Young, and Bernard Lafayette—came to Atlanta to work for the SCLC as aides to King.

   Bevel would later recall that in 1961, King didn't come across as especially competent in nonviolent tactics. The Nashville group of students had just picked up the Freedom Rides into Alabama and had been physically beaten and violently threatened. They had arrived in Montgomery, and King came from Atlanta to meet them. A leadership meeting was held, including Abernathy and Lawson and the Nashville students. As Bevel recalls, they turned to King in search of leadership in that important moment when they needed to decide whether to continue the Freedom Rides into dangerous territory in Alabama and Mississippi or not. Bevel recalled, "'Dr. King, what do you cats, as nonviolent leaders, propose to do?' And he said, 'Well, I don't know.' And we kept pumping him, and it became obvious to me that he had never really studied strategy and tactics of nonviolence." Bevel decided that henceforth King was a leader because of his ability to inspire courage, but not because of his tactical generalship: "After that, I understood that . . . strategically and tactically, he never could think. His nonviolence was philosophical, but never practically applied." Interview with Reverend James Bevel, by Katherine Shannon, July 6, 1968, The Civil Rights Documentation Project, transcript p. 15. In David Garrow papers, Pittsburgh, PA, Manuscript Collection 832, p. 36.

In effect, Bevel concluded that King was their leader but that he and the other activists would have to plan the actions of the movement themselves.

Diane Nash confirms this impression among the Nashville students that King was less experienced as a nonviolent leader than others, such as James Lawson:

> Martin King at that point and before did not have much knowledge of . . . non-violence as Gandhi developed it . . . later, I think he did a lot of reading and acquired it, but hadn't had the training that the Nashville group had. . . . Lawson was really the source of the non-violent philosophy, in terms of strategy and what to do and why.

Interview with Diane Nash by David Garrow, July 17, 1983, written transcript, p. 7. In David Garrow papers, Emory University, Atlanta, Box 8.1, Item 7.

Abernathy also moved to Atlanta to be King's second-in-command at SCLC. The leading SNCC activist in Atlanta was Morehouse student Lonnie C. King, no relation to the civil rights leader but a family friend who would play a central role not only in spreading desegregation outside the Alabama-based origins of the movement but also in impacting, without intending it, the election of the next president of the United States, John F. Kennedy, who, in turn, would be the president who finally led the charge against segregation.

3. Alex Haley, "Playboy Interview: Martin Luther King," *Playboy*, January 1965.
4. Interview with Michael Haynes, April 15, 2013.
5. Ralph David Abernathy, *And the Walls Came Tumbling Down* (New York: Harper, 1989), p. 434.
6. David Halberstam. "When 'Civil Rights' and 'Peace' Join Forces," In *Martin Luther King Jr.: A Profile*, ed. C. Eric Lincoln (New York: Hill & Wang, 1984 [1970]), pp. 187–211.
7. Lerone Bennett, *What Manner of Man* (Chicago: Johnson, 1976 [1964]), p. 187: "In fact, he often went for extended periods with as little as fours of sleep a night."
8. Marian Logan, *Eyes on the Prize* interview, December 9, 1988, http://repository.wustl.edu/concern/videos/mc87pv33b.
9. Howard Tilton Memorial Library, Tulane University, Andrew Young Oral History Collection, August 20–21, 1980, Box 138, Item 23, Side 1.
10. Reese Cleghorn notes,

> SCLC has a 1963 budget of about $450,000, up from $60,000 in 1960, when the staff numbered three. Fees from its affiliates amount to only about $15,000 of this. Dr. King himself raises about $100,000 with rallies, dinners, and other personal appearances. A surprising $150,000 or so comes through the mail, some spontaneously but most in response to appeals from Dr. King to a mailing list of thirty-five thousand people. . . . The National Maritime Union alone sent King more than $32,000 in the midst of the Birmingham crisis. About $100,000 of the SCLC budget is a grant by the Field Foundation to the home mission board of the United Church of Christ, which finances the citizenship school that SCLC administers. The remainder of the SCLC budget comes from periodic benefits, concerts, and assorted entertainment.

Reese Cleghorn, "Crowned With Crises," *Martin Luther King Jr.: A Profile*, ed. C. Eric Lincoln (New York: Hill & Wang, 1984 [1970]), pp. 122–123. Originally in *The Saturday Evening Post*, June 15 1963, pp. 15–19.

11. In a chronologically laid out summary document of Dr. King's "1961 speaking engagements" (King Center Archives, Box 12:65), one gets a good sense of the extent of his lecture and travel schedule. In that document, 71 lectures or speeches are listed in the calendar year, ranging from January 1 to December 14. Usually, he is traveling on the order of four to six times per month. The following partial list of visits can be cited to give a sense of the breadth and frequency of his travel:

January 12—the Knife and Fork Club, Sioux Falls, SD
January 15—Woodland Hills Community Church, Woodland Hills, CA
February 9—Newark State College, Union, NH
March 12—Temple Emanuel Forum, Worcester, MA

March 13—University of Bridgeport, Bridgeport, CT
March 15—Congregation B'nai Jehudah, Kansas City, MO
March 19—Duval County Citizens Benefit Corporation, Jacksonville, FL
March 24—Monterey Peninsula College, Monterey, CA
April 11—Dickinson College, Carlisle, PA
April 16—Williams College, Williamstown, MA; and Smith College and Amherst College, Amherst, MA
April 30—Mt. Holyoke College, South Hadley, MA
May 8—Temple Sharay Tefilo, East Orange, NJ
May 21—Dartmouth College, Hanover, NH
June 1–2—Billy Graham Crusade meetings, Brooklyn and Long Island, NY
June 6—Commencement, Lincoln University, Lincoln, PA
June 8–9—Billy Graham Crusade meetings, New York City and Bronx, NY
June 18—People's Independent Church, Los Angeles, CA
June 26–July 5—Speaker at six mass meetings in Indianapolis, IN; Jackson, MS; Pittsburgh, PA; Syracuse, NY; Hartford, CT; and San Francisco, CA
July 25—Wisconsin State College, Whitewater, WI
August 13—Riverside Church, New York City, NY
August 16—Lutheran Church convention, Miami Beach, FL
September 25—Local 1199, New York City, NY
October 9—Union College, Schenectady, NY
October 20—Congregation Mishkan Israel, Hamden, CT
October 22—White Rock Baptist Church, Philadelphia, PA
October 29—"Face to Face" TV program, London
November 8—Lewis and Clark College and Urban League of Portland, Portland, OR
November 12—Mankato College, Mankato, MN
November 24—Citywide fundraising campaign, Indianapolis, IN
December 6—San Jose City College, San Jose, CA
December 10—Chapman College, Los Angeles, CA
December 11—AFL-CIO convention, Miami, FL
December 14—Consumers League, New Orleans, LA

12. King Center Archives, Box 8:18. Another example of his high-energy typical travel schedule is provided by a 1963 article from *The Saturday Evening Post*:

> He is at home about ten days a month on average. More often he is traveling. A recent schedule took him to Chicago for four speeches on a Sunday, to the University of Minnesota Monday, back at his Atlanta SCLC office Tuesday with a church meeting at home that night; Wednesday through Friday there were meeting with the SCLC [Southern Christian Leadership Conference] staff; Saturday, counseling at his church and visits to hospitalized members; Sunday morning, preaching. And then on the road for New York, Connecticut, and Tennessee. Despite the pace, he almost always appears fresh.
>
> Cleghorn, "Crowned With Crises," pp. 113–127.

13. Halberstam, "When 'Civil Rights' and 'Peace' Join Forces," p. 189.
14. Ibid., p. 202.
15. The distance from the window to the ground is cited in Lawrence Reddick, *Crusader Without Violence* (New York: Harper, 1959), p. 60. Visitors to the King childhood home in Atlanta, which is now a federal site, can see for themselves what the distance is from the second floor windows to the ground below. Approximately 12 feet seems right. Visitors looking down likely would not assume that they would land uninjured if they jumped out of the second-story window. A fracture of an appendage would seem likely at the very least, at least in an adult, if not more damage depending on what part of the body hit the ground first. Children might be less injured due to lower body mass producing less acceleration and less overall force. The distance would matter to some extent to address the typical question of whether these jumps qualify as "suicide attempts" or whether the term "suicide" can be applied to them. The

writer who has discussed this matter in the most detail to date is the philosopher of religion, Frederick Downing, who uses quotation marks when using the term in the first part of his book but drops the quotation marks when returning to the jumps later in his book. Downing's interpretation is psychological, having to do with identifying with the grandmother (pp. 182–183) and viewing his grandmother's death as the "curse" that cast a shadow over King's entire life. Early death presaged his own death and influenced his constant concern with mortality. Downing devotes an entire chapter in his book to "Grandmother Williams" and her impact on King. This analysis is important and may be valid in many ways, but Downing doesn't raise the concept of depression and how it may produce suicidality. Frederick L. Downing, *To See the Promised Land: The Faith Pilgrimage of Martin Luther King Jr.* (Macon, GA: Mercer University Press, 1986).

16. In the King Center Archives (8:13), there is a book manuscript, which was later published, by Dr. Lenwood G. Davis, now a retired professor of history who taught at Winston Salem State University. Based on textual content, it seems that much of the early life of Dr. King in this source was based on interviews with family members, particularly A. D. King. Originally written in 1964, this contemporary manuscript is not influenced by later hagiography or controversy after Dr. King's assassination. The early suicide attempts are described in this work as follows:

> Even though Martin was a person of energy and probably could handle himself physically, he usually could talk himself out of most situations. Martin has always been considerate of others, however, he would always deal with himself violently. Before he was 13 years old, he had attempted suicide twice, and each time it was because of his grandmother and the love he had for her. A.D. once accidentally knocked his grandmother down unconscious while playing sliding down the banister from upstairs in the home. Martin was so preoccupied with the obsession that she was dead that he went to a second-story window and jumped out, falling some twelve feet to the ground. However, he did not injure himself. Another time he tried to commit suicide was on May 18, 1941, when he was twelve. He had slipped away from home to watch a parade, his grandmother suffered a heart attack while speaking at Mt. Olive Baptist Church, and on arrival to the hospital she was pronounced dead. When he heard about his grandmother, he ran all the way home as fast as he could. When he got home, he found the whole family crying. Feeling bad for slipping off to watch the parade, he went up to the second floor of the house again and jumped out of the window. He was shaken up a bit, but not hurt. This was the first time that anyone had died that was so close to him. . . . Martin was almost raised by his grandmother, she was like a second mother to him.

Manuscript titled "I Have a Dream: The Life and Times of Martin Luther King Jr.," by Lenwood G. Davis, Brooklyn College, 1964. This manuscript was later published in 1969 with the same title by Adams Press (Chicago) and reprinted in 1974 by Negro Universities Press (Westport, CT).

The jumps from the window were mentioned and described as suicide attempts in multiple contemporary sources in the early 1960s, including the *TIME* January 1964 Man of the Year article (available at http://content.time.com/time/subscriber/article/0,33009,940759,00.html), and in Cleghorn, "Crowned With Crises."

It is important to note that King Jr. did not publicly deny or refute the *TIME* magazine or *Saturday Evening Post* articles' descriptions of his suicide attempts.

Cleghorn wrote,

> He was sensitive, and twice as a young boy he seemed to lose control of himself in heartbreak. Once A.D., his younger brother sliding down a banister, knocked their grandmother unconscious. Thinking she was dead, Martin ran to a second-floor window and jumped out, but the fall was only ten or twelve feet and he was not injured. Later, when he was eleven, he learned that his grandmother really had died and took the same jump out the window—again escaping injury. (p. 117)

Note that Cleghorn does not use the word suicide and instead speaks of how he "seemed to lose control of himself in heartbreak." The *TIME* article, titled "America's Gandhi: Martin Luther King Jr." (January 3, 1964) was more explicit:

> Raised in the warmth of a tightly knit family, King developed from his earliest years a raw-nerved sensitivity that bordered on self-destruction. Twice, before he was 13, he tried to commit suicide. Once his brother, "A.D.," accidentally knocked his grandmother unconscious when he slid down a banister. Martin thought she was dead, and in despair ran to a second-floor window and jumped out—only to land unhurt. He did the same thing, with the same result, on the day his grandmother died.

The *TIME* article is written with direct quotations from interviewing King while on an airplane flight from Atlanta to Los Angeles. It also includes quotations from observations of King speaking in public. The unidentified author doesn't explain whether the personal history given comes directly from the interview with King Jr., from family, or from other sources. The book by Reddick is not referenced directly.

An analysis of the *TIME* article by the Stanford King Research Center and Institute notes the following:

> Although many of King's supporters celebrated the tribute, King was privately incensed by some of the comments in the story. His clothing style was described as "funereal conservatism," and he was said to have "very little sense of humor." King, who had garnered considerable fame from his speeches and oratorical skills, was criticized for his use of metaphors, which the author called "downright embarrassing." https://kinginstitute.stanford.edu/encyclopedia/time-magazines-man-year

The window jumps aren't mentioned.

17. Reddick, *Crusader Without Violence*, pp. 60–61.
18. Some clinical comments on suicidality from a psychiatric perspective are in order. One aspect of determining whether an act is suicidal or not is to assess the intent of the person and the lethality of the attempt. If the person did not intend to die and/or if the lethality of the attempt is low, clinicians sometimes use the phrase "parasuicide." This term typically is applied to minor actions, such as superficial cutting on the arms, often in the parallel direction to the arteries, which cannot be lethal. If such an action is conducted, for instance, in the next room from another person, with an open door, after an argument, then such a behavior would seem to have the intention of attention, not a wish to be killed in that moment. This type of parasuicidal behavior is common in conditions such as borderline personality, but it is not common in manic–depressive illness in the absence of borderline personality. The core features of borderline personality, such as childhood sexual trauma, are not known to be present in King's life history. Also, King's jumps were not repeated after the two attempts in adolescence. He did not engage in other parasuicidal acts later in his life.

    Hence, the typical features of parasuicidality are absent in King's biography, whereas the two jumps in preadolescence are consistent with suicidality. Regarding lethality, 12 feet would be high enough to potentially cause physical damage, possibly death if one landed on one's neck or head. The lower risk in children due to smaller body size is not something a preadolescent would have known or logically considered. Regarding intent, we cannot know for certain whether the young King wanted to die at that moment, but we also cannot assume he did not. Thus, the clear rejection of suicidality would not be supported by these facts, and the possibility of suicidality certainly exists. Perhaps the balance would be tipped in favor of using the "suicide" term when one takes into account that King's peers at the time, such as Lawrence Reddick, when they described these events after talking with King's family and with King himself, decided to use the term. The events were later dropped by King and his family in their description of his life, when the political implications of his biography had become important.

    Thus, King does not mention it himself in any of his writings or sermons in the 1960s, Coretta does not mention it in her 1970 memoir, nor does King Sr. in his 1980 memoir nor King's sister Christine Farris in her later memoirs.

Apparently relying on Reddick, Taylor Branch identifies the specific window as King's bedroom in the back of the house and Branch interprets the event as a suicide attempt. Describing the first event when A.D. slid down the banister and hit his grandmother, Branch writes,

> As her relatives raced to her . . . a far deeper panic seized M.L. He ran upstairs to his room at the back of the house and threw himself out the window. A new round of cries brought horror to the elder Kings . . . they had to run outside to their older son, who did not move until he heard that his grandmother was alive. Only gradually did it sink in that the shock of harm to the grandmother had driven M.L. blindly toward suicide.

Taylor Branch, *Parting the Waters* (New York: Simon & Schuster, 1988), pp. 48–49.

Branch describes the second jump after the death of King's grandmother with no new details other than what was present in Reddick's book, which again appears to be his main source for details regarding the jump (p. 57).

19. To summarize, the historical records written during King's life, and especially early in his career, call these jumps "suicide attempts." This is the language used in Reddick's 1959 book, and Reddick was very close to King, who cooperated with Reddick for the book. King's Morehouse College classmate Lerone Bennett's 1964 book (*What Manner of Man*) cites Reddick and repeats the phrase. Lenwood Davis' original 1964 manuscript, later published in 1969, also repeats the language as described above. Reddick and Bennett were longtime friends of King, and all three authors relied on the King family as their primary sources. Only later, after King's death, did his family, friends, and allies seek to downplay the childhood jumps. Family excepted, those persons typically did not know King early in his life, and of course they all tended to be concerned with protecting his image.
20. Martin Luther King Sr. with Clayton Riley, *Daddy King: An autobiography* (New York: Morrow, 1980), p. 26.
21. Taylor Branch, interview with Ralph David Abernathy, University of North Carolina Chapel Hill, handwritten notes of interview, November 19, 1984.
22. In theology seminary, during a student pastorship in Queens, New York, the ministerial evaluation reported "an attitude of aloofness, disdain, and possibly snobbishness . . . a smugness." MLK BU Archives, Box 1, Folder 2.
23. James Baldwin made the same observation:

> It is rare that one *likes* a world-famous man—by the time they become world-famous they rarely like themselves, which may account for this antipathy. Yet King is immediately and tremendously winning, there is really no other word for it; and there he stood, with an inquiring and genuine smile on his face, in the open door of his hotel room. James Baldwin, "The Highroad to Destiny," in *Martin Luther King Jr.: A Profile*, ed. C. Eric Lincoln (New York: Hill & Wang, 1970), pp. 90–112.

Bernard Lafayette also described King's ability to care about individual persons who might not be viewed as important:

> He paid attention to people, unlike many celebrities. For instance, he was speaking in Detroit at a rally. There was a fellow in the audience who had heard him speak a few weeks earlier in Birmingham, Alabama. When the speech was over, he went up to tell Dr. King that he had been at a rally with him in Birmingham (he happened to be visiting family in Alabama). Before he could say anything, Dr. King said, "Didn't I see you last week in Birmingham?" It shocked him. [King] was keenly observant, very attentive to details.

Telephone interview with author, January 15, 2013.

24. Interview with William Anderson, April 17, 2014.
25. Interview with Stanley Levison, February 14, 1970, by James M. Mosby Jr., Ralph Bunche oral collection, RJB 539, Moorland–Spingarn Research Center archives, Howard University, pp. 9–10.
26. Interview with Bernard Lee, by David Garrow, August 21, 1982, in David Garrow papers, Pittsburgh, PA, Manuscript Collection 832.
27. https://www.rabbinicalassembly.org/story/conversation-dr-martin-luther-king-jr.

28. Interview with Susannah Heschel, Newton, MA, May 15, 2013.
29. Interview with Wilhelmina Harris, Concord, MA, July 19, 2015.
30. Halberstam, "When 'Civil Rights' and 'Peace' Join Forces," p. 202.
31. Ibid., p. 202.
32. Reddick, *Crusader Without Violence*.
33. Interview with Michael Haynes, Boston, MA, April 15, 2013.
34. Lewis Baldwin has collected a large assemblage of King jokes. Lewis V. Baldwin, *Behind the Public Veil: The Humanness of Martin Luther King Jr.* (Minneapolis, MN: Fortress Press, 2016), pp. 259–320.
35. Interview, Tom Houck, Atlanta, July 2, 2015.
36. Michael Harrington, *Eyes on the Prize* interview, October 11, 1998, question 1, http://digital.wustl.edu/e/eii/eiiweb/har5427.0719.063michaelharrington.html.
37. Dr. Edwin Shirley, quoted in "Rev. King Had Quiet S. Florida Escapes: A Friend Recalls Times With Civil Rights Leader," *Sun Sentinel*, January 15, 2016, https://www.sun-sentinel.com/2006/01/15/rev-king-had-quiet-s-florida-escapes/
38. Cited in Baldwin, *Behind the Public Veil*, p. 311.
39. https://en.wikipedia.org/wiki/The_Other_America.
40. Michael Harrington, *Eyes on the Prize* interview, October 11, 1998, question 7, http://digital.wustl.edu/e/eii/eiiweb/har5427.0719.063michaelharrington.html.
41. Abernathy, *And the Walls Came Tumbling Down*, p. 468.
42. Interview, William Anderson, August 17, 2013. Here's another favorite from Anderson's recollection:

    > There was one joke that he particularly enjoyed: There was a time when Blacks were not able to be qualified as pilots of commercial planes. Eddie Richenbacher decided he was going to be a pilot; so he contacted Tuskegee to find someone who could fly a commercial airplane. They sent Sam Jones. Richenbacher asked Jones: Can you fly one of these twin jet planes. "Damn right I can fly that MF!" Eddie Richenbacher then said: "Oh no no no Mr. Jones, you don't understand, I'm talking a commercial pilot flying one of these planes with 200 people on it. You can't talk like that if you are going to be a commercial Eastern airlines pilot. We know you can fly a plane, so we're going to send you to charm school." So Sam Jones came back sharp as you can imagine, in a crisp white shirt, tie, a well-pressed uniform, and said, "I'm ready." So they assigned him to a plane. He got in, got onto the PA system, and said: "Good morning. This is your pilot. We will be flying at an altitude of 7,000 feet. Sit back and enjoy the flight." Then Jones forgot to turn off the speaker, and muttered to himself: "Now let me see if I can get this MF off the GD ground." The way King would tell that joke, you would just crack up.

    Abernathy gives an example of typical King mimicry:

    > One of the people he "did" was an Atlanta preacher named Hilly Thomas who had a stutter that became increasingly pronounced as he became more and more excited. Martin had a repertoire of Hilly stories that could keep people laughing for hours. . . . Martin used to recreate an entire sermon he once heard Hilly Thomas preach. . . . "Hilly began" Martin said, "by announcing, 'I'm going to preach this m-morning on the t-text 'God is Love.' And m-my subject is: 'is.' Now 'is' is not a noun; 'is' is not a verb. 'Is' is just 'is.' Like 'is you got your ticket?' 'Is you going?' 'Is' is just 'is.' " At that point Martin would be screaming, whooping, and waving his arms and the rest of us would be on the floor, holding our sides. He could continue the sermon until we gasped for breath and begged him to stop.

    Abernathy, *And the Walls Came Tumbling Down*, pp. 468–469.

3

"Expecting Great Things"

Martin Luther King Sr. was to Martin Luther King Jr. like an angry thunderstorm to a driving rain: They shared much in common, but only one of them had the power to frighten.

Senior was a large, loud, boisterous man. With his powerful build, close-cropped white hair, and small wire-rimmed glasses, he gave the impression of a coiled-up spring, constantly waiting to be unleashed. His son was a more soothing force.

King's Boston friend, Michael Haynes, recalled the difference:

> Daddy King, he was a little gruff. When he walked in the room, he acted like he was important. Mike King [King Jr.]—no. Celebrities make you often feel uncomfortable. Not him. Other people in civil rights would act like: Don't you know who I am? Not him. Never. Ever.

Even after becoming famous, Haynes stated, King was the "same guy, [the] same guy" that he had been as an unknown graduate student.[1]

The difference between King Sr. and King Jr. may have been partly temperamental, but it also was experiential. King Sr. was very gregarious, outgoing, talkative, somewhat arrogant, controlling—a larger-than-life presence. Said one friend of King Sr, who was also called Mike before his name change, "He was simply Mike King—always shaking hands, encouraging and demanding, making himself the center of attention in any room, full of claims for the past and promises for the future."[2] King Jr., as we'll see, had many of the same qualities as his father, although he was much tempered in how he expressed himself. King Sr., as befits his intensity, was a stickler for being on time, for instance. King Jr., in contrast, walked and talked slowly, and he was famous for being late. "Colored People's Time" was a joke King's aides applied to him with fondness and exasperation. On the day of his marriage, King Jr. procrastinated as usual, leading his

Soul on Fire. Nassir Ghaemi, Oxford University Press. © Oxford University Press 2026.
DOI: 10.1093/9780197657614.003.0004

father to yell in their house, "ML, boy, you're going to be late and it's your own wedding!"[3]

Yet the fact is, that for all his later tribulations, compared to his father, King Jr. had a much less stressful life until entering his public career in his mid-20s.

King Sr. was a classic self-made man.

Growing up in rural Stockbridge, Georgia, the son of a sharecropper, young Michael King was poor and barely literate. He left home when only 15 years old, after exchanging physical blows with his father, James Albert King, who had been in the process of beating up Michael's mother. His mother was no weakling; she had once beaten up a White millowner who had beaten the young King Sr., a tremendous act of courage that could have ended in her lynching. After the event, James King went to the millowner's house with a rifle to kill him and was met by a gang of White men on horses with rifles of their own. To avoid lynching, James then hid in the woods for some time until it was safe for him to emerge, after tempers had cooled.

Michael King came from valiant, even impetuous, stock; "Daddy King" would grow to embody that same unbridled courage.

After the run-in with his father James, his mother encouraged King Sr. to begin living his own life, and the adolescent boy jumped the railroads to Atlanta. King Sr. arrived in the big city without a means to make a living and without the ability to read or write. He had known the itinerant preachers of the countryside, and he had begun to wish to be like them. He worked in menial jobs for a number of years before realizing that if he was to become a preacher, he would need to be literate. He decided to enter college, but knew he would have to read and write first.

This decision didn't come easily. When he was 21 years old, 6 years after leaving the family home, James King came to Atlanta to visit his eldest son. James King needed help; he was getting older, the family was big; he needed his son to return to the farm to help feed the family. Michael King had to reject his father, to his face, to achieve his own dreams.

The young man registered at the Bryant Preparatory School and was assigned to the fifth grade level. There he sat for 5 years. Finally, in 1926, when he was 27 years old, he felt ready to apply to Morehouse College. He entered the office of the president, John Hope, to request admission. The admissions officer reviewed his academic history and declined him. The young King turned to walk away, and he thought of the years he had spent with children, laboriously learning in his twenties what he had never been taught as a child. He thought about his hard-working father whose entreaties to help his family he had rejected. He thought about his new girlfriend, Alberta Williams, daughter of one of the most prominent ministers in Atlanta, A. D. Williams, pastor at Ebenezer Baptist Church. He turned around and impulsively burst his way through the door of

President Hope. He blurted out his life story and pleaded with Hope to be given a chance to have a Morehouse education.[4]

John Hope looked at Mike King strictly. Born in 1868 of a Scottish father and a freed Black woman, a graduate of Brown University, Hope could have passed for White, but he spent his life trying to provide the best possible education to Southern Blacks. He was active in the National Association for the Advancement of Colored People (NAACP), and a close ally of W. E. B. DuBois. Hope looked over the young unsophisticated preacher wannabe. He turned to the admissions director and accepted Mike King for admission.[5]

If Martin Luther King Sr. would in later years be proud of who he was, he had reason to be.

King married Alberta Williams, whom he affectionately called "Bunch," and they had three children: first Christine, then M.L. Jr and last A. D. Williams King, their second boy. King took over Ebenezer Baptist Church from his father-in-law on the latter's death in 1931 and expanded the already well-regarded church into an even more successful ministry. King added a politically activist component to the church as well, and preached about civil rights. He soon became part of the top Black leadership in Atlanta, which negotiated with the mayor and White leaders to improve the lot of Black Atlantans.

Years later, his leadership role in the 1930s through the 1950s would be seen as mere history, as part of the "Old Guard" of Black leadership that was challenged by young students inspired by King Jr.

To his last days, King Jr. always showed great respect to his father, despite their differences in personality. After leaving Dexter Avenue Baptist Church in 1960, King's salary came as co-pastor at Ebenezer Baptist Church, adding up to less than $50,000 yearly in current value.[6] King Jr. would preach at Ebenezer once or twice a month, when he wasn't traveling. When he did preach, his father would sit to the side and say his favorite phrase to King Jr.: "Make it plain." In church, King Jr. always deferred to his father, even when he was a famed international civil rights leader.

* * *

As previously discussed, King Jr. not only had high physical energy, decreased need for sleep, and a very high general activity level but also he had manic traits of an excellent sense of humor, talkativeness, and perhaps excessively elevated self-esteem. His high energy level also applied to his sexual life, much of which was documented and reported by his enemies in the Federal Bureau of Investigation (FBI), whose records were revealed in the 1980s by historian David Garrow. In 1977, on behalf of the family, King's close aide Bernard Lee sued to have those records destroyed, but a federal judge instead sealed them for

50 years. Many of the transcripts have been made public but the full audio files are scheduled for release in 2027.[7]

There is tension in discussing this topic because some defenders of King's image view moralistic criticism from White historians as an expression of racism. Certainly it is the case that King's enemies, even during his lifetime, tried to use this aspect of his life to denounce him. Still, the truth of a message is not dependent on its messenger. In fact, the first published account of King's extramarital affairs, made public 2 years after his death, was written by John A. Williams, a Black writer-activist who, although critical of King as too moderate in his politics, respected him and supported even more radical approaches to ending racism.[8]

The approach taken here is both historical and, for the first time, medical and psychiatric.

Since the 1977 court order, the evidence on this topic has continued to grow. In addition to FBI records, close allies of King have gone on the record to describe his active sexual life. In 1989, just before his death the following year, King's best friend, Ralph Abernathy, described it in his ghostwritten memoir,[9] for which Abernathy was excoriated by many King allies at the time. A few years later, in 1995, one of the women Abernathy had described anonymously came forward with her story: Georgia Davis Powers, the first woman and first African American to be elected to the Kentucky state legislature, described her friendship and years-long romantic relationship with King. She was with him at the Lorraine Motel the night before his death. Soft-spoken and a devoted civil rights activist, she couldn't be condemned as seeking to undermine King's legacy.[10]

More FBI records also have been released regarding King via releases of previously classified records related to the Kennedy assassination. These records are transcripts of tapes, with romantic conversation, which if eventually verified would be rather definitive. They provide evidence that Southern Christian Leadership Conference (SCLC) staff member Dorothy Cotton was a long-time girlfriend, whom King often hosted at a little-known hideaway Atlanta apartment, as Cotton admitted later.[11] In his memoir, Abernathy revealed that King had been with two women the night before his death and that the second woman was angry with him because he had spent the entire night with the other. The two were Georgia Davis Powers and Dorothy Cotton; Abernathy's account has been confirmed by both women over time.[12] The FBI files newly reveal also that King had other long-term girlfriends in Washington, DC, and Los Angeles.[13]

In one of the recent FBI files, extensive wiretaps of Bayard Rustin were released. In that material, Rustin is having a conversation with someone whose name remains redacted. Rustin refers in 1965 briefly to a discussion with someone else, whose name also is redacted but who appears to have some clinical knowledge (perhaps a physician such as Dr. Arthur Logan). The conversation is about "the whole sexual angle," and the clinician is cited by Rustin as seeing that behavior as "an extreme form of neuroticism which only occurs during periods of intense fatigue." The term "neurotic" was used in that era as the opposite of "psychotic," the distinction between common abnormal feelings that may lead to psychological problems (neurosis, which was used to refer to what now tends to be called depression and anxiety) and less common, more severe feelings that tend to be more obviously insane (psychosis, which usually means delusions or hallucinations). In modern translation, the clinician was saying that King was not sick in the sense of delusions, but he did have significant anxiety or depression, which might drive his behavior.[14]

If it is true that King had a high amount of sexual activity, then various reasons can be given, the most common being the alpha male excuse: Once a male becomes powerful, females are attracted to him, and he can use his power to obtain sexual favors. In a way, this theory is that all power is, ultimately, about getting sex. It was well-known that ministers had special status in the Black community, especially in that era. As Abernathy would write years later, the aura of the Black clergy attracted female attention: "[The minister] had power and influence, more influence than anybody else in the community, and you don't have to chase women. The women will chase you."[15] This view could explain hypersexual behavior when King was famous and powerful, roughly 1957 (when the Montgomery boycott received attention) to 1968. But it wouldn't explain King's behavior if he was highly sexually active before 1957, when he was merely one graduate student among many, or just another seminary or college student. Of course, King wasn't married during that period, so that sexual behavior was not extramarital. The question is whether he had a high libido, greater than that of his peers, most of the time, even before he became an alpha male. Such appears to be the case. For instance, letters between King and his friends at Boston University theology school, Crozer Theological Seminary, and Morehouse College are full of sexual innuendo;[16] although we don't possess King's half of the correspondence in most cases, the tone in which his friends write him suggests that this kind of talk was common between them. Also, he had an active romantic and likely sexual life from the very beginning when he was at Morehouse College.

By the time he arrived at Boston University, King was an accomplished ladies man. His friends, such as Walter Raleigh McCall, teased him about it mercilessly. Once when one of King's Boston University friends, William T. Handy Jr., was in Atlanta and visited the King family, Handy mentioned "to Mrs. King how popular [King] was, how the girls were after him, how he wasn't doing anything wrong, but that he was very popular." Mama King became concerned and wrote "a sober letter" to her son: "Remember M.L.," she wrote, "we're expecting great things from you."[17] McCall, known as "Mac," was especially close to King and later wrote King to check on how he was doing with the important things, implying whether he was controlling his romantic life. McCall, who was close to King at both Morehouse and Crozer, competed with King in interviewing for King's first job at Dexter Avenue Baptist Church. (McCall would later be dean of a rural Georgia college.) While King was gaining national fame in Montgomery, McCall wrote letters about getting women pregnant and then wanting to stop providing child support because of too much attention from the mother of the child, and he wrote of the ease with which sexual activity could be satisfied in the role of a minister ("Gals are rushing me and I am staying clear of them down here. For I want no 'mess' from here out. Your Pal, Mac").[18] King, by then cautious, wrote back conservatively and courteously to his old friend in the late 1950s, and then they appeared to correspond increasingly less until King's death.

In summary, there is reasonably convincing evidence that King had an active sexual life not limited to his last decade of life when he had achieved international fame.

The alpha male explanation isn't the whole story. But it likely had a secondary role to play. As far back as the Montgomery years, King and his new best friend Ralph Abernathy apparently began to be tempted. The young preachers were more than average ministers; they were leading a new national movement. In the late 1950s, King and Abernathy attended a national Black Baptist convention. A leader of the group, Rev. J. Raymond Henderson, who also was a friend of King's father, wrote to them after the convention. He warned them that they were becoming famous and that with fame comes temptation:

> One of the most damning influences is that of women. They themselves too often delight in the satisfaction they get out of affairs with men of unusual prominence. Enemies are not above using them to a man's detriment. White women can be lures. You must exercise more than care. You must be vigilant indeed.[19]

Success was their main enemy now. King Sr. earlier had warned his son on the same matter after King Jr. gave a sermon in 1954 in Atlanta, soon after his return from Boston. Daddy King wrote his son a letter: "You see, young man, you are becoming very popular. As I told you, you must be very much in prayer. Persons like yourself are the ones the devil turns all of his forces loose to destroy."[20]

These social explanations, combined with constant travel, imply that King had voluntary control over his sexual behavior. If so, it would seem less explainable why he didn't curtail those activities in the face of consistent FBI surveillance. Abernathy expressed this logic to his friend, who simply refused to change.[21]

Even Abernathy, after raising the cultural explanation for his friend's sexual behavior, alludes to the need for another answer:

> We all understood and believed in the biblical prohibition against sex outside of marriage. It was just that he had a particularly difficult time with that temptation. His own principal explanation of that difficulty is one I choose not to repeat here.[22]

That explanation could not have been the mere availability of female attention, which Abernathy cites separately. The main implied option would be some sort of internal drive to sexual activity, although we cannot know for certain because Abernathy declined to be specific.

* * *

In addition to oral histories and FBI records, the other source of data on King's sexual activity is his medical evaluations. In fact, for a young man, King saw doctors frequently.

In early December 1961, just before joining the Albany movement and going to jail, King traveled to Philadelphia, without fanfare and without any scheduled public activities. Only *Jet* magazine took note of this personal visit, reporting that he had entered a hospital.[23]

King had arranged the visit through contacting one of the nation's most prominent Black physicians, Dr. Harold E. Pierce Jr., a dermatologist and plastic surgeon who worked at the Mercy–Douglass Hospital (a segregated hospital for Black patients that closed after desegregation). King stayed for two days; at some point, he was taken to an operating room and administered anesthesia.

A week later, just as King was about to go to jail in Albany, Dr. Pierce sent King a summary letter, never previously published, in which he discusses problems of pain, dribbling, and slowness of urination.[24] This description suggests that King decided to get a complete medical evaluation with a chief complaint of urinary symptoms. In a 61-year-old man, this complaint would not be unusual; enlarged prostate glands are common by that age. But at age 31 years, prostate problems are highly unusual. Also, urinary infections or other symptoms in men, as opposed to women, are uncommon; if present, they are typically caused by sexually transmitted diseases.[25]

* * *

However one understands King's adult relationships with women, his childhood female relationships appear to have been close and affectionate. Although the influence of father on son was huge and obvious, the role of the women in the King family is obscured in part by the sexism of that era. King's mother, Alberta, was quiet and unassuming, tending to stay in the shadows of her husband's presence. King and his siblings relate that Alberta was a loving influence, however, making her children feel wanted and appreciated. She is reported to have been in "constant good spirits,"[26] unlike her husband, whose moods were variable. The same is reported to have been the case for her mother Jennie Williams, who was the closest in the family to young King Jr.

Although King Jr.'s mother was very affectionate, the phrases he used for his mother and father—"Mother dear" and "Daddy"[27]—suggest somewhat closer ties to his father. She loved to play the piano, and she cooked excellent soul food meals that the family shared every Sunday at King Sr.'s home, even in later years. Alberta was deeply religious, the only child of A. D. Williams, who had founded Ebenezer Baptist Church and had built it into a powerful Atlanta church. The elder Williams was a member of the NAACP and a leading civil rights figure in Atlanta. Thus, King Jr. inherited his commitment to civil rights from both his father and his maternal side. Alberta played the piano at Ebenezer church throughout her life, and she was killed there during a service in 1972 when she was shot by a delusional Black man.[28]

King Jr.'s personality in terms of his emotional reactivity was said to be more like that of his mother than his father. King Sr. was reactive, whereas Alberta was calm. She "was the pacifist in the family";[29] King Sr. later recalled that the boy "was always a little sensitive in his response to even the most casual matters, and he was always one to negotiate a dispute instead of losing his temper."[30]

The other major mother figures in King's life were his grandmother, Jennie Celeste Williams, and his sister, Christine King Farris. As noted previously, the young King perhaps had no greater love than his maternal grandmother. When Jennie Williams died, little Mike apparently tried to kill himself. She was very affectionate to the young boy, and he felt her loss painfully.

When King Sr. would beat King Jr., as was common in that era, Jennie Williams would console the boy afterwards. The physical discipline sometimes involved spanking and sometimes apparently whipping. King Sr. later would recall how the boy would be teary but would resist the urge to cry. He viewed this experience "as peculiar and never forgot the scene or the trait" in his son. Jennie's consolations led the young boy to view her as a "saintly grandmother." She hated the spankings because "the child looked so pitiful."[31]

Christine was the first child and only girl in the family of three children. As often befits that birth order, she took a maternal role in relation to her younger brothers, even though she was only a few years older. Loving and supportive, Christine echoed her mother and grandmother in showering her brothers with affection. Throughout the years, she remained the most solid of the King siblings, marrying a stable and supportive husband, Isaac Farris, who was a major help to King Sr. and Coretta Scott King in later years.

In summary, the King household was composed of an extended family of loving parents and grandparents, an older sister who doted on King Jr., and a younger brother who kept him company.

There was only one problem. Mike King was limited to Black Atlanta; White Atlanta was off-limits. The young boy learned this lesson when he was approximately 7 years old when a White playmate stopped playing with him. His mother told Mike that she didn't want her son playing with a Negro. Confused, Mike's parents had to explain segregation to the child, who soon realized that his school was all-Black and his world was all-Black.

The routine horrors of segregation can't be underestimated, but overall, young Mike King suffered the evils of segregation like most of his peers. Because he was privileged economically, relative to many others in the Black community, the emotional impact of racist experiences might have been mitigated somewhat for him. In any case, it is probably fair to say that his personal experiences weren't particularly unusual.[32]

He attended Booker T. Washington High School, which was segregated, but it didn't prepare him well for college. Ambitious, young Mike skipped the 9th grade and the 12th grade, feeling an urge to attend college early, to be challenged more than he could in high school. Like his father, young Mike presented himself to Morehouse College, the most prestigious Black university in Atlanta, where the successor to John Hope as president was Benjamin Mays, who was also a friend of Daddy King. Mays admitted the young 15-year-old applicant, not knowing that approximately two decades later, he would be giving his eulogy. It was September 1944 when King Jr. entered his freshman year at Morehouse College.

* * *

In November 1966, at a key retreat of SCLC staff in Frogmore, South Carolina, James Bevel (one of King's staff and a youth activist) and King were standing in line waiting for food. As others in line listened discreetly, the two men discussed sex.[33] Bevel argued for open marriages, saying that love was boundless and shouldn't be limited. King disagreed, emphasizing that true love could occur only between one man and one woman. Bevel appealed to the nature of love; King cited the Bible. It wasn't lost on listeners that both men were struggling with their own sexual adventures, which were either openly known, in the case of Bevel, or an open secret, in the case of King. Bevel wanted to justify it with a new ethic and be freed of guilt. King accepted the old ethic and sought only forgiveness as a sinner.

Another possibility neither considered is that both may have had a version of manic–depressive illness, Bevel more severely than King, and that their high libidos could have been driven by their biology, not their psychology. They sought to rationalize ethically or understand theologically what may have been given to them simply by biology. For King, this probable biological reality would lead to a lifetime of spiritual guilt.

There obviously is a disconnect between King's morality-based politics and his apparently immoral sexual life. But there is a straightforward explanation that doesn't entail moral judgments. King was very talkative, had a very high level of physical energy, an excellent sense of humor, a large libido, and was extremely sociable. These personality traits also happen in the mood state of mania, as part of the high periods of manic–depressive illness (see Appendix 1). Usually those mood states last weeks to months, and one returns to one's usual personality. But, in many people, those manic traits can be part of one's personality; they are present to a mild degree all the time. This condition, mild manic traits as part of the personality, is called hyperthymic temperament: Traits include talkativeness, high energy, decreased need for sleep, high libido, high productivity and activity levels, and high self-esteem. These features, when all present together, are part of manic episodes. When present all the time, to a mild degree, they represent hyperthymic temperament.

People can also have depressive symptoms alternating with manic symptoms or frequently in combination. This type of mood temperament is called cyclothymia. King had frequent likely depressive episodes, but they were usually brief, lasting days. (Ralph Abernathy said, "Martin often fell into these moods of apprehension, but they never lasted long.")[34] The longer severe periods, lasting weeks or longer, were less common. The more common brief depressive states, along with constant manic traits, would be consistent most closely with cyclothymic temperament.

In other words, a key to the solution of the enigma of King's personality is that he may have had cyclothymic temperament. If true, his hypersexuality would be part of his biology more than his psychology, and moral and personal judgments on his character would be misplaced.

If this interpretation is correct, King never would have heard of it, nor did he know it. For him, the facts of his personality and life simply produced a major moral conflict. This is what he himself called his "inner civil war", and this is what James Bevel so clearly and forcefully expressed in an unpublished 1968 interview just after King's death.[35] The moral conflict had to do with the wish to remain faithful to his marriage vows and to Christian ethics, especially as a major religious leader himself, while he transgressed those ethics. This behavior would seem to make of this highly moral political leader a highly immoral human being.

The paradox would appear unsolvable, or perhaps could reflect incorrect premises. But there is a plausible explanation if he had a variety of manic–depressive illness.

Such an explanation would take the matter outside of the realm of morality, whether we as individuals accept those behaviors or not. It would make the matter part and parcel of who King was, a matter of the impact of his cyclothymic temperament on his strengths and his weaknesses. He would be due less praise for his positive qualities and less blame for his negative ones.

In fact, the latter might not matter as much as we might assume, in terms of his role as a leader. The Northern Black writer and activist John A. Williams was the first to publish about King's sexual activities, just 2 years after King's death, doing so with anonymous sources. Williams' book was received coldly, but he wasn't criticizing King; he was humanizing him. As Williams stated, "Martin King was no saint, but would a saint have fared better?"[36]

* * *

When examining a hero's childhood, most historians only focus on family relationships. Environment matters, but so does genetics. The child may be father to the man, but the genes are father to the child.

Daddy King certainly was opinionated and expressed himself forcefully. Even when doing something great, he revealed aspects of himself that could be viewed as weaknesses. For example, in 1960, he publicly endorsed candidate John Kennedy after Kennedy had helped release King Jr. from jail in Georgia. At a mass meeting, Daddy King said that he had planned to support Richard Nixon, partly because of reservations King had about the fact that Kennedy was a Roman Catholic. But now, King said if he had a satchel of votes, he'd send them all to Kennedy, a comment that may have had a national impact on a very close election. A few days later, Kennedy spoke with his aide Harris Wofford about Daddy King's comment in his support despite his Catholicism: "That was a hell of a bigoted statement wasn't it? Imagine Martin Luther King having a bigot for a father." But Kennedy's Irish humor came through, as he thought of the overbearing cyclone named Joseph P. Kennedy Sr.: "Well, we all have fathers, don't we?"[37]

Like his father and brother, A. D. King had also become a pastor, but he was a lifelong alcoholic and the opposite of his famous brother: A.D. moved from church to church without ever succeeding in establishing himself anywhere. He is commonly described as restless and unpredictable; he was sometimes depressed, although whether alcohol was cause or consequence of his depressions is unclear.

Daddy King saw himself in A.D.:

> I felt at times I was seeing much of myself in both the boys. A.D.'s angry response to being wronged, even slightly—I'd been there. . . . A.D. just

> backed away from [becoming a minister]. He was a child who was determined from his earliest days not to be what his father was.[38]

Daddy King describes taking the same attitude toward his own sharecropper father: anything but follow in his footsteps. A.D. was just like his father. He had a "robust extroverted temperament," Daddy King would recall later.[39]

A.D. also displayed hypersexuality. When King was in Oslo, Norway, accepting the Nobel Peace Prize in 1964, he asked Bayard Rustin to make arrangements for the trip for his family and his large entourage, which included many aides and friends with whom King was eager to share the experience. Among them was King's secretary, Dora McDonald, who one night was upset by the loud noise of the entourage; she called Rustin, as the group's organizer, to ask him to look into things. Rustin opened his door and saw "two guys . . . running down the hall chasing a woman and they're stark naked." One of the guys was King's brother, A.D. The woman was Scandinavian, scantily clad, and apparently stealing A.D.'s money and watch; there were apparently other "girls" there as well. Rustin called hotel security, who arrived on the scene and offered to give back the belongings to A.D. Rustin decided to let the women keep their loot so that they wouldn't talk to the press.[40]

A.D. would later move from church to church in the South, for a while in Birmingham, then Atlanta, then Louisville. He often was asked to leave by congregations that were concerned about his behavior. Alcohol was a major factor, but so was his sexual activity. In Louisville, where he was a pastor in his last years, he had a long-term mistress.[41]

Clifford Beal had married A. D. King's daughter, and Beal himself was a psychiatrist. He knew Daddy King well and had lived with him for some time. According to Dr. Beal, King Sr. was concerned about his son's alcoholism and likely depression. He thus sought psychiatric help and eventually A.D. was treated by a psychiatrist in Atlanta, Dr. Julius Ehik, a Hungarian immigrant who had fled the Nazi and Soviet occupations of his country.[42] Ehik published a paper about treating alcohol withdrawal with a new medication, thioridazine, which was mainly used at that time for schizophrenia.[43] It is possible that A.D. received such treatment at times. In the late 1970s, Dr. Beal asked Dr. Ehik about A.D.'s prior diagnosis and treatment; no records are available, but Dr. Ehik said that the diagnosis he had made was bipolar disorder.[44] If accurate, this report would provide genetic support for the possible diagnosis of manic–depressive illness for King Jr.

One year after King's assassination, while his wife and some of his kids were on vacation in the Caribbean, A.D. was at home with his teenage son. His adult daughter and son-in-law visited until approximately 1 a.m. When they left, he was sitting in his easy chair, watching television. At approximately 2 or 3 a.m., a neighbor's teenage son "reported hearing some splashing followed by the sound of coughing" coming from the backyard pool that had been installed a few weeks earlier. "Then the noise stopped."[45] A.D. was an excellent swimmer.

The next morning, at approximately 10 a.m., A.D.'s son found him in the pool in his underwear.

An autopsy was conducted and found a very high alcohol level of 0.27; the death was ruled an accidental drowning.[46] The absence of evidence of cardiac arrest in the autopsy would appear to rule out a heart attack. Some in the King family remain suspicious of homicide.[47]

Another possibility is suicide, especially given his alcoholism, past depression, and apparent past suicidal thoughts. According to Georgia Davis Powers, A.D. had repeatedly talked about wanting to kill himself throughout the years, especially when he was drunk. Alcohol is a major risk factor for suicide. Powers knew A.D. well when he was a pastor in Louisville from approximately 1965 to 1968. Once, King Jr. called Powers because he had gotten off the phone with A.D., who had threatened to kill himself. King Jr. was concerned enough that he asked Powers to go to his brother's house to check on him. She did so, and she concluded "it was the alcohol talking."[48] But many people drink alcohol without becoming suicidal. Depression usually is present.[49]

In short, both his father and his brother were highly energetic and extroverted persons, and in his brother's case, also hypersexual, alcoholic, and intermittently suicidal. These traits are consistent with mood temperaments similar to King Jr.'s cyclothymia—probably hyperthymia for King Sr. and cyclothymia for A.D. King. Because these mood temperaments are genetic and inherited, evidence for their existence in King's family strengthens the probability that King Jr. had cyclothymia as well.

This was the genetic and environmental endowment of young Mike King, as he navigated the world of childhood and adolescence. By 1945, he had skipped 2 years of high school and was ready to follow his father and grandfather to Morehouse College in Atlanta.

From there, he would far exceed them.

Notes

1. Interview with Michael Haynes, April 15, 2013.
2. Taylor Branch, *Parting the Waters* (New York: Simon & Schuster, 1988), p. 43.
3. Christine King Farris, *Through It All* (New York: Atria, 2009), p. 75.
4. Branch, *Parting the Waters*; Martin Luther King Sr. with Clayton Riley, *Daddy King: An Autobiography* (New York: Morrow, 1980), pp. 24–48.
5. King Sr. with Riley, *Daddy King*, pp. 77–78.
6. When asked about rumors that he had "amassed a personal fortune," King replied, "Me wealthy? . . . If I have any weaknesses, they are not in the are of coveting wealth." He went on

to enumerate in detail his personal finances: King took only a $1 salary as president of the Southern Christian Leadership Conference (SCLC). His Ebenezer salary was $6,000 yearly, which approximates $47,500 in current value. He kept approximately $4,000 to $5,000 yearly of honoraria from his constant lecturing and speeches, approximately $35,000 in current value. He gave the remainder of his lecture income, which was large at approximately $200,000 yearly, to SCLC (equivalent to approximately $1.5 million in current dollars), as he also did with book royalties. Alex Haley, "Playboy Interview: Martin Luther King," *Playboy*, January 1965; Reese Cleghorn, "Crowned with Crises," in *Martin Luther King Jr.: A Profile*, ed. C. Eric Lincoln (New York: Hill & Wang, 1970), pp. 113–127. Originally in *Saturday Evening Post*, June 15, 1963, pp. 15–19.

7. David Garrow, *The FBI and Martin Luther King Jr.* (New York: Norton, 1981), pp. 168–170. Garrow interviewed some Justice Department lawyers who had listened to the classified tapes. They were not only mailed in 1964 to King with a note recommending suicide but also shared with Attorney General Robert Kennedy and President Lyndon Johnson, as well as multiple journalists.
8. John A. Williams, *The King That God Didn't Save* (New York: Simon & Schuster, 1970).
9. Abernathy's memoir appears to have been ghostwritten. He was not known to be a powerful writer before the memoir, yet the book is written in beautiful prose. Abernathy acknowledges Thomas Landess as assisting him in research for the book. Landess was a White professor from South Carolina who became quite active in the Reagan administration as a conservative intellectual. He became close to Abernathy after the latter supported Reagan in the 1980 election. After Landess' death, one of his friends reported that Landess had ghostwritten the autobiography: https://www.washingtontimes.com/news/2012/jan/13/tom-landess-rip.
10. Georgia Davis Powers, *I Shared the Dream: The Pride, Passion, and Politics of the First Black Woman Senator from Kentucky* (Liberty Corner, NJ: New Horizon Press, 1995). Powers gave a gracious and honest interview about her relationship with King and her life to Tony Brown: https://www.tonybrownsjournal.com/mlk-affair.
11. https://theconversation.com/the-civil-rights-activist-so-close-to-martin-luther-king-jr-she-was-thought-of-as-his-other-wife-118750.
12. Ibid.
13. Much of this material was summarized by David Garrow in an article that generated controversy: David J. Garrow, "The Troubled Legacy of Martin Luther King," *Standpoint*, May 30, 2019, pp. 30–37, accessed at https://www.davidgarrow.com/2019-2.

    The FBI material regarding Dorothy Cotton was confirmed independently by Jason Miller, who had interviewed Cotton before her death. His article includes audio clips in which she describes her long-term intimate relationship with King. https://theconversation.com/the-civil-rights-activist-so-close-to-martin-luther-king-jr-she-was-thought-of-as-his-other-wife-118750. One example from the recent FBI files follows. King makes a long-distance call to a woman in Washington, DC, identified as Martha Carter:

    > Martin asks why Martha is not at work today. Martha reports that Martin Luther must be coming to town and remarks that Martin had to wait until the whole nation was coming to Washington before he could give Martha a call. Martha and Martin squabble about whether Martin has tried to call. . . . Martha then queries Martin: "Why you never call me, Babe?" Martin replies that he has. . . . Martha interrupts to say, "I will always love you. You can mistreat me. You can forget to call me, but I will always love you."

    This phone call is dated 4:54 p.m., August 23, 1963, and occurred during the lead-up to the March on Washington.
14. The FBI recorded a phone call on April 17, 1965, in which Tom Kahn and another anonymous person call Bayard Rustin:

    > Rustin: Incidentally, I got some new information on the Martin deal.
    >
    > [Name redacted]: I hope its better.
    >
    > Rustin: Well, it's worse. I've consulted with [name redacted] who feels the situation means about what you said, fatigue, but he's distressed with the whole sexual angle, that's more important than anything else.

> [Name redacted]: Well, it can be neurotic or psychotic and I don't think it's psychotic.
>
> Rustin: He said it's an extreme form of neuroticism which only occurs during periods of intense fatigue.
>
> [Name redacted]: Well, that makes a big difference, but no one can tell from a distance, but that's what it sounds like to me.

15. Interview, Ralph Abernathy, September 14, 1979, by David Garrow. David Garrow papers, Pittsburgh, PA, Manuscript Collection 832, Box 1.9, transcript p. 13.
16. One example is a letter from a Crozer friend, Horace Edward Whitaker, from 1952. He writes, "Dear Mike: Apparently you are still meeting these girls who are one-time wreckers. Watch the Doctor don't let one catch you with your shoes off [underlining in original]." *The Papers of Martin Luther King, Jr. Volume II: Rediscovering Precious Values, July 1951–November 1955*, ed. Clayborne Carson, Ralph Luker, Penny A. Russell, and Peter Holloran (Berkeley: University of California Press, 1994), p. 159. Whitaker would become a minister in New York and his native Virginia.
17. Rev. William Talbot Handy Jr. was a classmate of King at Boston University for one year and then left to become a minister in a church in Louisiana. Soon after leaving Boston, on November 18, 1952, Handy wrote the following letter to his old friend:

> Dr. M. L. King, Jr. (Not the real Doctor)
> 745 Commonwealth Ave.
> Boston 15, Mass.
> Dear M.L.:
> I imagine you were not expecting a letter from me at all, but I assure you that I have not forgotten you nor will I ever. The year we fellowshiped together has made a lasting imprint upon my heart and shall never be obliterated. Then too, if we did drift the relationship between Ruth and the other members of your family would always maintain some sort of tie.
>
> How is old B.U.? I miss the gang in the room solving the problems of the world, politically, socially, and in the theological realm. If only the people of the world would listen to us, there would be no trouble. How is Mac? Has he decided to relieve himself of his many responsibilities? Does he still jump up in the air and kick his heels together? I certainly hope he does something before he has a nervous breakdown. . . .
>
> I know you are now married? Which one was it? No, I know you are still galivanting around Boston, the most eligible and popular bachelor in town. I wonder how you are progressing without my steadying influence gone. Remember M.L., "we are expecting great things from you." The only element to restrain our expectations from bearing fruit will be M.L. himself. However I know that he will not allow himself or influences to bring failure about him or embarrassment to his beloved Father and Mother. I won't preach to you anymore.

To explain the quote in the letter, Clayborne Carson interviewed Handy:

> Handy later explained in a telephone interview that he was quoting a letter written to King, Jr., by Alberta Williams King the previous year. Handy had visited the senior Kings during one of his frequent trips to Atlanta to be with his wife, Ruth, who was teaching at an Atlanta school with Christine King. "We'd go by the [Kings'] house where they fed us and all that kind of thing. Once I went down there and said to Mrs. King how popular he was, how the girls were after him, how he wasn't doing anything wrong, but that he was very popular. . . . She wrote him very soberly and I remember that he shared the letter with me. She said I'd been there and that she'd heard some things about him and she just wanted to be sure that he gets there straight. And she wrote those words, 'Remember M.L., we're expecting great things from you' " (Handy, interview with Clayborne Carson, 1 July 1992). Alberta King's letter has not been located. https://kinginstitute.stanford.edu/king-papers/documents/w-t-handy-jr

18. MLK BU archives, Box 34, Folder 3, https://kinginstitute.stanford.edu/king-papers/documents/walter-r-mccall-0.

19. David Garrow, *Bearing the Cross* (New York: HarperCollins, 2004 [1986]), p. 109.
20. Branch, *Parting the Waters*, p. 119.
21. Ralph David Abernathy, *And the Walls Came Tumbling Down* (New York: Harper, 1989), pp. 474–475:

> I had only one real conversation with Martin on this subject. He was involved with a young woman and her closeness to Martin had been spotted by some of the reporters. . . . Martin and I were thrown in jail again and once more shared a cell, where we were left alone for most of the day. Realizing that I would never have a better opportunity, I brought up the matter. "Martin," I said, ". . . whatever your relationship with her, you need to cool it down. With Hoover's men hiding under every bed, you just can't afford to continue the way you have." Sitting there on the edge of the cot, he stared at the wall for a long time. . . . "Ralph, what you say may be right, but I don't care. Nor do I care what Mr. Hoover thinks or says. The FBI can do whatever they please, but I have no intention of cutting off this relationship." I nodded my head and changed the subject. I was disappointed in his reaction. . . . We never talked about the matter again.

22. Abernathy, *And the Walls Came Tumbling Down*, p. 471.
23. *Jet* magazine reported this hospitalization as follows: "The Reverend Martin Luther King Jr. was hospitalized at Philadelphia's Mercy–Douglass Hospital for a two-day 'physical check-up,' according to his personal physicians, Dr. Harold E. Pierce Jr. and Harry L. Thomas" ("Hospitalized Martin Luther King for 'Check-Up,'" December 14, 1961). Mercy–Douglass, a segregated hospital, closed on July 20, 1973. I found no access to any hospital records that existed there in the past.
24. King Library and Archives, The King Center, Atlanta, dated December 15, 1961, Box 7, File 24.
25. Dr. Pierce went on to describe evidence of diverticulosis (a common incidental finding in adults of small outpouchings in the colon, which can sometimes become infected, producing abdominal symptoms) and recommended not eating small seeds that might get stuck in the diverticuli, leading to infection. He also noted a scar on Dr. King's right chest, the result of stabbing, and recommended that nothing need be done to it unless it became painful. He ended by expressing his admiration: "I have decided to forego usual consultation fees and I join with many other friends and well wishers to wish you Godspeed in your noble fight to bring liberty and justice to all people in our time." The question of why King had urinary symptoms was left unwritten. King Library and Archives, The King Center, Atlanta, Box 7, File 24.
26. Cited in Lewis V. Baldwin, *Behind the Public Veil: The Humanness of Martin Luther King Jr.* (Minneapolis, MN: Fortress Press, 2016), p. 263.
27. Christine King Farris, *Through It All* (New York: Atria, 2009), p. 58.
28. King Farris, *Through It All*, 58, pp. 145–152.
29. Cited in Baldwin, *Behind the Public Veil*, p. 20.
30. King Sr. with Riley, *Daddy King*, p. 126.
31. Summarized in Baldwin, *Behind the Public Veil*, pp. 28–29.
32. Garrow, *Bearing the Cross*, p. 35.
33. Chuck Fager, *Eating Dr. King's Dinner: A Memoir of the Movement* (Durham, NC: Kimo Press, 2014).
34. Abernathy, *And the Walls Came Tumbling Down*, p. 478.
35. Rev. Vincent Harding, "Introduction to 'Unfulfilled Dreams,' in *A Knock at Midnight* (CD audio of 12 sermons), ed. Clayborne Carson and Peter Holloran (New York: Grand Central Publishing, 1998), https://kinginstitute.stanford.edu/encyclopedia/harding-vincent-gordon. Interview with Reverend James Bevel, by Katherine Shannon, July 6, 1968, The Civil Rights Documentation Project, transcript, in David Garrow papers, Manuscript Collection 832.
36. John A. Williams, *The King God Didn't Save* (New York: Pocket Books, 1971), p. 181.
37. Arthur M. Schlesinger, *Robert Kennedy and His Times* (Boston: Houghton Mifflin, 2002 [1978]), p. 218.

38. King Sr. with Riley, *Daddy King*, p. 127.
39. Ibid., p. 144.
40. Garrow, *Bearing the Cross*, p. 367.
41. Powers, *I Shared the Dream*.
42. https://www.ajc.com/news/local/julius-ehik-fled-nazism-communism/1D84FxzpMyA91GHWdkyxZL, accessed March 14, 2023.
43. J. Ehik, "The Use of Thioridazine in the Treatment of Acute Brain Syndrome Due to Alcohol," *Journal of the Medical Association of Georgia* 57, no. 7 (1968): 347–348.
44. Interview with Dr. Clifford Beal, by video, Atlanta, February 21, 2023. Beal stated that A. D. King likely had bipolar disorder, in his professional opinion, with symptoms of "mood swings" along with a "temper." His view was that "there's a lot of mood disorders in the [King] family," which he later defined as having "mood swings" and being "high energy people."
45. "Dr. King's Brother Drowns in Atlanta Home Pool," *The New York Times*, July 22, 1969.
46. https://www.nytimes.com/1969/07/30/archives/a-d-king-autopsy-finding.html.
47. https://www.seattletimes.com/nation-world/younger-brother-gets-lost-in-the-shadow-of-martin-luther-king.
48. Powers, *I Shared the Dream*, p. 176.

    > In between visits, M.L. telephoned me often, usually at night. One night he sounded very upset. "A.D. just phoned," he said. "He was drinking and he told me he was going to kill himself. Will you go over there and try to sober him up?" I rushed over to his brother's house. His wife, Naomi, took me to their bedroom. "A.D., what's wrong with you?" I demanded. "Why are you worrying your brother with such foolishness? Hasn't he got enough to think about?" "I was just kidding him," A.D. insisted. "I'll call him now and tell him I'm all right." He dialed the number and talked with M.L. for a few minutes. "I'm not going to do anything crazy," A.D. assured him. Then he handed the phone to me. "It's all right," I told Martin. "It was just his liquor talking." (p. 176)

    Powers explores A.D.'s psychology and describes conversations with his brother. She said,

    > "A.D. loves your father, but I think he has some underlying resentment of his unbending discipline. Your dad sounds like he was a dictator." "In our house he was the supreme authority," M.L. replied. "Do you think that overpowering force from your dad had a psychological effect on A.D., and caused him to drink excessively?" I asked. "A.D. would have to undergo extensive analytical psychotherapy to get to the root cause of his problem," he said. (p. 159)

49. In the next generation of Kings, less is known understandably because of the medical confidentiality that most living people maintain, but King's daughter has been open about a crisis when she contemplated suicide. John Blake, "Moving Out of the Dreamer's Shadow: A King Daughter's Long Journey," August 25, 2013, CNN, https://www.cnn.com/2013/08/25/us/bernice-king-profile/index.html.

4

Years of Glory

In the early 1960s, the Kennedy White House had become a key ally to the efforts of Martin Luther King Jr. and his circle. In November 1963, the president's assassination was not only a harsh blow to the civil rights movement but also a personal omen.

King was forlorn, losing his strongest ally in the government and realizing as well that if the president could be killed, then his own safety was hardly ensured. As King and his family watched that day unfold on television in their Atlanta home, King's daughter, Yoki, commented, "Oh, Mommy, we're never going to get our freedom now." Martin III, aged 6 years, asked, "Daddy, President Kennedy was your best friend, wasn't he, Daddy?" In a way, he was, commented Coretta Scott King after the death of her own husband.

Kennedy had become King's friend indeed, a friendship whose loss King would come to rue after he fell out with Lyndon Johnson over the Vietnam War. Faced with his children's insistent questions, King spoke the truth softly to his wife: "This is what is going to happen to me also. I keep telling you, this is a sick society."[1]

The following year would be the peak of the civil rights movement's activities but a tough one for King personally. King was the leader of a wildfire of a movement. In 1964, 115 Southern cities saw 935 demonstrations, 11 Southern states conducted more than 20,000 arrests of civil rights activists, and 35 bombings occurred throughout the South in relation to civil rights actions.[2]

In January 1964, *TIME* magazine chose King as Man of the Year, which was followed by news in October 1964 that he had been awarded the Nobel Peace Prize. King had come a long way. It seemed that fame wouldn't let him go: The more diffident King was, the more the world seemed to reward him.

But nemesis struck at the height of success. J. Edgar Hoover, the head of the Federal Bureau of Investigation (FBI), had been concerned about former communists in King's circle, throwing doubt on King's own loyalty to the United States. In 1963, after the March on Washington, Hoover and his top FBI

Soul on Fire. Nassir Ghaemi, Oxford University Press. © Oxford University Press 2026.
DOI: 10.1093/9780197657614.003.0005

lieutenants had concluded that King was "the most dangerous Negro" in the Nation.[3] The Nobel Prize was too much.

Hoover publicly denounced King for the first time. In an interview with reporters, he called King "the most notorious liar in the country" and said that the civil rights movement was "spearheaded by communists and moral degenerates."[4] King felt obliged to reply to deny the charges, and the back and forth was front-page copy in major media such as *The New York Times*.

Hoover decided to go on the attack. FBI agents put together a mix of explicit recordings and anonymously sent the summary tape to the Southern Christian Leadership Conference's headquarters in Atlanta, along with a letter implying that King should commit suicide.

The parcel sat unopened for some time and then was sent to the King home. Coretta opened it and listened to the tapes. She would say years later that it just sounded like "mumbo-jumbo" and she wasn't convinced it was sexual in nature. But the implication was clear when she read the accompanying letter:

> KING, In view of your low grade . . . I will not dignify your name with either a Mr. or a Reverend or a Dr. . . . King, look into your heart. You know you are a complete fraud and a great liability to all of us Negroes. . . . Clearly you don't believe in any personal moral principles. King, like all frauds your end is approaching. You could have been our greatest leader . . . not . . . a dissolute, abnormal moral imbecile.

The letter went on at some length in this manner, and ended thus: "You are an evil, abnormal beast. . . . King, there is only one thing left for you to do. You know what that is. . . . You better take it before your filthy, abnormal fraudulent self is bared to the nation."[5]

To the end of her life, according to those close to her, Coretta never believed that her husband had been unfaithful. She once said privately to King Papers historian Clayborne Carson, "If all that had happened, don't you think I would have known?"[6] She believed that the tapes had been forged by the FBI and that all the allegations of sexual indiscretions had been created by the FBI under the direct guidance of Hoover in an attempt to derail the civil rights movement when it had finally begun to achieve its goals.

King was hospitalized in Atlanta in October 1964 for one of his periods of "exhaustion"/depression, when he was notified of the Nobel award. He gave a press conference from the hospital.[7] Throughout the Nobel Prize period, King was an unhappy man. Much of his worry had to do with the increasing pressure from the FBI, but also other issues, such as a conflict with Ralph Abernathy and his wife Juanita, who believed that Abernathy should have received more recognition at the Nobel Prize presentation in Oslo, Norway.[8]

Coretta noted,

> Only Martin's family and close staff members knew how depressed he was during the entire Nobel trip. It was a time when he ought to have been happy. . . . We had to work with him and help him out of his depression. Somehow he managed all the official functions . . . and the public never knew what he was going through.[9]

King had left for Oslo in early December 1964, received the prize on December 10, and was back in the United States within a week. He received a hero's welcome by the mayor of New York; was flown to the White House for a private greeting by President Johnson; and was received in Atlanta by the choir of Ebenezer Baptist Church, which greeted him at the airport with Christmas carols amid a throng of reporters. By Christmastime, however, King was increasingly withdrawn.

One night, as he visited with his parents in their Atlanta home, King uncharacteristically left all of a sudden. He had been anxious and withdrawn enough that his mother was concerned about his sudden departure. Alberta King picked up the phone and called Atlanta's highest ranking Black police officer, Howard Baugh, who also had been a childhood friend of King Jr. Baugh later recounted that Mama King said her son "was very depressed." She and Baugh were "frightened to death" by his sudden departure from the house. Baugh spent the night searching the streets of Atlanta for King Jr. Eventually, he went to a factory where Black workers had been striking, an event that was prominent in the news, and which King supported. There, at midnight, he found the recent winner of the Nobel Peace Prize standing alone on the sidewalk. No one was around. Baugh asked King what he was doing. King said that he was waiting for the midnight shift to change so that he could speak to the workers. King didn't seem willing to go back home.[10] Baugh left King there, standing by himself.

* * *

Long before he became a public figure, the young King struggled with whether he should enter the ministry, like his father and grandfather. Like many young men, he was uncertain about what he should do with his life.

Every Tuesday morning, the young men of Morehouse College (it was all-male; its female counterpart was Spelman College) would gather to hear their president, Dr. Benjamin Mays, preach in Sale Hall. Being a Morehouse man was important to Mays. It meant being a professional who was well-educated, well-mannered, and devoted to helping the African American community. Three main kinds of professionals were trained: doctors, lawyers, and ministers. These were the leaders of the Black community.

The themes of May's Tuesday morning talks were that the young men assembled before him had an immense responsibility to undertake: They were the elite of the African American community, and they needed to lead that community toward freedom. Author of groundbreaking research on African American Christianity,[11] Mays taught a social gospel that viewed the Black Church as a means toward personal and political freedom. He wanted his students to be spiritually committed and socially aware. He sometimes talked to them about his meeting with Mahatma Gandhi, and he provided a Christian interpretation of the Indian leader's nonviolent methods. King would later talk about going "to Gandhi through Jesus."[12]

In the audience, young King Jr. soaked it in. He would go up to Dr. Mays after some talks and discuss certain aspects. He dropped by for "frequent chats," and bit by bit, over 3 years, May became what King later termed his "spiritual mentor."[13]

One influence Mays had on King was to convince the young man that his life calling was in the ministry. As King would say many times later, his great grandfather was a preacher, his grandfather was a preacher, his father was a preacher, his uncle was a preacher—his path seemed foreordained. But when he first entered Morehouse, King entertained the idea of going his own way. He loved the Black church, as exemplified by Ebenezer Baptist Church, but he was embarrassed by its emotionalism. The congregation shouted, stomped, sang, and laughed. His father preached to the emotions of his audience. It was all good, but the young King wondered whether it was respectable intellectually. Was it all sound and fury, an opium for the masses? Or was there any solid truth to it?

So King entered Morehouse doubting whether he should follow his father's example. He went through the list of professions: First, he wanted to become a doctor; then he wanted to become a lawyer; he hesitated about going into the family business. He decided to major in sociology, which had a requirement of a class in statistics.

King struggled and suffered; he couldn't make sense of the mean, the mode, and the median. He noticed that some of his classmates worked out the mathematical answers to statistical questions quickly. But the more he tried to be as quick as they were, the more quickly he was "flunking out of the course,"[14] as he later stated. One fellow in particular, Leif Cane, was a whiz at statistics, and young King was envious.

Finally, King realized that he couldn't handle statistics. He said to himself, "Now, Martin Luther King, Leif Cane has a better mind than you."[15] What took Cane[16] an hour would take King two or three hours, and even then King might not get it right.

This class in statistics taught King an important lesson. He had to recognize his limitations. He didn't have the intellect for mathematics or the sciences. He wasn't cut out for medicine; he also didn't really have a passion for the law. He had no sudden enlightenment, but by his last year at Morehouse, when he looked inside himself, he developed a gradual realization that ministry felt right.

Notes

1. Coretta King, *My Life With Martin Luther King Jr.* (New York: Holt, Rhinehart & Winston, 1969), p. 244.
2. John A. Williams, *The King God Didn't Save* (New York: Pocket Books, 1971), p. 151.
3. Assistant FBI director William C. Sullivan wrote an internal memo after the March on Washington in which he described King's famous speech there as a "a powerful demagogic speech." He continued: "We must mark [King] now, if we have not done so before, as the most dangerous Negro of the future in the Nation from the standpoint of communism, the Negro and national security." David Garrow, *The FBI and Martin Luther King Jr.* (New York: Norton, 1981), p. 68.
4. Ibid., p. 22. Garrow describes how top Hoover aides tried to specify to reporters that his personal attacks on King should be off the record, but reporters declined.
5. David Garrow, *Bearing the Cross* (New York: HarperCollins, 2004 [1986]), p. 373.
6. Clayborne Carson, *Martin's Dream: My Journey and the Legacy of Martin Luther King Jr.* (New York: Palgrave Macmillan, 2013), p. 118.
7. This hospitalization occurred at St. Joseph's Hospital in Atlanta, under the supervision of one of King's physicians, Dr. Asa G. Yancey Sr. According to *Jet* magazine,

   > Dr. King entered the hospital suffering from a severe virus condition, but his primary objective is complete rest. Said Mrs. Coretta Scott King, Dr. King's wife: "He delivered three major speeches in three different cities over the weekend. When he returned he was completely exhausted, tired and empty."

   "Why Dr. M. L. King Jr. Entered an Atlanta Hospital," *Jet*, October 29, 1964.
   During the hospitalization, King was noted as having "high normal" blood pressure, but no overall medical illness was identified. The article noted that the hospital was newly desegregated and Dr. Yancey was its first Black physician and King was its first Black patient. A local television newsclip captured the event: http://crdl.usg.edu/export/html/ugabma/wsbn/crdl_ugabma_wsbn_38277.html?Welcome.
8. These events are documented in Garrow, *Bearing the Cross*. It is notable that in his long autobiography, Abernathy omits any mention of the Nobel Prize or the trip to Oslo with King.
9. Garrow, *Bearing the Cross*, p. 366.
10. Ibid., p. 369.
11. Benjamin Mays, *The Negro's God* (Eugene, OR: Wipf & Stock, 2010 [1938]).
12. Garrow, *Bearing the Cross*, p. 75.
13. Of all his teachers and mentors, it is said that Dr. Benjamin Mays approximated the most complete role model for King. In his Crozer years, one can find some evidence that King was searching for a role model. The 20-year-old seminary student had been impressed by an apocryphal story about Mozart's first recital (when he was only a 12-year-old). He wrote it verbatim in his lecture notes, in his pencil handwriting. The young Crozer student wrote,

    > The story is told of how Mozart the great musician reacted at his first recital.
    >
    > It is said that when he was to give his first recital he became very nervous as all beginners do. He realized that all the royalty would be there. He realized the critics from every corner of the continent would be present. So he said to his master: "I can't do the job." But the master said: "You must. . . . I am going to sit in the balcony

> and every gesture I make you make every move I make you make." And so that night Mozart appeared before this audience and as he began to play, he placed his eyes on the master. Every move he made Mozart made, every gesture he made Mozart made, and as he played that night, the very souls of men were shaken.

MLK BU Archives, Box 1, Folder 2. The paragraph has been corrected grammatically.

14. These comments were made in what is probably his favorite sermon, "Three Dimensions of a Complete Life." He gave this sermon as his trial sermon when he was auditioning for his first job at Dexter Avenue Baptist Church in Montgomery, Alabama; it's also the sermon he gave in London on his way to receive his Nobel Prize. The specific quotes here are from the occasion when he is recorded as giving it on April 9, 1967, in the collection of sermons available in audio form as *A Knock at Midnight*, a CD audio of 11 sermons edited by Clayborne Carson and Peter Holloran (New York: Grand Central Publishing, 1998). The text of "Three Dimensions" can be found in the following transcript of his first presentation of it at Dexter in 1954, but it doesn't included the quotations in the text, which are from the 1967 audio version: https://kinginstitute.stanford.edu/king-papers/documents/dimensions-complete-life-sermon-dexter-avenue-baptist-church. The 11 sermons in the *A Knock at Midnight* audio collection are the most definitive collection of King's sermons and the best resource to hear and understand him. Each sermon is preceded by an introduction from a friend of King or other prominent ministers. The following sermons are included:

    February 28, 1954—Rediscovering Lost Values
    November 4, 1956—Paul's Letter to American Christians
    November 17, 1957—Loving Your Enemies
    1963—A Knock at Midnight
    July 4, 1965—The American Dream
    June 5, 1966—Guidelines for a Constructive Church
    April 9, 1967—The Three Dimensions of a Complete Life
    August 27, 1967—Why Jesus Called a Man a Fool
    February 4, 1968—The Drum Major Instinct
    March 3, 1968—Unfulfilled Dreams
    March 31, 1968—Remaining Awake Through a Great Revolution

15. "The Three Dimensions of a Complete Life," in *A Knock at Midnight*.
16. Leif James Cane graduated from Morehouse and became chief accountant at the Universal Life Insurance Company in Memphis, Tennessee (*Jet*, February 12, 1976, p. 21).

5

"His Ability Exceeds His Record"

In the Selma, Alabama, campaign of 1965, King experienced perhaps the greatest success of his leadership. The Selma movement had been started by James Bevel, a staff member of the Southern Christian Leadership Conference (SCLC). In late 1963, just after the Birmingham church bombing that killed four young girls, Bevel and his wife Diane Nash had come to the conclusion that something more needed to be done. As they watched the news on television about the deaths of the girls in Sunday school, Nash and Bevel fell to their knees and vowed they would respond.[1] They decided to move the struggle from desegregation to voting rights, and they joined others who had begun to take steps to register voters in the city of Selma, where the majority was Black but less than 1% of Blacks were registered to vote. The vast majority of the population lived below the poverty line. The literacy test was enough to prevent most Blacks from voting.

Bevel and others eventually convinced King and the SCLC to join the voter registration movement in Selma, knowing that massive protests would be needed.

King was reluctant to start another campaign in Selma. He told his friend Ralph Abernathy that he was convinced he'd be killed there. Abernathy wondered why King was so despondent. After he and Abernathy went to Selma and were imprisoned, King's mood became gloomier. When freed, he was invited to the White House. President Lyndon Johnson hoped to convince King to end the Selma campaign in return for a promise of a voting rights bill. King wasn't certain what to do. He suddenly fell ill, couldn't eat well, developed diarrhea, and was anxious and disturbed. He went into the hospital for a few days and lay in bed.

In the meantime, Bevel and other SCLC leaders moved forward in Selma. A young Black man, Jimmie Lee Jackson, was killed by state troopers. Bevel decided to organize a march from Selma to Montgomery, like Gandhi's famous salt march to the sea. The long days of marching would get the attention of the world.[2]

Soul on Fire. Nassir Ghaemi, Oxford University Press. © Oxford University Press 2026.
DOI: 10.1093/9780197657614.003.0006

King left his hospital bed to confer with SCLC and Student Nonviolent Coordinating Committee (SNCC) leaders in Selma. He couldn't lead the march, and it appears those around him didn't want him to do so either. Both King and Abernathy returned to Atlanta. By the time the initial march was planned, King was against it. Andrew Young and others called him in Atlanta, and King asked them to call it off. Young told him that 300 people were ready and they would just march to the end of the bridge, meet the state troopers, and then turn around once they were stopped. King gave his approval but wanted to avoid a scene. Don't send a bunch of people to jail, he advised Young.

Young and the other organizers decided that the marchers would move forward in formations of two persons, and they had to choose the two people to be in the first line. John Lewis said that because he represented SNCC, he should be one of the two in the front of the march. The other person could represent SCLC, and the top three SCLC members there—Young, Hosea Williams, and James Bevel—had to choose among them. The three men tossed a coin and Williams lost.[3] So although Lewis is seen beaten in his head in the terrible scenes that followed, the middle-aged man standing just as courageously next to him was World War II veteran Hosea Williams. Upon returning to the United States, still dressed in his military uniform, he was beaten and left for dead in Alabama when he drank from a Whites only fountain. Williams was ready for Selma.

The attack that ensued and was shown later on national television galvanized an outcry nationwide that led to the eventual march from Selma to Montgomery that King would lead with a large crowd of clergy and activists, Northern and Southern, Black and White.

When King gave his final speech in Montgomery at the end of that march, he wouldn't know that it would be his last final triumphant speech in the civil rights movement.

It was the high tide of the movement. From there, a gradual denouement would ensue that would end in a motel in Memphis.

* * *

James Bevel was very close to King and was a central leader in many major civil rights successes. "Bevel was the only man who consistently had King's ear," said Reverend Al Sampson, who believed that others around King envied Bevel for his access and influence.[4] Bevel was a key planner of the most successful mass direct action SCLC campaigns in the South, especially Birmingham (where Bevel organized children and adolescents to march in 1963, leading to the indelible images of fire hoses and dogs being used on them by Bull Connor's police), the 1965 Selma to Montgomery voting rights march (which also provoked police brutality in the classic Edmund Pettis bridge scenes), and King's 1966 Chicago campaign. Ralph Abernathy considered Bevel "the number three man in the movement" after King and himself; he added that "the civil rights movement would not have been as successful as it was, and Dr. King could not have done the things that he did unless he had a James Bevel."[5] Bevel insisted on wearing a yarmulke, although he wasn't Jewish, to honor the Hebrew prophets, he said, but also to trick Mississippi sheriffs. (Bevel wasn't unique; SCLC staff distributed yarmulkes to non-Jewish volunteers in Selma, "knowing the importance of Jewish support to the movement."[6]) "Those who knew Bevel well," biographer Taylor Branch writes, "like John Lewis and Bernard Lafayette, knew that he lived on the wispy edge between religious genius and lunacy." Branch reports that King "respected the 'voices' Bevel claimed to hear" and that "in moments of stress, Bevel served as a reminder that there was an essential element of craziness to the movement."[7]

In later years, as discussed in more detail in Chapter 18, Bevel was psychiatrically hospitalized. Perhaps it was his own personal experience that led Bevel to use the phrase "political psychiatry," the view being that the psychology of nonviolence was the only way to heal the racism that is a sickness in White America. As he said in a 1968 interview,

> The American White people are . . . the most savage, bestial, corrupt, murderous people on earth; and they engage in war games, killing, scheming, tricking all the time. They can't help that. It's not because they are mean. It's because they are mentally ill.[8]

This sounds, and is, harsh, but the perspective is one of the physician wanting to heal, and not denying the severity of the diagnosis. Of course it is a metaphor, but it's another twist to the psychiatric metaphors that characterized much of the thinking of leading civil rights leaders such as King and Bevel.

King was at his busiest in these years. He relied on many kinds of people, not just impulsive ones such as Bevel but also eminently calm ones, such as Stanley Levison, his New York–based alter ego, who helped run the SCLC office there and also was central to his intellectual think tank called the "Research Committee," which helped King analyze current affairs and helped him write his own books and essays.[9] On the SCLC staff, Andrew Young later recalled how he and Walter Fauntroy (the main SCLC representative in Washington, DC) were viewed as the sane and stable members of the SCLC leadership, whereas almost all others were "strong egos" —leaders who were courageous if not reckless, sometimes impulsive:

> Martin always said, look, normal people don't challenge the law of the land. He said you got to be strong enough to be creatively maladjusted.

> And sometimes he said, Andy, you're too well-adjusted. You can adjust to segregation and you can teach other people to accept it. And rise above it personally. But we need people around who can't be adjusted. People who have to upset things. He said then after it's upset, you can go in and help settle it. But you would never upset anything.
>
> And so there was this nice mixture of people. He'd normally put me and Walter Fauntroy in the category of people who were . . . rational and logical about things. And he said I'm not trying to play you down or dis [you]. . . . You have a role too. But we need people to disturb the troubled waters. And you're not going to trouble the waters. And that's true.[10]

Later, after nearly two decades as the elected Washington, DC nonvoting delegate to Congress, Fauntroy also began to act erratically, spending money excessively, leading to bad debts, after which he fled the country to unknown locations in the Arabian Gulf. He returned to the United States in 2016 and was arrested briefly as a fugitive (see Chapter 18).

According to Bernard Lafayette, King knew that Bevel was mentally unstable and yet brilliant. King probably sensed that something was awry in his own feelings at times: His depression made sense in the context of his political struggles, but he also spoke of the "schizophrenia in my soul," the "inner civil war" between his North and South, and his "Dr. Jekyll and Mr. Hyde." King knew there was something different about him: "I am conscious of two Martin Luther Kings," he said once privately, "I am a wonder to myself."[11]

* * *

The salvation of humanity lies in the hands of the creatively maladjusted, King believed. This was a great insight: It's not just any maladjustment but, rather, a creative kind that is most needed. Otherwise, maladjustment lies perilously close to a harmful insanity.

The hindsight of the historian is overly confident, however. Who can know when any person is too maladjusted or not maladjusted enough? At least, if we appreciate this notion, we can be prepared to accept the idea that being maladjusted can be good and being "adjusted," our central feature of mental health even today, can be harmful. Speaking at a college decades after King had spoken there on the maladjustment theme, Vincent Harding reflected: "In his wonderful way, [King] was challenging us to be maladjusted. We want to be adjusted to, in step with, the world. But can you really be a Christian and be 'adjusted' all the time? Was *Jesus* 'adjusted'?"[12]

The young King Jr. was in a hurry. He had sped his education up, taking enough credits to graduate in 3 years, effectively skipping his senior year so that he graduated college at age 18 years. In his final year at Morehouse, he took classes with the chair of the Department of Religion, George D. Kelsey, who was the first classroom professor to have an influence on King's thinking. In fact, Kelsey would give King the only "A" he ever received in his college studies. Kelsey's intellectual rigor, applied skeptically to the Bible and Christian theology, gave King a sense of inspiration. He developed the feeling that his Christian beliefs, obtained in the emotional cauldron of Ebenezer Baptist Church's stomping congregation, could be put through a process of scholarly analysis, and the results could be, as he later stated, both "intellectually respectable as well as emotionally satisfying." As King later noted, at Morehouse "the shackles of fundamentalism were removed from my mind."[13]

For the rest of his life, King would apply this dual approach to his spirituality: an emotional base filtered through intellectual analysis. He would be an "evangelical liberal" in religion—evangelical because he affirmed the personal and emotional nature of faith, but liberal because he rejected literal interpretations of the Bible and he accepted historical and sociological analyses of the Bible and of Christianity.

He would, like his father and grandfather and great-grandfather, become a preacher after all.

King Jr. always had known that his father hoped and prayed that the son would follow the paternal footsteps, become a minister, and take over the family business at Ebenezer. Kelsey and Mays showed young King Jr. that he could satisfy his father's hopes while being true to his own intellectual ambitions. Of his Morehouse mentors Mays and Kelsey, King would later write, "I could see in their lives the ideal of what I wanted a minister to be."[14]

King wanted to be part of the larger intellectual world, not just the world of the Black church. Like Mays and Kelsey, he wanted both. His Morehouse years showed young King that this new ideal existed, and he decided to devote himself to achieving it.

King Sr. was ecstatic. His prayers had been realized. Later, A.D. would follow in the same footsteps, although less successfully, but at least the family vocation remained intact. The father arranged for a trial sermon, King Jr.'s first pulpit sermon, in the younger man's last year at Morehouse. The line into the church that Sunday was so long that the venue had to be changed from the sanctuary to an auditorium. Eighteen-year-old Martin Luther King Jr. would preach for the first time in public. The sermon was well received by the congregation, and Daddy King was pleased. Most of it was taken from one of his favorite sources, the liberal New York minister Harry Emerson Fosdick.[15]

In the early spring of 1948, in King Jr.'s final months of college, his father had made arrangements for his ordination at Ebenezer as a Baptist minister, along with two ministers who were family friends and Morehouse professors (but who had not taught King Jr. in college).[16] King Sr. officiated the ceremony, prayed with his son, and discussed his beliefs. King Jr. expressed new liberal interpretations he had learned at Morehouse: He didn't accept the Bible as literal expression of God's words but, rather, historically as a document written by men. Hence, he rejected some fundamentalist doctrines, such as Bible literalism about the virgin birth. Although his father believed in the literal truth of such Bible stories, he and his colleagues still agreed to ordain young King. He was one of them, part of the Ebenezer home, even though he was liberal in his interpretations.

In addition to helping him reach decision about his life vocation, Morehouse provided young King Jr. with an active outlet for social life and his first adult experiences.

He engaged in college life with gusto.

* * *

There were 204 other students in King's class. Although he was a few years younger than others, and still lived with his parents, King jumped into social activities. He became president of the sociology club, joined the debating team and the glee club, and played on the Butler Street YMCA basketball team. He joined the student council and became a member of the college chapter of the National Association for the Advancement of Colored People.

King entered oratorical competitions, winning second prize twice. He also became increasingly socially conscious, writing a letter to the editor of the main Atlanta newspaper about some racial murders that had occurred.

For two summers, one before Morehouse and the other during college, he joined other students to work on a tobacco farm in Connecticut. This summer experience was meant to allow King to appreciate the lives of the working class, to experience farm labor; he could have had easier summer jobs, but he apparently took the tobacco farm work as a means of expanding his life experience with the poor. The trips to Connecticut also informed him for the first time about the differences in life in the North versus the South. When the train reached Washington, DC, he no longer had to sit in Black-only areas. When he returned South from his summer job, upon reaching the nation's capital, the ironically placed border of racial segregation, he moved from integrated to segregated cars.

Young King tasted the social freedom of the integrated North, and he grew even more disenchanted with life under segregation in the South.

In addition to deciding to become a minister, young King's main activity at Morehouse was to have fun. He earned the nickname "Tweed" because he dressed so stylishly. Despite the fact that his father opposed dancing and drinking on Southern Baptist religious grounds, King did both. Some who knew him thought he may suffered from "PK syndrome"—being a preacher's kid.[17] Because ministers had high social status in the African American community, their families were under great scrutiny. Their children in particular would be watched by the congregation to see if they lived up to Biblical standards. The result predictably would be either conformism or rebellion, as was the case most overtly with A.D. and to some extent with King Jr. Both danced and drank and partied, while King Sr. did his best to discipline them and control them. Once in college, however, the King boys were out of the orbit of their father's complete control, and they showed it. King Jr. had a lot of fun in particular with his friend Walter McCall, and the two "became almost inseparable friends," known as "Mac and Mike."[18]

Popular with both women and men, young King Jr. blossomed quickly at Morehouse. He was extroverted and funny and fun. His college years began a process that would be a truth for his future life: King would love to be around people, and people would love to be around King.[19]

He was known to have a number of girlfriends at Morehouse. Sexually popular even before becoming a powerful man, his romantic entanglements were numerous and often short-lived. His brother A.D. said of the college King, "He kept flitting from chick to chick. I don't think he ever kept one regular girlfriend for more than a year—two at most."[20] "He just loved to party. He enjoyed life," said McCall.[21]

The extent of King's focus on his social life as opposed to his studies was such that it led historian Clayborne Carson, who has spent more years studying the career of Martin Luther King Jr. than King was active during that career, to conclude that King "was never a strong student. He preferred to party and use his college years to hone his oratorical skills."[22]

That was Mike King Jr.—a funny, fun-loving man. But he was beginning to develop a serious side. He had decided to become a minister. Now he would enter the seminary.

* * *

First, he had to get accepted somewhere, and he had to do so with a less than stellar academic record. In 4 years of college at Morehouse, he had obtained only one A (from Dr. Kelsey in a course on the Bible).

He had 20 B's, 18 C's (including one in Church History), 1 D (in French), and 11 Passes. (He had 1 incomplete in statistics, which he later completed with a C grade.) His overall grade point average was 2.48, equivalent to a C+.[23]

King decided to apply to theological seminary at the mostly White Crozer Theological Seminary near Philadelphia. He chose Crozer because he wanted to go North for further education, like his mentors Mays and Kelsey had done. He had tasted some of the freedoms of the North, and he had begun to interact with White students in Atlanta through the Intercollegiate Conference, a group that met at Emory University once monthly. He wanted more interactions with Whites than he could have in the South, and Crozer was one of the seminaries that was well-known to encourage and accept Black applicants.

He would need excellent letters of recommendation to offset his middling grades, and he would need to rely on the willingness of seminaries such as Crozer to allow for lower grades among Black applicants, given backgrounds where they had started with fewer educational opportunities than their White peers.

King got the recommendations. Mays wrote of him and another applicant to Crozer that they had "good minds" and were capable of "substantial B work" but they were "not brilliant students." Kelsey noted of King in another letter that his record was "short of what may be called 'good' " but that he was "one of those boys who came to realize the value of scholarship late in his college career. His ability exceeds his record at Morehouse."[24]

Crozer accepted King in 1948, and from that point on, King's ministerial and public career would move forward in a straight line.

Notes

1. Interview with Diane Nash by David Garrow, July 17, 1983, transcript, p. 7. David Garrow papers, Emory University, Atlanta, Manuscript Collection 832, Box 8.1, Item 7.
2. Interview with Bernard Lafayette by James Findlay, interview 7, pp. 24–27, https://www.loc.gov/folklife/civilrights/survey/view_collection.php?coll_id=949. The fact that Bevel initiated the march from Selma to Montgomery is documented also in an interview of Ralph Abernathy by Randall Kryn: "The famous Selma to Montgomery march was conceived by Jim Bevel." Randall Kryn, "James L. Bevel: The Strategist of the 1960s Civil Rights Movement," in *We Shall Overcome: The Civil Rights Movement in the US in the 1950s and 1960s*, ed. David Garrow (Brooklyn, NY: Carlson, 1989), Vol. 2, pp. 517–535.
3. These details are provided in his *Eyes of the Prize* interview by Andrew Young, October 11, 1985, http://repository.wustl.edu/concern/videos/sf268667q. According to Young,

> We were all back in Atlanta when people began showing up in Selma to march from Selma to Montgomery. So they called me about nine o'clock in the morning, and, I jumped on a plane and went to Selma. And when I got to Selma, I saw, driving in from Montgomery, I saw all of the State Troopers on horseback, and I saw them with their teargas masks, but they were all standing around. There must have been a couple hundred of them, and they were all standing around, you know, in a very relaxed sort of manner, not looking menacing at all. And, so when I went, across the bridge going to the church, they didn't bother me and I didn't stop and bother them. But we called Dr. King, and we—he had asked us to call off the march. And we persuaded him that since there were about three hundred people there, maybe they could go ahead and march, that they weren't going to get far anyway, that we had seen the State Troopers and they were going to probably stop them and turn them around, or maybe they would, people would get arrested. So, he said, well, OK, go ahead and march, he said, but don't you all go to jail. And we thought that what was going to happen was that we would march over there and everybody would be arrested. So, John Lewis and Hosea

> Williams and I, and James Bevel, decided that only two should go. Well, John said, well, I represent SNCC, so I'll go, and one of you, you all decide which one will go. So we played odd man, and we flipped a coin and the odd man got to march, and the odd man was Hosea Williams. And—but nobody anticipated the kind of savagery and brutality that occurred.

4. Ben Joravsky, "James Bevel Turns to the Right: 20 Years Ago He Was One of Martin Luther King's Most Trusted Advisers. Now He's on Ronald Reagan's Side. Is He a Leader, or Is He Lost?" *Reader: Chicago's Free Weekly*, July 20, 1984, Vol. 13, No. 24.
5. Kryn, "James L. Bevel," p. 535. Like the manic–depressive General William Sherman, Bevel's creativity had a dark side. Bevel was intimidating; King and Andrew Young and many SCLC figures were nonconfrontational by nature, and Bevel sometimes needed serious confronting. Bernard Lafayette emerged as one person who could challenge Bevel. As Lafayette said,

> My approach to Bevel was to ask him questions to get him to think about what he was doing, not to argue with him. Some people said that I was the only person that could argue with Bevel. That's only partly true. No one could really argue with him. I got Bevel to argue with himself.

For example, Lafayette noted that when Bevel left King to go join the anti-Vietnam War campaign, his former SCLC friends noticed that "Bevel was coming up with strategies and decision-making that was highly questionable." He continued:

> King sent me up there to see if I could bring him back from New York to Atlanta. He had gotten an artist to draw a painting/poster with LBJ holding a Vietnamese baby in his mouth, blood dripping down his shirt. It was kind of gross. [Bevel] also wanted to get a ship to sail people to Hanoi [without any real plans about what would happen once they got there]. . . . So I said to him, "Suppose someone gave you a boat and knew it wasn't seaworthy, you'd be suspicious wouldn't you?" Once he heard my questions, he realized that there must be a better way. If you argued with him, you got nowhere.

Interview with Bernard Lafayette, January 15, 2013.

6. "I donned my movement uniform: still-stiff denim overalls, a matching jacket and, incongruously, a yarmulke. Another staff member, who understood the importance of Jewish support to the movement, had passed them out to us not long before." Chuck Fager, *Eating Dr. King's Dinner: A Memoir of the Movement, 1963–1966* (Durham, NC: Kimo Press, 2014), Kindle edition, p. 3.
In fact, a large part of SCLC funds came from liberal Jewish allies, organized in part by Stanley Levison in New York. Levison was the central leader of the SCLC office in New York, and he also was highly active with the American Jewish Congress, where he served as treasurer. He also had been in charge of funding for the Communist Party, according to the Federal Bureau of Investigation (FBI). New FBI documents assert that "from 1957 through 1962, Levison gave [SCLC] . . . a total of $76,500; the equivalent of $650,000 today." https://www.thebulwark.com/what-are-we-supposed-to-think-of-martin-luther-king-jr-now. This amount of funding would have paid the salaries of the entire administrative and field staff of SCLC for a full year (based on the 1963 SCLC budget). https://www.crmvet.org/docs/orgsdocs.htm#docssclc.
7. Taylor Branch, *Parting the Waters* (New York: Simon & Schuster, 1988), pp. 753–754. Bevel was a polarizing figure. Wyatt Tee Walker, brought in to organize the quarreling executive staff of SCLC, was an outsider from Virginia. Highly organized and efficient, Walker found Bevel to be the opposite of what he valued. Yet, he found that King and the top SCLC leadership valued Bevel almost no matter what trouble he caused. Wyatt said in an interview, "I never liked Bevel. I won't say I didn't like him; we didn't' get along. Bevel didn't like me. I liked him" (transcript p. 82) and

> I called [Bevel] at Dr. King's direction from Chicago and told Bevel to go to Clarksdale, or something, to see about the situation there. Bevel thought I was trying to get him out of Birmingham and he cursed me out in front of my secretary and called me some vile names. When I came back I proceeded to require some reprimand of him. Who do

> you think the executive committee called in? Bevel? No! They called me in. And that settled it! I was done then. (transcript p. 93)

Walker left his SCLC work thereafter. Interview of Wyatt Tee Walker by John Britton, October 11, 1967, in David Garrow papers, Pittsburgh, PA, Manuscript Collection 832.

A contrasting example of Bevel's impact on the rank-and-file comes from Chuck Fager, a young White activist, new to the SCLC staff in Selma:

> And when I met Bevel, I was spellbound. Bevel was short, serious-looking, and charismatic. He stood out among the suits of the other Executive Staff members, because he wore the movement field uniform of overalls all the time, though with carefully starched and pressed dress shirts beneath them. He also shaved his head, an unheard of practice in those days, and covered it with a colorful, elaborately beaded yarmulke, which I gathered came from Africa. His voice was high and almost squeaky, but he had a natural eloquence and energy that was very magnetic.

Fager. *Eating Dr. King's Dinner*, p. 70.

8. In 1995, Bevel became a central organizer of the "Million Man March" on Washington, DC, led by Louis Farrakhan's Nation of Islam. A few years later, one of his adult daughters accused him of sexually abusing her and other daughters throughout their childhood (dating to the mid-1990s); taped confessions were produced in a Virginia court, which led to his 2008 conviction at age 72 years and imprisonment for a 15-year term. After serving 7 months, while free on bail during appeal, he died of cancer. His conviction was posthumously upheld by the Supreme Court of Virginia.

   Les Carpenter, "A Father's Shadow," *The Washington Post*, May 25, 2008.

   Bill Brubaker, "Civil Rights Leader Convicted of Incest," *The Washington Post*, April 11, 2008. Timothy Noah, "Bevel's Second Children's Crusade," *Slate*, April 10, 2008, https://slate.com/news-and-politics/2008/04/the-rev-james-bevel-hero-of-the-civil-rights-movement-is-convicted-of-incest.html.

   An interview intended to be produced as a documentary, conducted just before his death, shows him to be recalcitrant, with flashes of his trademark charisma, but without apparent remorse. https://www.youtube.com/playlist?list=PL6kViTwgpokIJ8Ouu0C3fB0Iy9kTi7O2g.
9. David Garrow, *Bearing the Cross* (New York: HarperCollins, 2004 [1986]), p. 332. The Research Committee consisted of Levison, Clarence Jones, Bayard Rustin, Harry Wachtel, and Cleveland Robinson, with others sometimes coming. It met with King approximately once monthly, usually in New York. One can notice King's intellectual respect for Bevel for allowing him to participate in this group at times. This was not a group in which Abernathy or others such as Hosea Williams would participate. Levison, Wachtel, and Rustin had past connections to the U.S. Communist Party, and some others, such as Robinson, were trade unionists. These connections emphasize how King's intellectual thinking tended to be leftist-oriented.
10. Andrew Young, *Eyes on the Prize* interview, October 11, 1985, p. 5, accessed at https://americanarchive.org/catalog/cpb-aacip_151-db7vm43n05.
11. Garrow, *Bearing the Cross*, p. 289.
12. http://www.bethelks.edu/news-events/news/post/4257.
13. Clayborne Carson, *Martin's Dream: My Journey and the Legacy of Martin Luther King Jr.* (New York: Palgrave Macmillan, 2013), p. 124.
14. *The Autobiography of Martin Luther King Jr.*, ed. Clayborne Carson (New York: Grand Central Publishing, 1998), p. 16.
15. Based on an interview with Larry H. Williams, King's first sermon mainly was based on a published sermon by Harry Emerson Fosdick, "Life Is What You Make It." I was unable to find that sermon in Fosdick's works. It has been used by other preachers, however. For instance, in 2020, it was presented here: https://www.rivercityia.org/sermons/your-life-is-what-you-make-it.
16. Lucius M. Tobin and Samuel W. Williams. They were not close to King Jr. as professors at Morehouse, but they were friends of King Sr. David Garrow, "The Intellectual Development of Martin Luther King, Jr.: Influences and Commentaries," *Union Seminary Quarterly Review* 40 (1986): 5–20.

17. James Farmer describes this concept in his memoir, quoted in Keith D. Miller, *Voice of Deliverance* (Athens: University of Georgia Press, 1998), pp. 38–39. It also was brought up in relation to King by Wilhelmina Harris. Interview with Wilhelmina Harris, Concord, MA, July 19, 2015.
18. Branch, *Parting the Waters*, p. 61.
19. King's college friend was Walter McCall, who was 6 years older than King. McCall later recalled that he didn't think that King took his studies very seriously; instead, he "loved the lighter side of life." *The Papers of Martin Luther King, Jr. Volume II: Rediscovering Precious Values, July 1951–November 1955*, ed. Clayborne Carson, Ralph Luker, Penny A. Russell, and Peter Holloran (Berkeley: University of California Press, 1994), p. 122.
A later letter in 1954, 6 years after graduating from Morehouse, when King began his public ministry in Montgomery, gives a sense of how the two friends had interacted and how their relationships with the opposite sex had been an important part of their friendship:

> Dear Mike,
> It was good to hear from you the other day, and to know that all things seem to be going your way. I must admit, however, that I thought that you had forgotten the Ole Boy. Yet, I do understand what it means to keep busy. . . . By the way, things here from the lady angle. I am going to get married. . . . I would like to have you serve as the best man. [King did not attend.] I suppose [a friend] told you about my other chick from N.C. who was down visiting me in Feb. . . . Doc., really she is beautiful, but she does not have what this girl has. I hate to break off from her, but I am ready to be married, so I am not willing to continue playing the field. [*Name deleted*] has gone to California. I gave her fifty dollars with the idea of helping to support the child, but that support only gave [*Name deleted*] a ray of hope to win me over to marry her although I have told her again and again that I am not going to do that. She has already worried the very day light out of me by long distance phone calls and a host of letters. So, instead of continuing that support, I have cut it off already. Never do I expect to help in any fashion. Man, [*Name deleted*] will harass me to death if I give her the least o' consideration. Hate to take that attitude, but I think I am wise in so doing. . . .
>
> Your pal, Mac.
> (Mamie Thompson who received her M.A. from B.U. [Boston University] is on our summer school faculty. Tell me, what is it between you and her?)

The Papers of Martin Luther King, Jr. Volume II, p. 235. Also accessible at https://kinginstitute.stanford.edu/king-papers/documents/walter-r-mccall-0.
20. Jerry Tallmer, "A Man with a Hard Head," in *Martin Luther King Jr: A Profile*, ed. C. Eric Lincoln (New York: Hill & Wang, 1970), p. 3.
21. McCall, interview by Herbert Holmes, March 31, 1970. King Archives, Atlanta.
22. C. Carson, "Martin Luther King Jr.: The Morehouse Years," *Journal of Blacks in Higher Education* 15 (1997): 121–125.
23. Ibid.
24. Garrow, *Bearing the Cross*, p. 38.

6

Years of Suffering

During the decade from the late 1950s to the late 1960s, Martin Luther King Jr. was hospitalized approximately once a year for medical reasons that were unclear at the time. The most common explanation was "exhaustion," but a review of available medical records indicates that no physical cause was ever found for King's exhaustion. Instead, some of the records indicated "nervous" causes for his physical exhaustion and other somatic symptoms (e.g., diarrhea). During these periods, King was extremely tired but couldn't sleep well, couldn't concentrate, lost motivation in his usual interests, had increased appetite, and experienced markedly sad mood. These periods usually lasted weeks. By current definitions, these symptoms would meet the standard of clinical depressive episodes. Andrew Young commented that King "became physically ill when . . . he was . . . emotionally low."[1] It seems that King had a dozen or so brief hospitalizations in the 1950s and 1960s, in between his adolescent window jumping and his end-of-life despair.

King's close friend, Ralph Abernathy, described how those hospitalizations would occur often at times of high stress, in the midst of major campaigns, such as the Selma marches.[2] King's colleagues would create reasons why King was not publicly active. Others noticed, but they didn't know why; as the northern Black writer and activist John Williams wrote in his 1970 study of King: "The record revealed that during every demonstration in which King participated, at the key moment when he was most acutely needed to lead a mass confrontation, he was absent."[3] Williams implied a lack of courage, but no one discussed or considered depression.

Sometimes King's depressive episodes would occur even during good periods, as described previously when King was traveling in Europe to receive his Nobel Prize award (Figure 6.1). Coretta Scott King, his wife, noted a paradoxical "depression" at a time when King should have been purely happy. The truth was unknown to the public, and probably to King and his family and friends as well.

Soul on Fire. Nassir Ghaemi, Oxford University Press. © Oxford University Press 2026.
DOI: 10.1093/9780197657614.003.0007

f depression seemed less obvious in the period of the young King's lies. Despite his mediocre grades, Crozer Theological Seminary young Morehouse graduate, who found himself for the first time 'hite environment—a liberal White environment in which he was a disparaged, minority. King was greatly attracted to the liberalism Protestant perspective, and he put aside forever the evangelical of his roots. In the future, he would seek to meld the personal and onal approach to God that he inherited from the Black evangelical the liberal–rationalist approach to religion he learned at Crozer. ence was George Washington Davis, the teacher at Crozer with ook the most classes. Another important resource was Kenneth Christian ethics course, which King took, was the first that Smith a few years older than King, Smith would remain a lifelong friend, 70s, he published a searching personal examination of the theolog- s on King's thinking.[12]

hat King learned grew out of the philosophy of existentialism, a way at grew in popularity after World War II. Prominent theologians ink Christianity in an existential sense—as a matter of personal ot just abstract belief. This worldwide movement resonated with g's experience of the emotional religion of his father and the Black existential Christianity provided a way for King to combine the world's theology with his roots. At Crozer, he became attracted logians of this ilk, such as Paul Tillich (about whom King would dissertation), Reinhold Neibuhr (whose political theory greatly ng's nonviolent methods), and Edgar Brightman (a leader in "per- logy, who viewed the relationship of man and God as being be- alities).

ar Philadelphia, in the town of Chester, Pennsylvania, Crozer was stant seminary, steeped in the teachings of the "social Gospel" and hese approaches interpreted Christianity in a modernized, liberal t was viewed as a man, not a God, who came to Earth to help the rejected. He abjured wealth and worldly success. Christianity is personal salvation—although it is partly that: It is equally about ice in society, including with political revolutions if needed. This Gospel perspective. The rationalist aspect was the view that re- mere emotion; it had to be consistent with reason and science. instance, can be shown to be written in a historical time, by dif- beings, with various alterations. Hence, it isn't simply God's word. e aspects of Christian belief, such as miracles, need to be rejected with scientific knowledge. The reasons for faith are as important

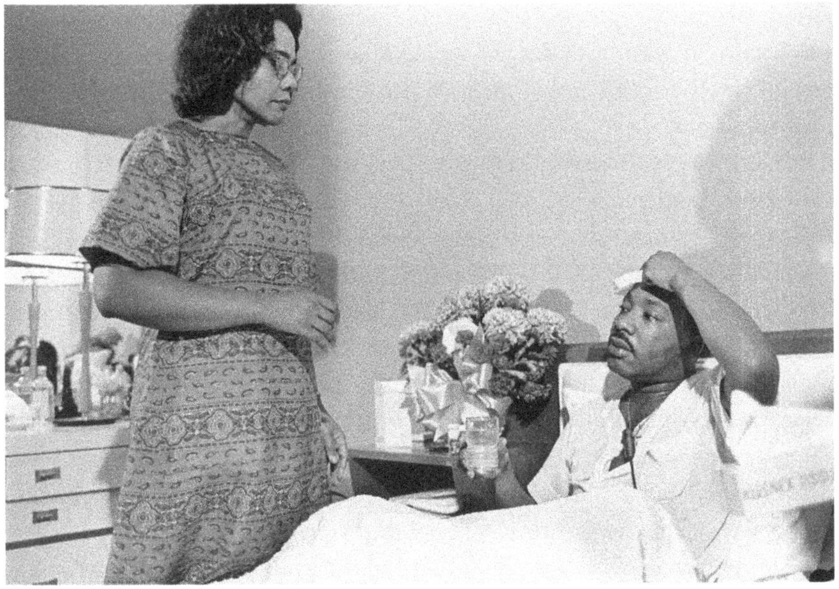

Figure 6.1 Martin Luther King Jr. with his wife Coretta, his only photographed hospitalization, in Atlanta 1964, when he was awarded the Nobel Prize.

King's hospitalizations may be the best proxy for possible depressive episodes. The late Ralph Abernathy wrote in his memoir that King's hospitalizations tended to occur at the height of stressful situations, such as during the march from Selma to Montgomery, producing some embarrassment and lack of leadership at crucial moments. Abernathy denied that the hospitalizations were due to stress or a mere "nervous stomach," because he cited the presence of physical symptoms such as fever and chills.[4] But Vincent Harding, who knew King from the 1950s onward, viewed those hospitalizations as related to stress:

> Periodically, he simply went into the hospital to get out of the normal processes of living his life. In a lot of ways, that was one of his retreats. He would go maybe once or twice a year, and stay maybe 3–4 days.[5]

Unless King had some serious medical illness that is still unknown to the public (as in the case of John Kennedy's Addison's disease, which was hidden from the public), it is difficult to explain, on purely medical illness grounds, the occurrence of multiple regular hospitalizations for an otherwise healthy man in his 30s. However, "somatic" symptoms of depression are common, and the decade of the 30s is the primary age at which episodes of depression begin to occur. Brief hospitalizations, under medical auspices, would provide the relief from stressors in the environment that could help reduce the severity of a depressive period. Depressive episodes resolve spontaneously, with or without treatment, thus being consistent with King's hospitalization rate of one or two times yearly. Except for Abernathy, in his memoir, no one has described these common hospitalizations.

When asked, Bernard Lafayette, one of King's Southern Christian Leadership Conference (SCLC) aides, remarked of King, "Usually he would be hospitalized medically, every couple of years or so. He needed to rest and slow down and sleep, to take a little mini-vacation. It usually lasted a few days."[6] Dr. William Anderson, a leader of the Albany, Georgia, civil rights movement, also confirmed this matter. Anderson knew King since adolescence, growing up in the same circles in Atlanta. Years later, Anderson would become a physician, the only medical man among the many preachers who were active civil rights leaders in the 1960s. He led the Albany desegregation movement, going to jail with King. He thus knew King well from the time King was an adolescent boy to the peak years of King's political activities. He also served as one of King's personal physicians. Thus, there are very few people as well placed as Anderson, alive today, who can discuss King's mental health. As noted previously, Anderson observed that King was, most of the time, highly energetic, active, sympathetic, and extroverted. But there were times when his high energy would end, and he would suddenly become tired and down and would need to get away from everyone. And these periods happened repeatedly throughout his life. Says Anderson,

> [King] was in remarkably good health and always he was mentally in control. He knew his limits; annually he would come up to Detroit and check into my hospital, for a day or two. There was the Park Statler Hotel and he would stay there 2–3 days. Usually like January or so. . . . There are those who say about me: nervous energy. The more stressed I got, the more I wanted to get out of the situation. Stress gave me the energy to go on another day. Martin was the same way: His energy was at the highest point when he was in the most stressful situations. Selma, Birmingham—he would reach a peak of energy and then he had to stop and he had to take time off. I was with him in New York once on a whirlwind: He spoke at 7 different churches one night. He thrived on what he was doing. If you had stopped him from doing it, like going to jail, that's when he became depressed.[7]

Anderson is describing an alternation between high energy and activity and low energy and depressed mood, with brief yearly hospitalizations in Detroit, not previously documented in other sources or archives but consistent with the reports of Abernathy, Harding, and Lafayette. Confirming these oral reports, there is

available documentation for medical ho
"exhaustion" in 1964 and 1965.[8]
One can give some detail on a specifi
King had a full medical evaluation at the
porary newspaper article provides the co
lead a 2½-mile march on city hall with a
ging downtown during rush hour. King w
"had been treated for exhaustion at the
and for a while it was doubtful that he w
had been exhausted by his three-day cam
the parade."
The record notes that King had fatig
some apparent diarrhea attributed to "n
not extreme (systolic 158 mm Hg/diast
the bronchitis; thus, neither finding co
of his examination was basically normal
fatigue and apparent diarrhea were due
plex injection—which has no proven s
nervous tension, and thus was essentiall
Exhaustion due to nervous tension n
cause one is stressed—or it can mean, w
that one is prone to major decline in ph
varied stressful life experiences. That des
ical depression, which is a disease (see A
These hospitalizations or urgent e
only lasting a day to a few days. Full cli
months. If these hospitalizations represe
they would not be traditional full clini
pressive states as part of cyclothymic te
consistent presence of manic and/or de
mild, but sometimes more severe (furth
It does not appear that King ever had
ical evaluation in his life, at least that has
a psychological analysis of his handwriti
As discussed later, King's depressive
life, and his personal physician, Dr. Arth
chiatric consultation. But for most of h
and active, and these constant manic tra
day or a few days of exhaustion and fatig

* *

That future c
graduate stu
admitted the
in a largely W
a valued, not
of this Whit
conservatism
highly emoti
tradition wit
A major infl
whom King
Smith, whose
taught. Only
and in the 19
ical influence
Some of w
of thinking t
began to reth
experience, n
the young Ki
church. This
larger White
to White the
later write hi
influenced Ki
sonalist" the
tween person
Located n
a liberal Prot
rationalism.
manner. Chri
poor and the
not just abou
fighting injus
was the socia
ligion wasn't
The Bible, fo
ferent human
Similarly, som
if they conflic

as the emotions behind faith. In short, philosophy, based on reason, needs to undergird religious belief.

These were the teachings given to King at Crozer; he already had learned these ideas at Morehouse (where he imbibed rationalism) and somewhat at Ebenezer Baptist Church (where the social Gospel was taken for granted). At Crozer, these basic ideas were annealed in King's mind to the point where they would serve forever as his basic way of thinking in life.

This intellectual progress came perhaps at the cost of a temporary tension with the more emotional Black church experience of King's past. The young man did a pastoral internship at a Black church in Queens, New York, as part of his Crozer coursework. One of Daddy King's friends was the minister who oversaw King Jr.'s visit, and he wasn't impressed. He gave King Jr, an overall B grade and remarked that he had "an attitude of aloofness, disdain, and possibly snobbishness . . . a smugness."[13]

* * *

As Patrick Parr has detailed wonderfully, King's experience at Crozer was central to his personal development as a young adult. He experienced the freedom of the North much more fully than in his prior brief trips there. He had a White girlfriend, as described further below; could travel with White and Black friends to Philadelphia; lived in an integrated dormitory; and interacted with highly sympathetic and liberal students and teachers. The Crozer campus was almost heaven.

Not everything was perfect. King began to experience racism as an adult in a way that was frequent enough, and scary enough, to make him even more determined to end it. Two incidents stand out. When he had recently arrived at Crozer, a new Southern White student named Lucius Hall confronted King over an apparent prank played on Hall in their dormitory, and Hall pulled a gun on King. Another Black student, Marcus Wood, intervened. The administration later got involved and admonished Hall, who later dropped out of Crozer.

On another occasion, King and his friend Walter McCall went to a diner in New Jersey with two female friends; it was late at night and McCall asked for beer. The diner owner, who was a German immigrant, got angry, left, and returned with a gun, shooting in the air. King and McCall and their friends hurried away in their car. King filed a lawsuit against the owner, with the help of the local National Association for the Advancement of Colored People (NAACP), which was King's first civil rights act in his life. The owner was found guilty of illegal gun possession, but the discrimination suit was later dropped when only McCall ended up testifying.[14]

At Crozer, King turned a corner. In the 3-year seminary program, there is a progression. In his first year, he continued to perform similarly as he had at Morehouse, with mostly B's and C's—acceptable but not stellar. (He had five B's, four C's, and three A's.)[15] It is notable that he received two A's related to "homiletics," the practice of preaching sermons. He had been practicing sermons for years. Two of his C's were given for "public speaking," an ironic fact for a man who would become famous as perhaps the greatest American orator of the modern age.

In his second year, his grades began to improve, with no C's, seven B's (five of which were B+'s), and two A's. And in his third year, he scored all A's in eight courses.[16] By graduation, he had won a scholarship award.

In short, Mike Jr. was becoming more serious about his academic work. His friend McCall noted, "The dramatic change came in him when he entered the seminary. He began to take his studies more seriously. . . . He devoted time to his books night and day."[17] A White classmate later commented, "He was very studious; he spent a lot more time on his lesson assignments than most of us did."[18]

King had become very popular and was elected class president. He did the best among his peers in his written and oral comprehensive examinations, and he was highly regarded by the faculty.

He carried himself with the mien of duty and respect that would stay with him the rest of his life. One time, when he was displeased with another Black student drinking beer and acting too casually, King commented, "Don't you know you carry the burdens of the entire Negro race on your shoulders?"[19]

But King had fun too. He especially liked to play pool with his classmates, cigarette dangling from his lips, in the basement of the main Crozer building. One time, when his father and his paternal uncle Rev. Joel King were visiting for a Baptist convention in nearby Philadelphia, King Jr. brought them to the pool table, pulled out his cigarette, and calmly began to play. Joel King was shocked and expected his temperamental older brother to explode. Daddy King rejected alcohol, tobacco, dancing, and a host of other vices. He likely never had seen his namesake smoke a cigarette before. But the elder King said nothing, much to his younger brother's surprise.[20]

At Crozer, King was one of 11 Black students out of a total student body of approximately 90 persons. For the first time in his life, he was in a mostly White environment. He was only 19 years old when he entered in 1948—as usual, a number of years younger than most of his peers. Living in the North for the first time, in a different environment, King was given a lifeline to his origins through a family friend, J. Pius Barbour, a Black minister who had graduated from Crozer and pastored a Black church in Chester. Barbour had attended Morehouse and was in King Sr.'s large circle of friends. When his son was accepted at Crozer, King Sr. contacted Barbour to ask him to serve as a father figure during the Crozer years.

As with Mays, King Jr. found in the older man an excellent role model of intellectual depth and religious skill: "He is full of fun, and he has one of the best minds of anybody I have ever met," the younger man wrote his mother.[21] Barbour, largely unknown to historians, had a major influence on King Jr.

Barbour would tutor King and other Black Crozer students on the nuances of preaching in the Black church tradition. The Crozer students learned about the concepts of theology in their classes with White professors. Then on weekends they would study at "Barbour University" and learn how to explain and apply those concepts to a Black church audience. King's life was very much to follow this pattern: take ideas from the larger world, such as Gandhian nonviolence, and explain/apply them in the Black world of the South.

* * *

King's first experience of life in a mostly White area of the North was punctuated by an important emotional event: He fell in love with a White woman. Betty Moitz was the daughter of the school cook, and she lived on campus. In the course of their 6-month relationship, King seriously talked of marrying her. He was dissuaded by his friends and the strong intervention of Rev. Barbour. They convinced him that his professional career would suffer too much from having a White wife. Recently interviewed, Moitz said, "We were madly, madly in love, the way young people can fall in love."[22] King had even brought Betty with him to Barbour's house and asked the older man why he simply could not marry them right now.[23] Eventually, King relented when Barbour organized a group of local ministers to meet with the young man and convince him how harmful this marriage would be to him.[24] Barbour thought the breakup had a long-lasting effect: "He was a man of a broken heart—he never recovered."[25] Some of his friends thought that in a different era, the two likely would have married.

When King was stabbed in 1958, Barbour would joke about King's relationship with Moitz:

> I was not concerned about your stabbing as I always felt that you would not die. The only thing that bothered me was the thought that perhaps one of your old girlfriends had decided to take vengeance on you. If that woman had been White, I would have fainted, unless I had seen her name.[26]

Despite his consistent efforts for integration, King only spoke once briefly with his friend and biographer Lerone Bennett in 1964 about his own personal experience of being in an interracial relationship. Such mixed marriages occurred occasionally at that time, but they were very controversial. They were illegal in many places, unfavorable with more than 90% of Whites according to polls at the time, and not acceptable in Black churches.[27]

Moitz remained silent all her life about the relationship until Patrick Parr talked to her in 2016 in her sole interview about King before her death soon thereafter at age 89 years. She had nothing but affectionate memories.[28]

Integration for King was a social concept and a personal one. But, when it came to marriage, it was a line he couldn't cross.

The North had been very good to King. After Crozer, he moved farther North to Boston for 3 more years of fun and learning. But he always knew that he would return back South. Despite the many professional opportunities he would have had in Northern universities and churches, he still had the weight of the entire Black race on his shoulders. He famously returned South in 1954 after his studies, and the next decade would be full of his Southern actions against segregation. By 1966, however, he turned his attention North again, and even moved temporarily to Chicago, seeking to expand his movement from desegregation to an attack on institutional racism. He was done with the South.

But the South wasn't done with him. Memphis, Tennessee, beckoned, and before Memphis, James Meredith forced King to make one last big march in the South. It would turn out to be the last great march of the civil rights movement.

* * *

Meredith, a Mississippi native, had concluded that victory in the South could not be declared yet. The laws were beginning to change, but attitudes had not. Blacks still feared for their safety if they challenged segregation laws. Meredith declared a "March Against Fear," and, with only a few companions, began a 220-mile trek from Memphis to Jackson, Mississippi. They started on June 5, 1966; one day later, a gunman wounded Meredith with a shotgun.

Meredith, the first Black student to desegregate the University of Mississippi in 1962, was a civil rights leader without a party. He didn't coordinate with the SCLC, the NAACP, the Student Nonviolent Coordinating Committee (SNCC), or any other organization. He just did what he thought he needed to do. It was June 1966: Voting rights had passed Congress, and the civil rights bill had ended segregation. But change was too slow for Meredith; racism had ended, but racists abounded.

The "Meredith march," as it would be known, would turn out to be the last hurrah of the civil rights movement. The civil rights organizations that had not been part of Meredith's plan felt forced to continue his march after he was shot. They all picked it up and continued for approximately 3 weeks, until ending in Jackson with a rally of 15,000 people. For the last time, King as leader of the

SCLC was joined by the SNCC, headed by Stokely Carmichael, and leaders of the Congress of Racial Equality, the NAACP, and the Urban League.

It would be the last unified march of the civil rights movement.

The march was hot and grueling; despite state national guard protection, there was constant fear that someone would get shot, like Meredith had. The marchers were stressed and afraid, and although they obeyed King's nonviolent tactics, they were not very nonviolent with each other. They would fight verbally, and sometimes physically, with each other; women were struck by men and demeaned. Physician volunteers, such as Dr. Alvin Poussaint, had to use psychiatric medications like antipsychotics to calm some marchers.[29]

In addition to the fear of personal harm during the march, there was a larger division. Carmichael and the student activists of SNCC had long been more radical than King's SCLC; now, with legal goals in the South achieved but much informal racism remaining North and South, Carmichael and the SNCC were increasingly attracted to the image of Malcolm X rather than King.

Approximately 10 days into the march, in Greenwood, Mississippi, Carmichael was arrested briefly. When he left jail and rejoined the marchers, surrounded by many young SNCC supporters and media, he raised his fist and chanted, for the first time, for "Black Power." As a witness described it, seeing a crowd of SNCC activists and assembled media outside the jail, "Stokely let it all hang out":

> "This is the twenty-seventh time I have been arrested—and I ain't going to jail no more!" The crowd exploded into cheers and clapping. "The only way we gonna stop them White men from whuppin' us is to take over. We been saying freedom for six years and we ain't got nuthin'. What we gonna start saying now is Black Power!" . . . The crowd was right with him. They picked up his thoughts immediately. "Black Power!" they roared in unison.[30]

The next morning, King met with Carmichael and tried to convince him to drop the Black Power slogan and replace it with King's slogan, "Freedom now." Carmichael refused. It was the beginning of the end of the civil rights movement, as SNCC and other Black radicals gave up on nonviolence and split from King's leadership.

Five months after Carmichael raised the Black Power slogan during the Meredith March, King gathered all the SCLC leadership and staff for a retreat in Frogmore, South Carolina. For days, they debated what the nonviolent movement should do next, in response to the challenge of young radicals from SNCC and also in response to the problem of providing leadership to Northern Blacks.

King began to make a shift, not away from nonviolence but away from the limited goals of desegregation and voting rights. He now wanted the civil rights movement to fight against poverty and capitalism, an economic fight:

> We must honestly face the fact that the Movement must address itself to the restructuring of the whole of American society. . . . This is often a difficult point. . . . Now this means we are treading again in very difficult waters, because it really means that we are saying that something is wrong with the economic system of our nation. This is what it means, really. It means that something is wrong with capitalism.

King went on to state clearly in private at the SCLC retreat what he avoided saying in public: "There must be a better distribution of wealth, and maybe America must move toward a Democratic Socialism."[31]

The American socialist leader Michael Harrington had recognized this aspect and expressed it to King years earlier.[32] But not all of King's aides felt comfortable with the transition from fighting segregation in the South to fighting capitalism in the North—both in the name of opposing racism.

Although he tried to direct the civil rights movement in the direction of an anti-war and anti-capitalism movement from 1966 onward, King had not arrived at those commitments overnight. As early as June 1956, in the middle of the Montgomery bus boycott, he presaged those ideas in a speech to the national NAACP convention in San Francisco. He denounced "the madness of militarism" and "an economic system which takes necessities from the masses to give luxuries to the classes" (a common refrain in many sermons during the next decade). "I have no doubt," he foretold with acute foresight, "that by 1963 we will have won the legal battle" against segregation.[33] These were courageous words, because the NAACP was completely organized around the struggle in courts to change the laws of segregation. King signaled from the very start of his public life that he wanted more: He wanted to transform America into a nation that refused to fight wars and refused to allow poverty. Only then could racism itself, and not just racist laws, be vanquished.

Racism, materialism, militarism—King clearly identified the true axis of evil in our society. He had been struggling with just the first; now he realized that to defeat it, he would have to challenge the other two.

On April 4, 1967—exactly one year before his murder—King came out most strongly and publicly against the Vietnam War in his famous speech at the iconic liberal Riverside Church in New York City.

The denouement had begun.

President Johnson and his allies in the Black and White liberal communities turned on King. Respected Black journalist Carl Rowan pilloried King in a widely read *Reader's Digest* article, subtly accusing him of communist sympathies. King responded publicly by charging Rowan with McCarthyism.[34] Even Bayard Rustin privately disagreed with King and pulled away from him.

In mid-September 1967, SCLC staff met in a retreat at Airlie House in Warrenton, Virginia. King wasn't sure what to do next.

Then, to protest economic hardship, Marian Wright of Mississippi presented an idea to hold a fast and sit-in, composed of King and other religious leaders along with some poor citizens, at the offices of the U.S. Secretary of Labor in Washington, DC. The idea sparked King's interest, and he took it further. Why not organize waves of protestors to come to Washington, demanding jobs and justice? The Poor People's Campaign, King's final act, was born.[35]

A few months later, in late November 1967, King and SCLC staff returned to Frogmore, South Carolina, for another retreat. King had become more convinced that his proposal for radicalization of their efforts, presented there the prior year, should move forward:

> The decade of 1955 to 1965, with its constructive elements, misled us. Everyone underestimated the amount of rage Negroes were suppressing, and the amount of bigotry the white majority was disguising. . . . Nonviolent protest must now mature to a new level . . . to mass civil disobedience.[36]

King had returned to the very first place he had heard about nonviolent resistance, the essay "On Civil Disobedience" by that incorrigibly honest and sincere New England loner, Henry David Thoreau-except Thoreau launched a protest of one. In the prior decade, King had led a movement of protests in one area of the country, the South. Now he wanted to have mass civil disobedience throughout the nation, sparked by one huge action in the nation's capital, the Poor People's Campaign.

At the end of these twists and turns, King might have become president—or at least run a campaign for it.

In fact, throughout 1967, anti-Vietnam War activists tried to convince King to run for president, with pediatrician and anti-war activist Dr. Benjamin Spock as his vice presidential candidate. When King would visit college campuses, he would be greeted with handwritten signs: "King–Spock." King wasn't entirely uninterested, apparently.

On August 31, a few weeks before the SCLC retreat in Warrenton, Virginia, King attended the "National Conference for New Politics" convention in Chicago. The convention was the product of about a year of grassroots organizing to find an anti-Vietnam War alternative to President Lyndon Johnson.[37] The convention specifically wanted to explore and promote a third-party King–Spock ticket, and King was invited to be the keynote speaker.

The event was an important marker of the 1960s era because it was the only time that the period's protest movements tried to come together: the predominantly White and college student-based New Left, the civil rights movement headed by King, and the growing anti-Vietnam War movement. The effort would fail, in terms of the mass movements and also in terms of its narrower political goal of running a successful anti-Vietnam War candidate in 1968.

King began to speak from a third-floor platform, looking down on the delegates below, who were shouting against nonviolence. He became nervous, fearing for his safety, and uncharacteristically started repeating himself in his speech, which fell flat. He left quickly by a back door and immediately flew back to Atlanta.[38]

The convention ended up debating mostly about how much voting power to give its Black delegates, and in the end it didn't endorse a third-party campaign. It ended disorganized and without consequence.[39]

The effort failed, but the notion that King could be viewed as a plausible presidential candidate, under any circumstances, two decades before Jesse Jackson's campaigns and four decades before the first Black American president, is itself notable.

The convention was a sign of what was to come in King's last 6 months of life. He would make efforts here and there—New Politics, anti-Vietnam War speeches, the Poor People's Campaign, Memphis—but he wouldn't gain traction.

Could King have pulled back? Should he have listened to some of his advisors, such as Levison and Rustin, who warned him against his new radicalism? Or maybe to his concerned father, who had cautioned him years earlier that he needed to slow down, after his return to Atlanta from Montgomery in 1961:

> ML had come back home. I again urged him to cut back on his activities, take a long look at the way things were developing before he exposed himself to the constant danger that gathered around him. Several times we argued. I'd grow angry, telling him how bullheaded he was being. He'd been scarred by the struggle in very serious ways. His schedule—the speaking, the organizing, the meeting—had exhausted him.[40]

Perhaps King should have realized that the civil rights movement was, after all, as Lyndon Johnson and Democratic hawks believed, a matter of freeing Southern Blacks. It really didn't apply to the Northern states, much less to the rest of the world. Perhaps King could have taken the presidency of a divinity school at Howard or Harvard or Boston University and spent some time on the manicured lawns of a pretty university campus.[41] Or maybe he could have just taken the pulpit of some nice liberal church. At the Warrenton retreat, friends heard him confess his wishes in private, saying "he wanted just to be a preacher, and he was sick of it all. . . . The Lord had called him to be a preacher, and not to do all this stuff . . . he wanted to leave it and he was tired. . . . He had a couple whiskies in him . . . [and] he was just really saying it."[42] Or maybe after the Poor People's Campaign, he thought he could go to Africa for a year and rest, write, recharge, and then come back.[43]

If he had survived to take his Africa trip, or if he had called off the Poor People's Campaign and just took a breather, he might have re-entered the political arena when the country proved ready, maybe when Jimmy Carter had been elected president a mere decade later. It could have been him, not his father Martin Luther King Sr., who would have given the benediction at Carter's inaugural. It could have been him, not Andrew Young, who would have been Ambassador to the United Nations. It could have been him in his mid-50s, not Jesse Jackson, who would have run for president in the 1980s, and maybe even been elected. Or he might have lived into his late 70s to see Barack Obama elected president in 2008. Or maybe by then he finally might have agreed to run himself.[44]

Notes

1. Andrew Young, *Eyes on the Prize* interview, p. 15.
2. Ralph David Abernathy, *And the Walls Came Tumbling Down* (New York: Harper, 1989), p. 323.
3. John A. Williams, *The King God Didn't Save* (New York: Pocket Books, 1971), p. 153.
4. Abernathy, *And the Walls Came Tumbling Down*, p. 491.
5. Interview with Vincent Harding, December 28, 2012.
6. Interview with Bernard Lafayette, January 15, 2013.
7. Interview with William Anderson, August 17, 2013.
8. 1964: Hospitalized at St. Joseph's Hospital, Atlanta, under the care of Dr. Asa Yancey ("Why Dr. M. L. King Jr. Entered an Atlanta Hospital," *Jet*, October 29, 1964). 1965: Visit to Williams Clinic, Chicago (King Center Archives, Box 7:24).
9. Thomas Fitzpatrick, "King Leads Loop March," *Chicago Tribune*, July 25, 1967. I thank Jonathan Eig for unearthing this article and the timing and context of the Williams Clinic visit.
10. There is no date on the medical record at the Atlanta archives because the first page is missing. Apparently, it was removed before the record was put in the archives. The first page of a medical record typically will have the "chief complaint" or the reason for the medical visit. The Williams Clinic was a popular family run medical center in Chicago, a kind of Black Mayo Clinic, founded by three African American physician brothers (Jasper, James, and Charles Williams) to serve the Black community. Jasper F. Williams, MD, was an obstetrician (https://www.chicagotribune.com/news/ct-xpm-1985-04-17-8501220730-story.html). His brother James B. Williams, MD, was King's physician when King lived in Chicago briefly in 1966 (https://www.thehistorymakers.org/biography/dr-james-williams-41). The clinic was very popular in the Black community until it closed sometime after the 1960s. Here is one reminiscence on an internet site:

    > My family was extremely close to the Williams brother[s]. If you only needed a GP [general practitioner], you went to Dr. Charles. Needed surgery, Dr. James and if you were having a baby, Dr. Jasper was your guy. Charles Jr. and his brother also were doctors, but it wasn't CJ's passion. If I remember correctly, he left medicine for

technology. Every member in my family went there, and if someone was too sick to go to the clinic, they would come by your house—especially James and Charles. https://www.sixthward.us/2012/12/the-former-williams-clinic.html

The signature line of "JFW:dt" was standard for the secretary typing the dictation being DT and the doctor doing the dictation being JFW. Given the above summary of the usual roles of the three brothers, it is likely that Jasper Williams was King's physician on this admission. King mainly showed up on short notice, and Jasper was the doctor available to see him. This is supported by the contemporary *Chicago Tribune* article "King Leads Loop March" by Fitzpatrick.

11. There are no publicly available written documents assessing King's psychiatric condition or mental health. The closest material, which is only tangentially relevant but worth documenting here for completeness, is a handwriting analysis done on April 13, 1964, by a handwriting analyst, Patricia Lavin of Chicago (King Center Archives). The context is unknown; her letter to King is as follows, with no response documented:

> Dear Dr. King: I thank you for your response to me. This is the analysis that I will submit on you. (You might let me know if this is you.)
>
> Dr. King's writing reveals the strength of his character. He has the rare ability suffer and to sublimate himself. His tall letters show his capability, enthusiasm, pathos, that he is a leader and a gregarious person, who likes to be around people, and who works well with them. His writing is that of an actor or an orator—stars of stage, movies and television—write like Dr. King. It is in the height of his upper letters that his idealism is betrayed, and it indicates his ambition and drive also. He is tenacious, holds on for dear life, the hooks at the beginning words, surely NOT just a predisposed tendency, but a powerful characteristic. He has breeding; is a conventional person. . . . He is compliant, yet he has a scorching will power—shown in his long "t" bars. He is sympathetic—the right slant—he seeks approval, and yet has a firm mind without conflict or confusion—general layout of his letter, the margins and spaces between words and lines. . . . Relates unusually well to people, goes all the way over to the right of his paper. Dr. King's writing reveals that he is without material drives, no fat lower loops; he is discreet; knows how to exercise prudence and caution. The true nobility of Dr. King is shown by his signature, which is simple, not a bit inflated. Most of us inflate our signature. But not Dr. King. If one ever doubted Dr. King's character, study graphology. It is all "here." This is DR. KING. Sincerely, Patricia Lavin.

Despite many parts of the analysis that are consistent with the medical records and oral histories reviewed in this book (King's extraversion, gregariousness, energy and drive, ambition, and sociability, along with his humility and empathy), the absence of any attempt to describe any negative characteristics suggests the graphologist was somewhat star-struck, and it severely limits the scientific utility of this analysis. Overall, this graphology must be considered meager and of minimal scientific merit.

12. Kenneth L. Smith and Ira G. Zepp, Jr., *Search for the Beloved Community: The Thinking of Martin Luther King Jr.* (Valley Forge, PA: Judson Press, 1998). See also Patrick Parr, *The Seminarian: Martin Luther King Comes of Age* (Chicago: Lawrence Hill Books, 2018).
13. David Garrow, *Bearing the Cross* (New York: HarperCollins, 2004 [1986]), p. 42. Parr discusses this grade and relates it to his newfound intellectual skills and theological knowledge, which he found difficult to bring into his pastoral work with Black parishioners. Parr, *The seminarian*, p. 120; Kindle edition, p. 171. Later in his life, of course, King grew quite skilled at the combination of intellectual depth and emotional connection in his sermons. Parr also notes that Rev. William E. Gardner, the pastor of the Queens church and a friend of Daddy King, gave the lowest grades to King Jr., three C's, in "Willingness to accept suggestion and criticism," "Understanding of group work techniques," and "Concern for individuals in group."
14. These events are well described and documented by Parr. Parr, *The Seminarian*.
15. Clayborne Carson, "Martin Luther King Jr.: The Crozer Seminary Years," *Journal of Blacks in Higher Education*, no. 16 (1997, Summer): 123–128.

16. Ibid.
17. Interview with Walter McCall by Herbert Holmes, March 31, 1970, King Atlanta archives.
18. Interview with Dupree Jordan by David Garrow, January 14, 1984, Atlanta; cited in Garrow, Intellectual Development.
19. Parr, *The Seminarian*, Kindle edition, p. 168.
20. Parr, *The Seminarian*.
21. Carson, "Martin Luther King Jr.: The Crozer Seminary Years."
22. Parr, *The Seminarian*, Kindle edition, p. 120.
23. Ibid., p. 152.
24. Parr, *The Seminarian*. Parr quotes this point from Marcus Garvey Wood, *And Grace Will Take Me Home* (Baltimore, MD: Gateway Press, 1998), p. 50.
25. Garrow, *Bearing the Cross*, p. 41.
26. Rev. J. Pius Barbour to King Jr., November 19, 1958, MLK BU archives, Box 34.
27. Parr, *The Seminarian*.
28. Ibid.
29. Interview with Alvin Poussaint, May 15, 2013.
30. Stokely Carmichael, quoted in "Stokely Carmichael, Black Power," by Kalen M. A. Churcher, https://voicesofdemocracy.umd.edu/wp-content/uploads/2010/07/churcher-carmichael.pdf.
31. Address at Southern Christian Leadership Conference staff retreat, Frogmore, SC, November 14, 1966. King Center Archives, Box 119.
32. Michael Harrington, *Eyes on the Prize* interview, October 11, 1998, question 2:

    > When I talked to Dr. King about politics and ideas . . . the name socialist . . . didn't bother him at all. My feeling when I talked to him about it was that it would have been criminal if I had asked him to identify himself as a socialist. I really thought that he had problems enough without adding that one. But I certainly felt that he not only agreed with my immediate program but that he agreed with my concept that what is needed is a new utterly democratic society committed to freedom that goes beyond the capitalist welfare state.
    > http://digital.wustl.edu/e/eii/eiiweb/har5427.0719.063michaelharrington.html

33. Garrow, *Bearing the Cross*, pp. 77–78.
34. Ibid., pp. 576–577.
35. Ibid., p. 578.
36. Ibid., p. 581.
37. https://www.marxists.org/history/etol/document/swp-us/idb/ysa-nec-min/NEC%201967/60-national-conference-new-politics-jul-13-1967-YSA.pdf.
38. Interview with Septima Clark by David Garrow, December 28, 1983, transcript p. 23:

    > There was a convention in Chicago . . . there were blacks and whites walking up and down the aisle . . . saying that they could not stand that nonviolence. Dr. King was way up on the third floor, and he looked down and he saw a whole group. He said, "I know they have me now." But they took him out another door and put him on the plane and sent him back to Atlanta. So they missed him. I could tell that he was disturbed because when he knew he was speaking, he had a way of repeating quite a bit, and I knew that due to the fact the he must have been pretty nervous about the people whoever sitting there.

    In David Garrow papers, Pittsburgh, PA, Manuscript Collection 832, Box 8.2.
39. Garrow, *Bearing the Cross*, p. 577. A good summary of the content and meaning of the convention is found in Simon Hall, "On the Tail of the Panther: Black Power and the 1967 Convention of the National Conference for New Politics," *Journal of American Studies* 37, no. 1 (2003): 59–78.
40. Martin Luther King Sr. with Clayton Riley, *Daddy King: An Autobiography* (New York: Morrow, 1980), p. 172.
41. As early as 1957, immediately after the success of the Montgomery bus boycott, King could have cashed in his celebrity for comfort. Wrote his friend Lerone Bennett,

> Offers by the dozen poured. . . . In the days after the boycott, ten-, fifteen-, twenty thousand dollar a year offers, the pastorship of a large Northern white church, professorships, and even a a deanship of major white universities. Even more tempting were opportunities to earn more than $75,000 a year as a professional lecturer.

Lerone Bennett, "When the Man and the Hour Are Met," in *Martin Luther King Jr.: A Profile*, ed. C. Eric Lincoln (New York: Hill & Wang, 1984 [1970]), p. 106.

42. Garrow, *Bearing the Cross*, p. 578. The speaker is Joan Baez, who attended the SCLC retreat along with some celebrity fundraisers, such as Harry Belafonte. The interview was conducted by Will Leventhal and published in 1972. Also known as Willy Segal-Leventhal, he was a White activist who participated in Hosea Williams' SCOPE program in the mid-1960s.
43. Interview with Bernard Lee by Walter Burrell, June 23, 1977, transcript p. 219. In David Garrow papers, Pittsburgh, PA, Manuscript Collection 832.
44. Although King never predicted a Black president, he did predict that by 2000, the civil rights movement would have made great progress. Referring to the "great struggle for human freedom . . . within the framework of a democratic society," he said, "I believe that before the turn of the century, if trends continue to move and develop as presently, we will have moved a long, long way toward such a society." Alex Haley, "Playboy Interview: Martin Luther King," *Playboyl*, January 1965.

7

Boston Years

Upon deciding to obtain a PhD, the young Martin Luther King Jr. applied to Yale University, the University of Edinburgh, and Boston University (BU). Edinburgh and Boston accepted him, but Yale, his first choice, turned him down. Yale required a standardized test, the Graduate Record Examination (GRE). Despite excellent grades and recommendations, if King didn't do well on the GRE, he would be rejected automatically by Yale. That's what happened.

King's overall GRE score in March 1951 placed him in the lowest third of test-takers. He scored well in literature but did poorly in the sciences, fine arts, and social studies.[1] This pattern was not unusual for many Black students from the South, where their education in the natural sciences was limited.[2] Furthermore, King's education at Crozer Theological Seminary had included no sciences or mathematics, so it wasn't likely rational to expect that he would do well in those fields. Still, King did poorly even in the advanced test in philosophy, where he scored in the lowest third.

Given who he became, perhaps there is no better argument against standardized testing.

King's closest faculty advisors, such as Kenneth Smith and George W. Davis, preferred BU in any case, and after King decided against going to Europe, he went to BU. He knew that it was a theological school especially open and friendly toward Black students, and he looked forward to studying with the leader of the "Personalist" school of liberal Protestant theology, Edgar Brightman.[3] (The Personalist school viewed the relationship of man and God as between two persons; it emphasized the need for a concrete personal relationship with God, as opposed to viewing God as an abstract Being beyond human reach. In his later sermons, King often referred to this personal relationship with God, which of course dovetailed with the traditions of the Black church.)[4]

He got to study with Brightman for a year, and began to delve into Georg Hegel and other influences, before Brightman passed away. King then shifted his

Soul on Fire. Nassir Ghaemi, Oxford University Press. © Oxford University Press 2026.
DOI: 10.1093/9780197657614.003.0008

mentorship to Brightman's successor, Harold DeWolf, who would remain a lifelong friend and later would be keynote speaker at King's funeral.

King's PhD was in "philosophical theology." Most of King's BU coursework remained in philosophy proper (e.g., Plato, Immanuel Kant, and Hegel), whereas the rest was in philosophy of religion, Christian theology, and the history of other religions. He supplemented this work by auditing a course at Harvard University on the philosophy of Plato, who, along with Hegel, would be a lifelong favorite philosopher of King.[5] King's college notes reveal a very serious struggle with this work, as the young man developed his own worldview, a finely tuned empathic interpretation of Christian theology as primarily aimed at reducing suffering in this world, at both personal and social levels. He remained, throughout his life, self-identified as someone who valued and was trained in philosophy, not just in ministry.

As King wrote in one of his university folders of notes, "a mild mysticism" was his goal, achievable only with a great crisis of personal experience.[6] King was all too aware he had never experienced such a crisis. His life had been comfortable, planned, organized, well-to-do. And yet, from all he was learning, if he was to have a truly personal relationship with God, he would need to have a personal crisis of faith. And he might need a little abnormal moodiness too. In his Crozer class notes, he wrote, "<u>These are candidates for mystical experience</u> [underlined in original]. 1. Unusual degree of nervous and mental excitability. 2. A sufficient degree of ill health."[7]

Reading King's Crozer and BU class notes and papers, one comes away with the sense that this was a serious young man grappling with major existential themes, not only for himself but also with an eye to making an impact on the world.

Once a week, 22-year-old King Jr. would sit on the couch, along with his roommate Philip Lenud, a divinity student at Tufts University. Their Commonwealth Avenue apartment would become a hub for philosophical debate. As cigarette smoke wafted through the air, other Black students from throughout Boston's many universities would show up, ready to debate what Hegel meant, how Kant could be properly understood, what recent research about the life of Jesus meant for understanding the Bible—all with an eye to translating this academic knowledge to the real world of life in segregated America. William Talbot Handy, another BU student, later recalled wistfully in a letter to King a year after Handy had graduated, "How is old B.U.? I miss the gang in the room solving the problems of the world, politically, socially, and in the theological realm. If only the people of the world would listen to us, there would be no trouble."[8]

There they were, in one of the freest cities of the North, as far as Blacks were concerned, getting the best education that America could offer them. Their study of Hegel, Kant, Plato, and Aristotle wasn't segregated; it was the same study for

Blacks and Whites. They could travel with Whites in the buses and trains of the city; they could go to Revere Beach side by side with Whites; they could eat in the same restaurants. Everything that was taboo in King's hometown of Atlanta was freely given in Boston.

For Blacks, the North and the South were, essentially, two different countries.

But almost all of King's peers were transplanted Black Southerners, and although some would stay North after graduation, most would return to their roots, to their homeland, the South, where, with all its racism, they still felt most at home.

The job they envisioned for themselves was how to transplant the freedom of the North into the at-homeness of their feeling for the South. One method was to take their freedom to study very seriously and to use their new knowledge to shed light on their dilemmas in achieving freedom and equality in the South.

So King and his friends took their "Philosophical Club," held after hours outside the usual curriculum, quite seriously. They invited their teachers, such as DeWolf and others, to join and discuss and debate with them. This was a thoughtful group of students, the avant-garde of a new generation of leadership, who would, unlike their fathers and grandfathers, succeed in defeating Southern segregation.

* * *

King's personal life was busy and active, and his academic life was just as serious and rich. Yet years later, a Stanford University team led by Clayborne Carson, the official historian of the King papers, unearthed evidence that many of King's university papers and his dissertation were plagiarized partly, and without adequate attribution. King would footnote and reference sources, often without using quotation marks. This unwelcome finding may reflect various things, possibly including King's high amount of activity in his Boston years and soon after returning to the South, when he finalized his PhD thesis. He simply may have cut corners.[9] Still, as a reader of those writings, it is clear that the young man was earnestly struggling with the ideas he faced. Throughout his life, in the sermons that all agree are among the highest in quality, King continued to refer to those ideas and thinkers he studied at the university: Hegel, a personal God, the dialectical conflict of ideas, the problem of evil.

In the ministry, Black and White, as the scholar Keith Miller has described in detail, there is a tradition of repeating sermons given by others, in part or in whole. A preacher may add or subtract material of their own. This process is called "homiletic borrowing," and it is a generally accepted tradition in the ministry. The most popular ministers whose material would be most borrowed by others—such as the great Harry Emerson Fosdick, who was a favorite source for

King—don't tend to complain, and instead view imitation as flattery.[10] As Miller stated, "For Fosdick and many others, the notions of plagiarizing sermons had as much meaning as the notion of stealing air."[11] This process is even formalized in yearly handbooks, called the *Minister's Manual*, consisting of daily sermons that ministers can give without any expectation of scholarly attribution in the pulpit.[12]

This tradition is the exact opposite of academia and the worlds of journalism and literature, in which the slightest repetition of phrasing can be career ending. King took multiple courses in preaching; he learned standard sermon types, which he and others would repeat.[13] He also learned academic scholarship and the need for citation and documentation. The two lived in an uneasy tension but one that mattered little because King was not a university scholar but, rather, a preacher and social activist. Again, Miller explains the matter best:

> King adapted material in a highly creative way. No matter what he borrowed or how often . . . he paradoxically . . . sounded exactly like himself. His long training in the folk pulpit accounts for his extraordinary ability to use other's language to become himself. . . . His borrowed lines fit his persona more closely than did the words of ghostwriters.[14]

The young preacher was making his way, not with the highest standards of scholarship, but in such a way that he was arriving at a philosophy of action for his life and for his people.

* * *

In Boston, the blossoming philosophy/theology doctoral student had begun to grow into his role as a Black minister. Under the tutelage of Rev. William H. Hester, at Roxbury's Twelfth Street Baptist Church, King was connecting with the Black community in Boston. He attended Sunday services there most weeks for approximately 2 years and preached on a number of those occasions. Rev. Michael Haynes, then a young theology student and youth minister at the church, told me that when he first heard King preach, his immediate reaction was "Wow!"

King had learned to blend "Hegel with Hallelujahs," as an observer remarked,[15] and he had learned "how to speak to the PhDs and the no Ds."[16] Dr. Mervyn Warren was a young divinity student who conducted his dissertation on King's homiletics with King's involvement in the late 1960s. He found that King had created his own personal mix of ideas and emotion, mixing his Black church heritage with the White European education he received. Eighty-seven percent of the words in his sermons were one or two syllables. Ninety-two percent of his sentences were declarative, and 72% were simple sentences.[17] Thirty-nine percent of his quotations were to the Bible but more—49%—were to secular persons (thinkers, historians, philosophers, and poets). He cited the New Testament three times more often than the Old Testament.[18]

Through his oratory, King was already well on his way to being a leader of masses.

From 1951 to 1954, King completed his doctoral courses at BU, practiced his ministerial abilities in Roxbury, and found his future wife in Coretta. He would forever speak of his "Boston years" with great fondness. His path was made clear. Haynes thought to himself that this polished PhD in theology from the South could easily call up a Northern university, such as the University of Chicago, and become its chaplain. He could have stayed North and lived a calm and fruitful academic life. DeWolf recommended King to a number of Northern universities seeking faculty.

But King was explicit from the start that he sought the PhD not to become an academic scholar; he sought it to establish even better credentials than the average Southern Black minister (most of whom had bachelor's degrees from Black seminaries). He wanted to be a leader to his people in the South, and the PhD was the beginning, not the end, of that process.[19]

So King began to look into Southern churches seeking pastors. He avoided Atlanta and his father's church, Ebenezer Baptist, to which he could easily have returned as co-pastor (his eventual lifelong official job); he didn't want to be in his father's shadow. When Dexter Avenue Baptist Church in Montgomery, Alabama, emerged as a possibility, King won the job, beating out his old friend "Mac," Walter McCall. Apparently, the church leadership had settled on McCall but had invited King already, so they allowed King to give his trial sermon as a formality. King's sermon, on his favorite topic of "Three Dimensions of a Complete Life" (derived from a classic 19th-century sermon from the Boston clergyman Phillips Brooks),[20] was a hit; his oratory swayed some of the deacons. The president of the church board still supported McCall, however, and Mac was invited to give another sermon 2 weeks after King. He gave a sermon called "Four Dimensions of a Complete Life," but he couldn't compete in oratory with his old friend, and as the two buddies discussed the matter in letters, Mac generously deferred to Mike:

> If you are interested in getting [underlining in original] that church, I would be glad to put in a plug for you. You may inform me. Take it from me, that is a Great Church, Mike. Much honor will go to the man who gets it.[21]

* * *

Dexter Avenue Baptist Church was the church of the "upper classes" of Montgomery Black society (mainly faculty at nearby Alabama State College). Dexter Avenue was the main central street of Montgomery, leading to a circle around the state capitol. The church literally was on a corner of that circle, looking sideways directly at the capitol building. Another block up and to the right was the first Confederate White House, where Jefferson Davis presided over secession. Dexter sat at the heart of Confederate country, and its parishioners wanted to be seen as the best of the Black community: polite, educated, courteous, calm. They wanted an educated preacher who would discuss ideas, not a social activist who would propel emotions.

The job came open because the church deacons finally had fired their prior pastor, Dr. Vernon Johns, "God's bad boy."[22] Johns had come from Virginia to minister at Dexter. He had been polite and calm when first hired, but gradually he became intolerant of the suffocating segregation of Montgomery. He challenged the congregation to take a stand; he harangued them; he demanded action. Five years before Rosa Parks sat on the bus, Johns did the same thing.[23] But his congregation didn't respond.

Johns had made it acceptable to preach radical change in the South; he had opened the door to a promised land he would never enter but which soon would be taken by his successor, after the Dexter congregation fired him and hired a nice young academic PhD from Boston.

It turned out that Johns was the John the Baptist[24] of the civil rights movement, whose messiah had just arrived. But no one realized it yet.

Ralph Abernathy also had arrived in Montgomery as a new pastor and had been mentored by Vernon Johns. Abernathy became fast friends with the young King, whom he had met briefly while they were both college students in Atlanta when a date canceled on Abernathy, claiming illness, and then she showed up at a party with King, at which Abernathy was also present.[25] The friendship between the two men would prove to be closer than any other friendships either one had, and they would become inseparable, the earthy Abernathy playing the stolid Sancho Panza to King's mercurial Don Quixote.

Abernathy was a short man with a big torso and large facial features. He was a native Alabaman from a farm family and a military veteran. He spoke plainly, thought simply and clearly. He was reliable and solid, but he also had his own ambitions. Over time, he would become second in command in King's civil rights organization (the Southern Christian Leadership Conference [SCLC]), always marching side by side with King. He went to jail with King, ate with King, traveled with King, and slept in the same hotel rooms as King. He and his wife Juanita sometimes would vacation together with King and Coretta. He was the first to King's side in Memphis when the assassin's bullet arrived. He took over for King as leader of SCLC and lived another two decades, writing, just before his own death, a memoir that would lead to his public condemnation by many in King's circle.[26]

But that was all in the future. In 1954, King and Abernathy were two young ministers in their mid-20s, ready to make a mark on the world together.

King met the expectations of the Dexter congregation for the first year of his ministry there. He was very busy as pastor, not as social activist. In June 1955, King flew to Boston to receive his official PhD degree. In August, he was speaking in a church at an event organized by the National Association for the Advancement of Colored People (NAACP). In the back of the church sat an old union activist, Edgar Daniel Nixon, long the leader of the small NAACP branch in Montgomery and an activist in the Brotherhood of Sleeping Car Porters (headed by A. Philip Randolph, later the leader of the 1963 March on Washington). As the new minister finished speaking, the old activist turned to a friend and said, "You know that guy made a heck of a good talker." "He sure did," his friend replied. "I don't know how I'm going to do it," Nixon mused, "but one of these days I'm going to hang him to the stars."[27]

The rest of the story of the Montgomery bus boycott is well-known. Rosa Parks sat on the bus; Nixon finally found a spark to organize the city for a boycott. He just needed a leader. He thought about the young new preacher, who spoke so well and had no enemies in town. King was reluctant. Meeting that afternoon in a local church to plan the first mass meeting rally that night of December 5, 1955, Nixon challenged the assembled ministers: You have "lived off these washwomen for the last hundred years and ain't never done nothing for them." He questioned their courage: "We've worn aprons all our lives. It's time to take the aprons off. . . . If we're gonna be mens, now's the time to be mens."[28] King spoke up: "Brother Nixon, I'm not a coward." Just then the assembled group chose King as the leader of the boycott. As Nixon recalled years later, "[On] December the 5th, I hung him to the stars."[29]

We cannot know whether that comment by Nixon was hyperbole in retrospect, spoken a decade after King's death, seeking to generate more credit for his role than he tended to receive. But it's true that Montgomery would turn a young man of promise into an international star overnight.

King had prepared all his life to be ready to give that first mass meeting speech. After the church basement meeting, King had exactly 1 hour to go home and prepare himself for what would be, in retrospect, the most important speech of his life. Holt Street Baptist Church was full with approximately 1,000 people. Prior speakers had been incendiary already. E. D. Nixon had warned the crowd, "This is gonna be a long drawn out affair. . . . Before it's over with, somebody gonna die. . . . It may be me for all I know."[30] The crowd was fired up.

King spoke slowly and calmly.[31] He praised Rosa Parks and then for the first time publicly insisted on nonviolence:

> And you know, my friends, there comes a time when people get tired of being trampled over by the iron feet of oppression. [sustained applause] There comes a time, my friends, when people get tired of being plunged across the abyss of humiliation, where they experience the bleakness of nagging despair. (*Keep talking*) There comes a time when people get tired of being pushed out of the glittering sunlight of life's July and left standing amid the piercing chill of an alpine November. (*that's right*) [applause] There comes a time. (*Yes sir teach*)

By now the audience was applauding strongly; the speech could have become mere demagogy. But King slowed down:

> We are here, we are here this evening because we are tired now. (*Yes*) [applause] And I want to say that we are not here advocating violence. (*No*) We have never done that. (*Repeat that, repeat that*) [applause] I want it to be known throughout Montgomery and throughout this nation (*Well*) that we are Christian people. (*Yes*) [applause] We believe in the Christian religion. We believe in the teachings of Jesus. (*Well*) The only weapon that we have in our hands this evening is the weapon of protest. (*Yes*) [applause] That's all.

King ended quietly, simply, thoughtfully, anticlimactically even. He knew that meeting was just the beginning of a long, arduous task.

Notes

1. King's GRE scores were as follows, on a maximum score scale of 800:

   Overall: Verbal 350 (second lowest quartile), Quantitative 270 (lowest 10%)
   Subjects: Physics 310, Chemistry 280, Biology 360, Social Studies 320, Fine Arts 340—all lowest quartile. Literature 470 (top quartile)
   Advanced test in philosophy: 58 (out of 100)—placed in lowest third

   The Papers of Martin Luther King, Jr. Volume I: Called to Serve, January 1929–June 1951, ed. Clayborne Carson, Ralph Luker, and Penny A. Russell (Berkeley: University of California Press, 1992), p. 407.
2. Patrick Parr, *The Seminarian: Martin Luther King Comes of Age* (Chicago: Lawrence Hill Books, 2018).
3. Ibid.
4. https://www.britannica.com/topic/personalism.
5. When asked in 1965 which single book he would take to a deserted island, besides the Bible, King chose Plato's *Republic*: "I feel that it brings together more of the insights of history than any other books. There is not a creative idea extant that is not discussed, in some way, in this work." Alex Haley, "Playboy Interview: Martin Luther King," *Playboy*, January 1965.

6. Here is a sample of 1949 class notes on mysticism with Rev. George W. Davis. King writes,

> There must be a detachment from these things if the self is to be united with God [underlined in original]
> Pride
> Hatred
> Presumtion [sic]
> Evil desires
> Family substitute for God
> Desire of riches
> Desire of a name amongst men
> Passion of fame
> If we do have no mystical experience it is not God's fault, but our failure to properly purge our lives.

MLK BU Archives, Folder 4 Term III February 22–May 6, 1949.

7. MLK BU Archives, Folder 4 Term III February 22–May 6, 1949.
8. William Talbot Handy, letter, November 18, 1952. https://kinginstitute.stanford.edu/king-papers/documents/w-t-handy-jr.
9. The policy of using material from other sources without referencing them would continue in King's adult life. Many of his sermons were drawn directly in content or theme from other ministers of prior decades, especially Harry Emerson Fosdick and also J. Wallace Hamilton, George Buttrick, and the 19th-century minister Phillips Brooks. All these ministers were White, but King took ideas from them and applied them to the experiences of his life and of Black America. These sources for his preaching are well documented by Keith D. Miller, *Voice of Deliverance* (Athens: University of Georgia Press, 1998).

   He also pulled from his mentor Dr. Benjamin Mays, the president of Morehouse College. Ralph Abernathy later recalled sitting with Mays' wife, reading newspaper accounts of King's sermons and recognizing Mays' words: "It annoyed her that Martin didn't give Dr. Mays credit for the original ideas. It wasn't exactly plagiarism, she said, but it wasn't quite honest either." Ralph David Abernathy, *And the Walls Came Tumbling Down* (New York: Harper, 1989), p. 480.
10. Miller describes this topic in detail. Miller, *Voice of Deliverance*, pp. 122–136.
11. Ibid., p. 191.
12. There are different versions of *Minister's Manuals*—for instance, *Nelson's Minister's Manual*, *Christian Minister's Manual*, *New Minister's Manual*, and *Minister's Annual Manual*. All are accessed easily via internet search.
13. As Miller describes from the content of King's Crozer course in homiletics with Professor Robert Keighton, these basic types included the Ladder, Jewel, Roman Candle, and Classification sermons. Readers can find the details in Miller's book. The point is that homiletics includes repetition of certain sermon types, and thus it is different from scholarship, in which originality is emphasized. Miller, *Voice of Deliverance*, p. 123.
14. Miller, *Voice of Deliverance*, p. 195.
15. Mervyn A. Warren, *King Came Preaching* (Downers Grove, IL: Intervarsity Press, 2001), p. 121.
16. Ibid., p. 144.
17. Ibid., pp. 143–145.
18. Ibid., pp. 96–97.
19. King's informal mentor at Crozer, Rev. J. Pius Barbour, also advised King against being in Alabama. Soon after his arrival there, Barbour wrote the following (July 21, 1955; all capitals in original):

> Dear Mike . . . I warn you. Don't get stuck there. Move on to a big metropolitan center in THE NORTH, or some town as ATLANTA. You will dry rot there. I feel sorry for you with all that learning. I wrote a two hundred page thesis on RELIGION AND PHYSIOLOGICAL PSYCHOLOGY and with the exception of lectures to colleges have been unable to use ONE SINGLE IDEA in the Baptist Church. The country Negroes have swept into town and REDUCED the intellectual level of RELIGION. This is the day of Mass preachers except in certain spots. Hurry and get one. . . . Hurry

> up and reply. You (and) Coretta are going to rue the day you have children. The Catholics are right. Preachers should be celibates. Your old friend, JPB.

The Papers of Martin Luther King, Jr. Volume II, pp. 322–323.

20. Miller, *Voice of Deliverance*, p. 75. See also https://en.wikipedia.org/wiki/Phillips_Brooks.
21. Letter from McCall to King, January 17, 1954. https://kinginstitute.stanford.edu/king-papers/documents/walter-r-mccall. McCall is an interesting character. He keeps appearing and reappearing briefly in King's life, but given that they were the closest friends in college at Morehouse, and then remained very close in seminary at Crozer, it is interesting that it seems that King began to distance himself from his old friend after Montgomery. They traded some letters in the 1950s as King came to prominence in Montgomery, while McCall had taken a position as dean and chaplain at Georgia's Fort Valley State College from 1951 to 1957. As McCall's letters suggest, he seems to have been active romantically with others. It's unclear how and if these activities affected his employment. In 1957, McCall moved to Atlanta, where for the next two decades until just before his death in 1978 he was the pastor at Providence Missionary Baptist Church. He also was acting director of Morehouse's School of Religion from 1965 to 1969.

    It is interesting that despite living in the same city throughout the 1960s, McCall and King did not re-establish or continue their earlier close relationship of the late 1940s to early 1950s. Instead, King viewed Ralph Abernathy as his closest and best friend.

    McCall seems to have been very extroverted, rather happy-go-lucky, and had a healthy libido, based on his letters in the 1950s to King. William Talbot Handy's 1951 letter to King at BU hints at these character traits: "How is Mac? Has he decided to relieve himself of his many responsibilities? Does he still jump up in the air and kick his heels together? I certainly hope he does something before he has a nervous breakdown." https://kinginstitute.stanford.edu/king-papers/documents/w-t-handy-jr.
22. https://www.historynewsnetwork.org/article/vernon-johns-an-often-forgotten-controversial-civi.
23. Abernathy, *And the Walls Came Tumbling Down*, p. 116.
24. Abernathy made this analogy in an interview: "John the Baptist. He was not Martin Luther King, but we would have never had a chance to do what we did if it had not been for Vernon Johns." Interview with Taylor Branch, May 5, 1984, transcript, p. 4, University of North Carolina Chapel Hill archives.
25. Juanita Abernathy, November 14, 2014, Southern Historical Association, http://www.c-span.org/video/?322686-1/juanita-jones-abernathy-civil-rightsmovement.
26. Abernathy, *And the Walls Came Tumbling Down*.
27. Edgar Daniel Nixon, *Eyes on the Prize* interview, 1979 (exact date not provided), question 2, http://digital.wustl.edu/e/eop/eopweb/nix0015.0307.078ednixon.html. Nixon said,

    > On the second Sunday, in August of 1955, Reverend King was a speaker for the NAACP. A man who honored the professors of [unintelligible] college, Professor Jay E. Pierce and I was sitting in the back of the church when he got through talking. I said, "Pierce?" And he said, "Yes?" I said, "You know that guy made a heck of a good talker." He said, "He sure did." I said, "I don't know how I'm going to do it, but one of these days I'm going to hang him to the stars." And that was on the second Sunday in August, 1955. And on the morning of December the 5th, I hung him to the stars.

28. Taylor Branch, *Parting the Waters* (New York, Simon & Schuster, 1988), p. 136.
29. Edgar Daniel Nixon, *Eyes on the Prize* interview, 1979 (exact date not provided), question 2, http://digital.wustl.edu/e/eop/eopweb/nix0015.0307.078ednixon.html.
30. Ibid.
31. https://kinginstitute.stanford.edu/king-papers/documents/address-mia-mass-meeting-holt-street-baptist-church.

8

"Shattered Dreams"

It would be his last sermon at Ebenezer Baptist Church in Atlanta, the home church of his childhood, his father's church, and his grandfather's church. It was Sunday, March 3, 1968. He had a month to live. His father stood behind him. His mother sat in the choir. His wife and children sat in the first pew.

For the last time, in front of his mother and father and sister and wife and kids, Martin Luther King Jr. had a confession to make.

He looked out on his church family, cleared his throat, and spoke in his trademark baritone: "I want to preach this morning from the subject: 'Unfulfilled Dreams.' "[1]

David, King noted, was a great Hebrew king, and he wanted to build a temple in Jerusalem, but he died before it was finished: "So many of us in life start out building temples: temples of character, temples of justice, temples of peace. And so often we don't finish them. Because life is like Schubert's 'Unfinished Symphony.' " King paused: "Like David, [we] find ourselves in so many instances having to face the fact that our dreams are not fulfilled."

His audience listened and thought, perhaps, back to the most famous speech of King's life. He spoke now about his unfulfilled dreams, whereas 5 years earlier he had announced to the nation in front of the Lincoln Memorial that he had a dream. Now reaching the end of his life, an end he had been sensing for some years, he was announcing the failure of his dream.

"Now let us notice first that life is a continual story of shattered dreams."

The churchgoers didn't hear the perennial optimist of 1963 but, rather, the depressed realist of 1968: "Life is a long, continual story of setting out to build a great temple and not being able to finish it."

Why? King finds the cause in the Biblical concept of a constant struggle between good and evil. This fact is not only Biblical but also psychological. King is as personally explicit as he could be about his own experience:

Soul on Fire. Nassir Ghaemi, Oxford University Press. © Oxford University Press 2026.
DOI: 10.1093/9780197657614.003.0009

> In every one of us this morning, there's a war going on. (*Yes, sir*) It's a civil war. (*Yes, sir*) I don't care who you are, I don't care where you live, there is a civil war going on in your life. (*Yes it is*) And every time you set out to be good, there's something pulling on you, telling you to be evil. It's going on in your life. (*Preach it*)

King turned to psychiatric and then literary metaphors:

> There is a schizophrenia, as the psychologists or the psychiatrists would call it, going on within all of us. And there are times that all of us know somehow that there is a Mr. Hyde and a Dr. Jekyll in us.

This psychological inner civil war, for King, might have involved the manic and depressive sides of his own character, an important cause of his shattered dreams. But he found solace in faith:

> This brings me to the basic point of the text. In the final analysis, God does not judge us by the separate incidents or the separate mistakes that we make, but by the total bent of our lives. In the final analysis, God knows (*Yes*) that his children are weak and they are frail. (*Yes, he does*) In the final analysis, what God requires is that your heart is right. (*Amen, Yes*)

The audience connected with him. Maybe some wigs were flying, as sometimes happened in the emotional interchange between the preacher and his audience.[2] They knew he was talking about them, but also about himself.

This concept of an inner civil war, of a constant tension within everyone, is central to King's view of human nature, leading to his philosophy of nonviolence. There's some good and some bad in everyone; therefore, we all should be able to empathize with each other. King's alternating moods may have given him special insight into this aspect of human nature.[3]

For decades afterward, King's old friend Vincent Harding reflected on that last Ebenezer sermon. In an introduction to an audio recording of that sermon,[4] Harding reflects on King's need to confess, perhaps with a premonition of his coming death, to his family and friends in his home church:

> Our brother needed to share these words of self-reflection, confession, and hope . . . the schizophrenia in his soul. . . . He needed to confess how deeply he had failed himself and his own best possibilities, not only in the great public arena . . . but he needed to share the torment of his soul . . . his inner civil war.

Harding, like so many of King's friends, had seen a deep psychological change in King in his last years—a change that, in retrospect, reflected a profound clinical depression. King's friends, and historians after them, never had the clinical knowledge to be able to name it, but they saw and clearly described the depression that could take no other name:

> Many of us had seen the evidence of his internal conflict in his face, heard it in his voice. We recognized it partly because it so resembled many of our own struggles. In that last year, Martin looked more beleaguered, harassed, and desperate than I'd ever seen him before. And it was clear that more than external enemies were at work.

Years later, when asked what he meant by "more than external enemies," Harding replied, "I suspect that some of it was probably related to his relationships with women, and I think that's as much as I'm inclined to say."[5]

Harding suffered along with his friend, and he experienced a visitation:

> Several years after his death, I saw my friend [Dr. King] in a dream: All the tension, all the dividedness, that had been in his face, in his eyes, were gone. Instead there was a quietness, a heartfelt peace that I had not seen since my first meeting with him in 1958. And in the dream, as he looked at me, even though he did not speak a word, I somehow knew he was saying: "It's all right, Vincent, it is well with my soul."

Four decades would intervene before Harding himself died. In all those years, his old friend never visited him in a dream again.

* * *

King never liked Memphis, always dreaded it, avoided it. When his staff tried to start a Southern Christian Leadership Conference (SCLC) branch in Memphis in the early 1960s, King was reluctant. In retrospect, his friend Rev. Harold Middlebrook, who was from Memphis, thought that King had a "phobia" about the city: "There was always that feeling that something was wrong with Memphis that he just couldn't explain." Whenever he had to go there, to speak at a convention or a meeting, Middlebrook recalled, he never stayed long, not more than a day or two: "He always flew in, spoke, and got out as quickly as he could."[6]

Middlebrook later recalled that members of King's group all suspected King would be killed soon, but they thought it would be in Washington, DC, during the Poor People's Campaign. But approximately 48 hours before his death, "he realized that it was not going to be Washington but Memphis."[7]

Middlebrook was with King in Memphis on his final visit. This fear of Memphis might be a matter of hindsight, or maybe it was a real premonition.

That final time, when King arrived at the Memphis airport, he was met by a policeman serving a court order. As the order was read to him, Middlebrook noticed that King looked away into space, seeming nonchalant, unconcerned, sadly contented. Maybe, Middlebrook thought, he knew he was coming to Memphis to die.[8]

* * *

A few weeks before he was killed, King ran into his old college and seminary friend, Walter McCall, on an Atlanta street.[9]

"Mac, where are you going?" King asked.

McCall was stunned to see his old friend walking alone on the street, heading toward SCLC headquarters on Auburn Avenue.

"Don't ask me where I'm going. . . . You have no business being out here by yourself. Fool, don't you know you could get your damned head blown off?"

They laughed.

"Shucks, man," King replied, "even if I'm with everybody I could get my head blown off."

They laughed again.

"We need to get together," King told his old friend, "We haven't seen each other in a long time."

They agreed to get together, to be in touch.

They never got together.

Notes

1. The sermon here is transcribed from the audio version available in the *Knock at Midnight* collection. "Unfulfilled Dreams," in *A Knock at Midnight* (CD audio of 11 sermons), ed. Clayborne Carson and Peter Holloran (New York: Grand Central Publishing, 1998).

   The written version in King's published selected sermons, *Strength to Love*, is quite different. For instance, it quotes frequently from the Persian poet Omar Khayyam, which isn't in the actual oral sermon. Most important, it isn't anywhere as personal as the oral sermon. "Shattered Dreams," in Martin Luther King Jr., *Strength to Love* (Philadelphia: Fortress Press, 1981 [1963]), pp. 87–97.
2. The young White Northern Episcopal student minister Gurdon Brewster, who interned at Ebenezer Baptist Church in 1962, describes a sermon reaching its peak:

   > The people shouted as Dr. King rose to his highest level of intensity. Suddenly a woman cried out, and seizing her hair in her hand, pulled off her wig, and threw it in the air. This was followed by another and then another. Soon cries came from everywhere and wigs flew high in the air all over the sanctuary. . . . I recalled Lilliam [a parishioner] telling me . . . "You'll know he's preaching, Brewster, when the wigs begin to fly."

   Gurdon Brewster, *No Turning Back: My Summer with Daddy King* (Maryknoll, NY: Orbis Books, 2007), p. 213.

3. Psychologist Charles Collyer, a leading teacher of nonviolence, when asked, expressed this view:

> King's depression was not a major determinant of what he ended up saying and writing—[but] it may have given him insight into the importance of some of the things he was saying, like human nature being a mixed bag involving internal struggle. I think he had first hand experience of that.

   Interview, September 9, 2015.
4. Vincent Harding, "Introduction to 'Unfulfilled Dreams,'" in *A Knock at Midnight*.
5. Interview with Vincent Harding, December 28, 2012.
6. Middlebrook stated,

> I remember as far back as 1961. . . . There was always the feeling that there was something wrong in Memphis that he just couldn't explain. That is why Dr. King never worked here in Memphis, when Dr. King was speaking here in Memphis for conventions and this kind of thing and for the board meetings, he always flew in spoke and got out as quickly as he could. He never spent any time in Memphis never over a day or two days at the most.

   Interview with Rev. Harold Middlebrook by Joan Beifuss and Bill Thomas, July 18 and 21, 1968, in David Garrow papers, Pittsburgh, PA, Manuscript Collection 832, Box 1.9, transcript p. 5.

   Middlebrook was a Memphis native who worked for Ebenezer Baptist Church and the SCLC in the 1960s. While a student at Morehouse College, he lived with King Sr. in his house for some time and thus knew the King family quite personally.
7. Middlebrook stated,

> All of us suspected that Dr. King was going to be killed but we suspected it would be in Washington on the Poor People's Campaign. I think that about 48 hours before his death he realized that it was not going to be Washington but Memphis.

   Interview with Rev. Harold Middlebrook by Joan Beifuss and Bill Thomas, July 18 and 21, 1968, in David Garrow papers, transcript p. 6.
8. Middlebrook said,

> Well when Dr. King came back to Memphis on Wednesday he was first met at the airport and served a copy of the injunction. It was later reserved on him at the Lorraine motel. . . . As they were reading the injunction to Dr. King, Dr. King was looking off into space . . . and just nodded and say um hmm oh yes. Which was not like Dr. King.

   Interview with Rev. Harold Middlebrook by Joan Beifuss and Bill Thomas, July 18 and 21, 1968, in David Garrow papers, transcript p. 6.
9. Interview with Walter McCall by Herbert Holmes, 1970, p. 23. Oral History Project of the Martin Luther King Jr. Center for Nonviolent Social Change. King Center Archives, Atlanta.

9

In the Kitchen

Martin Luther King Jr. always had been in the bullseye.

He traveled hundreds of times yearly, usually with his aide Bernard Lee, but often without bodyguards or security. Once in a Birmingham, Alabama, meeting, a White neo-Nazi jumped out of an audience and punched him in the face. He walked at the front of hundreds of marches, often with hundreds or thousands of jeering White racists no more than a dozen feet away. Once, in a march outside Chicago, one of them threw a rock, which hit him in the head. Andrew Young asked Dr. Alvin Poussaint, a medical volunteer to the civil rights movement, to march a few paces behind King on marches, carrying a black first aid medical bag, to provide immediate care in case King was shot or attacked.[1] The large young Southern Christian Leadership Conference (SCLC) activist, James Orange—6 feet 3 inches and more than 300 pounds—would stand near King and would place other young men in marches around King to make it more difficult for a sniper to get a clean shot at him.[2]

King was stabbed, punched, stoned. If a single White racist had ever just pulled out a pistol and aimed it at him, King would have been an easy victim almost anytime, anywhere.

From the very beginning of his public life until its end, a decade of life from his late 20s to his late 30s, he was an ambulating victim. His assassination should not have been a surprise at any time, but it kept getting delayed.

Biographer David Garrow uses the metaphor of "bearing the cross" to describe King's attitude and mission in life. But the cross is born to the site of crucifixion. King's Gethsemane kept receding; he kept eluding death, as Kennedy fell, and then Malcolm X. He was left standing, but increasingly depressed, severely depressed, tired of bearing the cross. By 1968, he seemed unwilling to carry it any further.

It had been a decade-long journey. In 1961, when the young Freedom Riders from Nashville, Tennessee (including Diane Nash, James Bevel, and others) first met King, they pressured him to join them. Ralph Abernathy tried to deflect the

Soul on Fire. Nassir Ghaemi, Oxford University Press. © Oxford University Press 2026.
DOI: 10.1093/9780197657614.003.0010

pressure, saying that if King got on a Freedom Ride bus, "he would surely die." They persisted, saying that danger shouldn't be a deterrent.

King exploded: "Do not tell me when my time has come! Only God can tell me that!" And then: "I think I should choose the time and place of my Golgotha."[3]

Bevel wasn't impressed. He thought the great leader turned out to be a little afraid.[4] By 1968, Bevel knew better. The leader wasn't afraid. He just was searching for the right time and place. He knew the time: It would be before he turned 40 years old.[5] He didn't know the place yet, he didn't know where his Golgotha would be; but he sensed it; he sensed something about Memphis, Tennessee.

* * *

On March 25, 1968, at approximately 8 p.m., King visited the Upper West Side Manhattan brownstone home of Dr. Arthur and Marian Logan. One of the most prominent African American physicians in the nation, Logan, whose grandfather was a Confederate officer, was tall, blue-eyed, and very light-skinned. The debonair 57-year-old physician ran a hospital for the poor in Harlem but also counted many Black celebrities—such as King Jr., Duke Ellington, Billy Strayhorn, and Jackie Robinson—among his patients. King was coming to visit his wife, a member of the SCLC board and prominent civil right activist, but Dr. Logan also had an agenda.

"Uncle Martin!"

Dr. Logan's 7-year-old son ran to the door and led King to the kitchen.

"Let's play horsey!"

A moment later, the Nobel Prize winner was on all fours, young "Chip" on his back.[6] King crawled around the floor, with Chip holding on.

If that night was like others that Marian later would recall, King would say, "Marian, you aren't treating your leader very well."

"What's wrong?" she would reply.

It turned out he was looking for a drink, and Marian would comply.[7]

That evening, King and Marian launched into the beginning of what would be hours of discussion and debate about the Poor People's Campaign. As they debated, King smoked cigarettes and drank. The Logans were joined by two other lawyer guests, who were close friends: Stanley Levison and Clarence Jones. With black plastic glasses and thinning hair combed over his balding head, the 55-year-old Levison looked the part of the archetypal Jewish intellectual. Independently wealthy, and a former top supporter of the U.S. Communist Party, he had become King's closest political strategist.[8] King and Levison shared the same political values, and King trusted Levison's strategic instincts—except now. J. Edgar Hoover, the director of the Federal Bureau of Investigation (FBI), was convinced that Levison was King's Rasputin, the true power behind the throne.[9]

The other participant during that evening was 37-year-old Clarence Jones. He had married a White woman during an age when interracial marriage was uncommon, and he had represented celebrities in Los Angeles for some years until King had convinced him to join the civil rights effort. Now he was devoted to King, and, after moving to New York, he had become close to Levison too.[10]

Marian Logan had written an open letter to the SCLC board, in opposition to the Poor People's Campaign. Her view was that the event was likely to devolve into violence, which would harm the movement. Levison was sympathetic, concerned that the civil rights movement would lose much of its wider support in the country if it became too radical, moving away from more limited anti-segregation objectives.

Eventually, after hours of debating, King couldn't convince Marian, Marian couldn't convince King, and Levison wasn't willing or able to create a compromise.

Midnight had long passed.

King wasn't giving up on trying to convince Marian Logan. He kept talking and talking. By then, the quiet Dr. Logan had become annoyed and spoke up.

"Martin, leave her alone," he said. "She's not going to change her mind; she believes in this very strongly. And I think you should accept it. Can't you see she's exhausted?"

"Well, darlin'," King replied, looking at Marian. "I'll just have to pray for you. Just have to pray for you so you come around."[11]

Marian finally went to bed.

Sometime that evening, according to a later recollection by Clarence Jones, Dr. Logan and Jones had a conversation.

"I'm going to recommend that [King] see a psychiatrist," Logan said. "I'm going to strongly urge him to seek counseling. . . . I'm a physician offering him a professional opinion."

Jones doubted that King would agree, but Logan kept pressing: "And what in his heart will keep him from neglecting his mental health? [King] is sophisticated enough to realize psychotherapy has nothing to do with any emotional or moral shortcoming."

King does not appear to have had stigmatized attitudes about mental illnesses.[12] Still, Jones responded that King would reject the idea because "given the FBI surveillance into every aspect of his life, any psychiatric treatment will be used to further besmirch his character."[13]

As discussed previously, we now know that King had been hospitalized many times in his life for medically unexplained "exhaustion," lasting a day or days, quite the opposite of his high energy baseline, which would be consistent with the diagnosis of cyclothymic temperament. Sometimes his "exhaustion" periods lasted weeks, which would be consistent with full clinical depressive episodes. In the last year of his life, his depressive symptoms certainly lasted at least months, if not up to a whole year. In addition to markedly low energy, he had no motivation for his usual activities, was in poor spirits, and had increased appetite and weight gain. His sleep was always low in his usual cyclothymic state, but when his depressive periods became very severe, he would sleep excessively for a few days or weeks.

Psychiatrist Dr. Lonnie MacDonald, Coretta's college friend, also lived and practiced in Manhattan. It is possible that Logan planned to ask MacDonald to treat King. When I asked him decades later, MacDonald denied treating King but commented with some reluctance and no elaboration that King was "depressed most of the time."[14] After King's death, Andrew Young recommended to Coretta that his children receive psychiatric assistance, and she asked MacDonald to help them professionally, which he did in person for a few weeks during a visit to Atlanta.[15]

Of those present for the conversation, only Jones remains alive to tell what happened in Dr. Logan's house. Until recently, this story was never revealed, and Jones is only partially forthcoming.[16] We do not know for certain if Dr. Logan diagnosed depression per se, nor do we know if Dr. Logan spoke directly with King or only spoke with Jones. We do know that Levison, Jones, and King discussed Logan's recommendation and decided against accepting it.[17] It was approximately 8 a.m. when King left Logan's house.

A long eventful night had ended with neither King nor Marian nor Dr. Logan getting what they wanted.[18]

* * *

The drawn-out evening at the Logan house was a Monday night. The next day, Tuesday, King called again to speak with Marian, and again on Wednesday, and more than once each day. By then he was in Memphis. King and his supporters marched on Thursday, March 28. The protest went badly. Apparently, young Black radicals belonging to a gang called "the Invaders" waited until the march started, joined in the back, and, only approximately three blocks into the march, quickly broke off to riot, break windows, and loot stores. King was at the front of the march with Rev. James Lawson, Abernathy, and others. They heard windows break.

"*What was that?*" King asked.

"*Call off the march!*" he yelled to Lawson.

The crowd began to disperse. Police were responding violently, clubbing, pushing, and shooting people. Bernard Lee, always at King's side, arranged to get King and Abernathy in a car, and with police assistance, they were taken to a hotel. Overall, police killed one young Black protestor, injured approximately 60 others, and arrested approximately 280.[19]

For the first and only time in King's public career, a march he had led had turned into a riot.

King was despondent. He called Marian later that night.

"Martin," she advised, "I think you need to get your ass outta Memphis."

"Well, darlin'," he replied tiredly, "We can't turn around now. You know we have to keep going. This is our movement."[20]

Marian tried to convince him that the people in Memphis hadn't been trained well in nonviolence. King replied that his SCLC staff was coming to Memphis to ensure the next march stayed nonviolent.

King also called Levison that night, with FBI agents listening, and expressed his frustration:

> All I'm saying is that the Roy Wilkinses [head of the National Association for the Advancement of Colored People], the Bayard Rustins [who supported Johnson's Vietnam policy] and that stripe—and there are many of them. . . . Their point is: "I'm right; Martin Luther King is dead; he's finished; his nonviolence is nothing. No one is listening to it."[21]

* * *

Everything always led back to Montgomery, where it all began. The road to Memphis started with Montgomery.

From December 5, 1955, until December 20, 1956, when the U.S. Supreme Court ruled that segregated buses were unconstitutional, the Montgomery bus boycott had thrust King into a firing line he would face forever—serious and repeated threats on his life. "Some days more than forty telephone calls would come in, threatening my life," he later recalled, "the life of my family, the life of my child."[22]

King had been willing to take up the Montgomery movement leadership, and he wanted to help end segregation in the South, but he was now faced with the personal cost: the risk of being killed. "When I was arrested for the first time in Montgomery," he later confided, "I thought I was going to be lynched."[23] After a few weeks, as the death threats multiplied, he began to worry: "I felt myself faltering and growing in fear."[24]

It was the first set of threats, in Montgomery, that would give him perhaps the deepest and most personal experience of faith in his life. It was in the kitchen of his Montgomery home where he would have that mystical experience that he had read and wondered about in his Boston University classes. And it was there that he would meet and accept the threat of death, at the very beginning of his public career, knowing that it would follow and shadow him for all the rest of it.

David Garrow and other biographers have taken to calling it the "kitchen experience." It was quite the experience indeed, in a normal 1950s era kitchen. Garrow considers the spiritual experience that King described that night as "the key to understanding Martin King's own understanding of his life, his role, his burden, and his mission."[25]

King had been arrested for the first time in his life, spent a night in jail, and was then released. At home, his 2-month-old infant was sleeping in a crib in the bedroom. Coretta was in bed, sleeping soundly. It was January 27, 1956.

The phone rang. King picked it up.

"Nigger we are tired of you and your mess now. If you aren't out of this town in three days, we're going to blow your brains out, and blow up your house."[26]

Click. Dial tone.

King was rattled. His hands shook as he put the phone down.

Not knowing what to do, he got into bed, tried to sleep, couldn't sleep. He got up, turned down the short hall, walked into the dining room and across into the small kitchen of the parsonage. The tiles were 1950s burnt yellow. The square table in the middle was plastic. The stove was old and worn. A coffee kettle was in the corner. King boiled some water, added some coffee. It was past midnight.

King was scared.

"I started thinking about many things," he recalled in one of his sermons approximately a decade later. "I was ready to give up . . . I tried to think of a way to move out of the picture without appearing a coward."

He reminisced about how great his life had been and how terrible it could become:

> The first twenty-five years of my life were very comfortable years, very happy years. I didn't have to worry about anything. I have a marvelous mother and father. They went out of their way to provide everything for their children . . . life had been wrapped up for me in a Christmas package.

He paused and then went on.

"Everything was done [for me] . . . and if I had a problem I could always call Daddy—my earthly father. Things were solved."[27]

But no longer.

Could he really give that life up? Could he now consciously give up all his comfort and safety to put his own life at risk for a political movement?

He thought about his religion. He believed in God, he really did; but it was an inherited religion, received from his mother and father, from his grandfather. He thought again about his beautiful baby, so new to the world, so innocent. Was it fair to put her life at risk? She could be taken from him in a moment. His wonderful wife could be taken from him in a moment.

He recalled many times in sermons how he had a turning point that night. Uncertain what to do, he did what he had been taught to do when he was confused. He knelt in prayer, his hot coffee cup sitting in front of him.

He prayed out loud: "Lord," he murmured, "I'm down here trying to do what's right. I think I'm right. I think the cause we represent is right. But Lord, I must confess that I'm weak now. I'm faltering. I'm losing my courage."

King had heard about the need for a spiritual experience to make religion real. He'd never had it. Now, at the weakest and most fearful point in his life, it happened. He knelt silently, confessing his weakness, and then heard "an inner voice" saying to him: "Martin Luther, stand up for righteousness. Stand up for justice. Stand up for truth. And lo, I will be with you. Even until the end of the world."

King trembled as he recalled "the voice of Jesus, saying still to fight on. He promised never to leave me alone, never to leave me alone. No never alone! No never alone!"[28] He paused, as he recalled the scene in a later sermon, and repeated, more quietly: "No, never alone. He promised never to leave me alone."

King talked about this experience movingly many times in later sermons (and in private conversations).[29] Listeners can hear the fear in his voice, the confusion, and the determination at the end.

Visitors can go to the little parsonage house in Montgomery. They can go to the little kitchen in the back and stand around the table in the center. There, they can take a picture and wonder about a young man standing there in the mid-1950s, holding a cup of coffee, and asking God to speak to him in the face of threats on his life.

That was quite a little kitchen.

* * *

A few days later, the phone callers made good on their promise.

Coretta Scott King was sitting in the living room of her house, the parsonage of Dexter Avenue Baptist Church, talking with a friend. Her husband was at a political meeting at the church; their 2-month old baby, Yolanda, was in a bedroom in the back of the house.

Crash!

A brick slammed through the front window, spraying glass at the women. Coretta and her friend ran to the back bedroom to the baby.

Bang!

A loud explosion rocked the house and glass shattered everywhere. Coretta fell to the floor, covering the baby's body. After a few minutes, she came back to the front of the house and saw the shattered door and front windows. She pulled the door open and saw a small crater in the front porch, an exploded bomb smoldering underneath.

She went back inside and called the church. In a few minutes, her husband arrived, as dozens of neighbors surrounded the house. Police came too, and they tried to cordon off the area. The citizens who came to the house were furious. Some were shouting, yelling; a few had guns and knives. Police restrained a man challenging Whites to a shootout. The police worried a riot would break out, and they spoke with King.

The young pastor checked on his wife and baby, composed himself, and came out to the front yard to speak to the mob, by then a few hundred people. The mayor had arrived, and the police commissioner. Flanked by the mayor and police commissioner, King began by saying no one was hurt and then continued:

> Don't get panicky. . . . Don't get your weapons. . . . He who lives by the sword dies by the sword. . . . We are not advocating violence. We want to love our enemies. I want you to love our enemies. Be good to them. Love them and let them know you love them. . . . We must meet hate with love.

King had calmed the crowd. He now reassured it:

> I did not start this boycott. . . . If I am stopped, our work will not stop. For what we are doing is right . . . is just. And God is with us. . . . Go home and sleep calm . . . don't worry . . . I am all right and my wife is all right.

The crowd wouldn't leave, however, until they saw Coretta. She came outside. The angry mob began to disperse. A White policeman turned to a comrade, and whispered, "We'd sure enough be dead if it wasn't for that nigger preacher."[30]

Quietly, along with Ralph Abernathy, King applied for a gun license.[31] King and Abernathy were turned down, even after meeting with Alabama's governor. But others in their entourage had pistols, and for some months, the new apostle of nonviolence kept a gun under a cushion in his living room. Prodded by Glenn Smiley, a White activist for the Fellowship of Reconciliation (FOR; a pacifist New York–based group), and FOR leaders, King eventually put the guns aside.[32]

Years later, King recalled that he had "accepted the word of the bombing calmly. My religious experience a few nights before had given me the strength to face it."[33]

That night, when the bomb landed on the front porch in Montgomery, would prove to be symbolic of the rest of King's life.

* * *

Until then, King had been preparing, and doing so in relative safety. Atlanta, Crozer Theological Seminary, Boston: Those were all safe places where the struggle against racism was being prepared in abstract. Now he was in Montgomery; it was concrete and real, and his life and those of his wife and child had been threatened. Many normal humans would have retreated, taken a few steps back, maybe gone in another direction. The Northern churches and professorships all still could be had.

Word had spread.

That night, King and his family slept at the house of friends. He didn't sleep calmly, in contrast to what he said in his speech. There was a rapping at the door. Everyone stayed still. Were King's persecutors following him? A moments later, the rapping was repeated. Finally, King's friend peeked outside: It was Martin Luther King Sr. He had driven in the middle of the night from Atlanta 2 hours away. A little while later, Coretta's father arrived from his home about an hour away in Marion, Alabama. Both fathers were anxious for their children.

Daddy King asserted himself as he always had.

"Come on back to Atlanta. I need you at Ebenezer."

King Jr. replied by saying there hadn't been much damage, and he needed to stay for the boycott. King Sr. was fuming.

"It's better to be a live dog than a dead lion."

The son wouldn't be moved; the father pleaded and prodded.

Obadiah Scott, Coretta's father, exerted similar pressure. He made his daughter nervous, but Coretta refused too:

"I will not be returning home," she said. "I would not be happy if I left. I am going to stay here with Martin."[34]

King Jr. was moved. If Coretta had wavered, if she had done her father's bidding and taken their child away with her, what would he have done? Could he have stayed to lead the movement alone? He thanked Coretta tearfully; she was as committed to the movement as he was.

It's important to recognize Coretta's central role at the beginning of it all, as she would take up the mantle at the end. It was Coretta who would organize the King Center in Atlanta; she would spearhead the King national holiday; she would build the legend and burn it into the national imagination. For four decades after his death, Coretta would keep his dream alive. But she also was there at the very beginning, giving him the courage and support to start to dream at all.

The son broke with the father that day, and so did the daughter. The Kings would stay in Montgomery and fight on, knowing all the while that they were faced with death not as a remote end but, rather, as definite fact.

The only question was when.

Glenn Smiley of the Fellowship of Reconciliation rushed to Montgomery to meet and help this new unknown leader of nonviolent change. A month after the house bombing, Smiley wrote back to New York headquarters that a meeting with King represented "one of the most glorious, yet tragic interviews I have ever had." But he had a foreboding:

> I believe that God has called MLK to lead a great movement here and in the South. But why does God lay such a burden on one so young, so inexperienced, so good? King could be a Negro Gandhi, or he can be made into an unfortunate demagogue destined to sway from a lynch mob's tree.[35]

* * *

King suffered from severe clinical depression in the final year of his life. It was obvious to almost everyone around him. Andrew Young, among others, has described the change:

> In the later years, he was given to a kind of depression that he had not had earlier. He talked about death all the time.... He couldn't relax. He couldn't sleep.... Even when we were away on trips, he'd want to talk all night long.... He was spiritually exhausted.[36]

King drank alcohol more regularly and excessively during that last year, probably also making him more impulsive. Normally very self-controlled, he exploded at his aide Bill Rutherford and humiliated him publicly, shocking himself and those who observed the unusual behavior. Roger Wilkins found King "very tired and drained," "profoundly weary and wounded"; Wilkins dated the change to 1966, observing "a profound sadness" since then. King was heckled during a talk in Michigan one month before his death with taunts of "commie" and "traitor." Another staffer commented, "He was dark, gaunt, tired. He felt that his time was up.... He said that he knew they were going to get him." And yet he continued to decline bodyguards.[37]

The evidence of severe depression was overwhelming. Said Ralph Abernathy, "I had never seen him so depressed. Dr. King was greatly, greatly disturbed." He slept even less than he usually had: "I've been getting two hours a night sleep for the last ten days." "It was unbelievable ... the depressed mood that he was in."[38] Abernathy later noted, "He was just a different person. He was sad and depressed." And he stated to another interviewer, "He was a completely different person."[39] Relative strangers saw the marked change. Said Michael Harrington, the socialist,

> In all the previous times I'd met him, he was an extremely ebullient, relaxed, even exuberant man, very warm, funny, good-humored. . . . But at that meeting [in 1967] I felt that a lot of that had left him, and that the tactical situation . . . had put him in an almost despairing mood.[40]

Stanley Levison had advised King against seeing a psychiatrist, but he and Bayard Rustin both began to worry about King's preoccupation with death. Rustin later recalled, "Stanley and I had some very serious talks because we thought Martin was becoming a little too concerned about the possibility of death."

Once when Rustin expressed this concern, King replied, "You think I'm paranoid, don't you?"

"Sometimes I do," Rustin replied.[41]

Like her husband, Marian Logan saw King's growing depression: "He was very depressed," she later recalled, beginning with the negative reaction to his 1967 speech against the Vietnam War. She stated,

> I think he stayed depressed and he got progressively more depressed as he went along. He'd have these up times, I mean you could make him laugh and joke. . . . But I think innately he was a very unhappy, distressed person. . . . And it depressed him terribly and I, I began to see him, you know, going down.[42]

When Dr. Logan recommended that King see a psychiatrist, he was only drawing a conclusion that what was obvious to everyone. There certainly were reasons for King's depression—especially the constant threats to his life for a decade—but identifying causes doesn't negate the experience: King was severely depressed for the final year of his life.

King was frustrated by civil rights conservatives, who opposed his attempt to broaden the movement and oppose capitalism and imperialism, and he was frustrated by civil rights radicals who opposed nonviolence. He realized he was losing the mantle of leadership because some of his followers within the civil rights movement and even within his own SCLC were no longer following.

One day after a meeting of his New York circle, before he went to Memphis, Harry Belafonte noted that "Dr. King was highly highly agitated. His shoes were off, his tie was open, he was walking up and down the living room talking." King said: "I'm really very very concerned. . . . This integration movement is beginning to unfold things that I never quite envisioned. And I wonder if we are not in fact integrating into a burning house?"[43]

One of the last general SCLC staff meetings, which happened in Atlanta in early 1968, was, in retrospect, a kind of Last Supper between King and his disciples, except in this Last Supper the Christ-figure was rageful instead of forgiving.

King expressed anger at the lack of support for his Poor People's Campaign from many of his aides, especially James Bevel and Jesse Jackson. He railed at Jackson in particular in a way that was so out of character that Ralph Abernathy took him aside and asked, "Martin, tell me what is bugging you?"

It was obvious that King was upset by his political failures, but the level of anger and sadness he expressed went beyond what his closest friends believed was called for by the circumstances. Was it depression? Premonition of death? Both?

King walked out of the meeting without ending it, leaving Abernathy behind to finish it, and took refuge with Dorothy Cotton at his Atlanta hideaway apartment.[44]

Notes

1. Interview with Alvin Poussaint, May 15, 2013.
2. White activist Chuck Fager noted,

> That was one of my early tasks as a rookie civil rights worker: to stay close to Dr. King when we filed through the Selma streets. There were three or four of us who shared this duty, and we kept him pretty much surrounded. We were the point men, his bodyguards. Unarmed, of course, and in my case at least, no great physical threat to any direct assailant. But without weapons and muscle, how were we supposed to provide protection? Simple: Our bodies were visual obstructions, blocking the aim of any sniper crouched on nearby rooftops, trying to draw a bead on Dr. King through the scope of a high-powered rifle. The job was explained to me by big James Orange, who had been around the movement a lot longer. I grasped its function at once. But I also had a question: What if the sniper fired anyway, hoping for a lucky shot, and hit me instead? James Orange answered my query first with a characteristically broad, hearty grin. Then he shrugged, slapped me on the shoulder and said, "Hey, don't worry about it, Chuck. If you get killed, we promise—Dr. King will preach at your funeral!"

Chuck Fager, *Eating Dr. King's Dinner: A Memoir of the Movement, 1963–1966* (Durham, NC: Kimo Press, 2014), p. 2. See also https://en.wikipedia.org/wiki/James_Orange.

3. This scene is based on the reports of David Halberstam and James Farmer. David Halberstam, *The Children* (New York: Fawcett, 1998), pp. 272–273. Farmer describes the scene in his memoir, quoted in Keith D. Miller, *Voice of Deliverance* (Athens: University of Georgia Press, 1998), p. 173.
4. Interview with Reverend James Bevel by Katherine Shannon, July 6, 1968, The Civil Rights Documentation Project, transcript p. 15, in David Garrow papers, Pittsburgh, PA, Manuscript Collection 832.
5. Bernard Lee confirmed this aspect—that King expected to be killed; he just didn't know the right time and place. When asked whether King said anything about the possibility that he might be killed, Lee replied,

> He answered that question very early in our relationship. That question was solved years ago. Long before he reached Memphis. It simply became a matter of fact: One

> day, some place, somewhere he knew that he would be assassinated. He used to say so often that he knew he would never live to be 40.

Interview with Bernard Lee by Walter Burrell, June 23, 1977, transcript pp. 209–210, in David Garrow papers, Pittsburgh, PA, Manuscript Collection 832.

6. Interview with Warren "Chip" Logan, May 20, 2013.
7. Marian Logan, *Eyes on the Prize* interview, December 9, 1988, http://repository.wustl.edu/concern/videos/mc87pv33b.
8. They were the leading fundraisers for the party and attended and participated in key strategy sessions and conventions. In the process, Stanley Levison had gained a great deal of experience in radical politics. Disillusioned with communism, especially as it had played out in Stalin's Russia, Levison joined many ex-communists in drifting away from the party. He never rejected his socialist convictions, but he had concluded that a communist revolution would never happen in the United States. Instead, he had been intrigued by Gandhi and Nehru's nonviolent socialism in India, and as soon as he had heard of this young minister who had challenged segregation in Montgomery, Alabama, in 1955, Levison had reached out to him. That was a lifetime ago, it seemed, although it had only been a dozen years. Now that young minister was a worldwide hero, and Levison was still at his side, one of his few White advisers.
9. Hoover had tried for years to convince anyone who would listen that Levison was still a communist—even though he had left the party in the 1950s—which painted King as a communist stooge. Those charges had caused King some trouble with President Kennedy for a while, and they were resurfacing in the Johnson administration, ever since King had come out against the Vietnam War. He had, in effect, become supportive of the communist North Vietnamese, in Johnson's eyes. The president's aides reminded him that there was this Jewish communist in New York, who was King's close adviser.
10. A few years earlier, Jones had been living a comfortable life in Los Angeles, practicing law for the affluent, living with his White wife in a fancy large home with a retractable roof. He had gone to Alabama to help King on a legal problem, and on a visit to Los Angeles, King had come to his home. Impressed by Jones' affluence, King made a point to mention it in a sermon that Sunday in Los Angeles, to which he had invited the young Jones. Chastened, Jones had decided to join King's circle, to devote himself to something larger than himself. He had gotten to know Levison, then moved to New York, and now he was part of King's New York "kitchen cabinet." King, constantly traveling, was in New York almost as much as he was in his hometown of Atlanta, and when in New York, he always consulted with his kitchen cabinet.
11. Marian Logan, *Eyes on the Prize* interview, December 9, 1988, http://repository.wustl.edu/concern/videos/mc87pv33b.
12. King had advanced views regarding mental illness, as demonstrated in a 1958 *Ebony* column response to a reader, who asked for advice regarding her alcoholic husband: "First, let me say that the person who becomes an alcoholic is victimized with a real sickness. The Yale studies on alcohol reveal that the alcoholic has a disease which is as serious as any other organic disease, and consequently the alcoholic is in need of sympathy and understanding rather than scorn."
    King archives, Atlanta, April 6, 1958, Box 87.
13. Tavis Smiley, *Death of a King* (New York: Little, Brown, 2014), pp. 107–108. This dialogue is based on a personal interview between Tavis Smiley and Clarence Jones that occurred in August 2013, according to documentation I received from Smiley and his assistants. Dr. Jones provided the information presented in email form to me on March 13, 2013.
14. Interview with Lonnie MacDonald, August 19, 2016.
15. Email from Charles Bowles, December 12, 2016, who was conducting an oral history with Dr. Lonnie MacDonald:

    > Andrew Young suggested to Mrs. King that the kids receive psychiatric assistance after hearing it helping the Kennedy family. Mrs. King selected Dr. MacDonald due to their friendship and he went down to Atlanta to spend time with the kids for a few weeks.

16. Dr. Jones told me in writing about this event in Dr. Logan's house for the first time in 2013; it had never been revealed in any prior historical work on King. However, citing lawyer–client

confidentiality, Dr. Jones refused to meet with me or provide any further information beyond what is presented in this chapter.

17. Email from Clarence Jones, March 13, 2013.
18. Here is Marian Logan's description in the *Eyes on the Prize* interview, December 9, 1988, http://repository.wustl.edu/concern/videos/mc87pv33b:

 "[Interviewer:] And you had a long evening with you and your husband and Dr. King.

 [Marian Logan:] Right.

 [Interviewer:] Can you tell us about that night?

 [Marian Logan:] Well, it was an horrendous evening. He came around eight o'clock in the evening. And he stayed until I guess it was almost 7:30 a.m., eight o'clock the next morning. We sat up and talked and had drinks, but mainly Martin was trying to turn me around, to change my mind about my opposition to the war—I mean the, not the war, the Poor People's Campaign. And finally my husband said, Martin, leave her alone, you know. She's not gonna change her mind, she believes in this very strongly. And I think you should accept it. Martin left, you see, just to . . . I don't think he could ever accept it because at the end of that . . . that was on a Monday night, he called me every night, every day, sometimes twice day, Tuesday, Wednesday and Thursday, and Thursday was the night he was killed.

 [Interviewer:] You were upset at the end of that night?

 [Marian Logan:] Oh, Lord, yes. Oh, I was devastated by it. And I've always felt if only we had a little more time to talk, not that I would've changed his mind, but maybe we could have come to an adjustment of our feelings about it so that we wouldn't be as rigid. I was hoping that he would really understand my feelings and why my decision was as it was. And I also was hoping, more importantly, that I could make him know that I understood his position and how he felt it was so necessary that he do this. . . .

 [Interviewer:] How did your husband finally end that evening, and what did Dr. King say?

 [Marian Logan:] Well, by that time Arthur was really getting very annoyed. We, we had been up all night, and Martin just wouldn't let up. So, Arthur finally said, Martin, leave her alone. Can't you see she's exhausted? She's not gonna change her mind. So, Martin said, Well, darlin', like he often said, I'll just have to pray for you. Just have to pray for you so you come around. Martin could put such a hurtin' on you, you know, make you feel so guilty. And I would get so angry. Sometimes I would give in, but just a little bit 'cause I was not about to let him think [laughs] he had won completely, you know. But I loved just tinkering with his brilliance and testing his mind, you know. And challenging him in things."

19. Flip Schulke and Penelope McPhee, *King Remembered* (New York: Pocket Books, 1986), pp. 240–241.
20. Marian Logan, *Eyes on the Prize* interview, December 9, 1988, http://repository.wustl.edu/concern/videos/mc87pv33b: "Well, I'll tell you. I did tell him he oughta get his ass outta Memphis. Those were my very words. And he said, Darlin', we can't turn round now. He said, We have to keep going. I said, OK, Martin.
21. https://www.nytimes.com/1985/09/15/us/wiretaps-reveal-dr-king-feared-rebuff-on-nonviolence.html.
22. David Garrow, *Bearing the Cross* (New York: HarperCollins, 2004 [1986]), pp. 57–58.
23. Ibid., p. 640, note 39, quoting from William Peters' 1956 article in *Redbook*, "Our Weapon Is Love."
24. Martin Luther King Jr., *Strength to Love* (Philadelphia: Fortress Press), pp. 113–114.
25. David Garrow, "Martin Luther King, Jr., and the Spirit of Leadership," *Journal of American History* 74 (1987): 438–447, quote from p. 447.
26. Garrow, *Bearing the Cross*, pp. 57–58.
27. Ibid., p. 57.
28. Ibid., p. 58.

29. King's description of the experience in his sermons was not meant just for public consumption. Others describe that he explained this experience in private conversations as well. For instance, Gurdon Brewster, *No Turning Back: My Summer with Daddy King* (Maryknoll, NY: Orbis Books, 2007), p. 68.
30. Garrow, *Bearing the Cross*, pp. 59–61; Taylor Branch, *Parting the Waters* (New York: Simon & Schuster, 1988), pp; 165–166.
31. Coretta King, *My Life with Martin Luther King Jr.* (New York: Holt, Rhinehart & Winston, 1969), p. 130.
32. According to John A. Williams, another incident also had an influence: "He gave up the gun when friends serving as bodyguards almost shot up a newsboy who had rustled a bush by laying his bike against it." John A. Williams, *The King God Didn't Save* (New York: Pocket Books, 1971), p. 24.
33. Garrow, *Bearing the Cross*, p. 60.
34. King, Coretta Scott, "Coretta: My life, my love, my legacy" (p. 50). Henry Holt and Co., 2017.
35. King Center archives, 10:15 and G68.
36. Garrow, *Bearing the Cross*, p. 602.
37. Ibid., pp. 596–602.
38. Ibid., pp. 609–613.
39. Taylor Branch, interview with Ralph David Abernathy, University of North Carolina at Chapel Hill, handwritten notes, November 19, 1984.
40. All citations except the prior endnote are from Garrow, *Bearing the Cross*, pp. 596–599.
41. Garrow, *Bearing the Cross*, p. 602.
42. Marian Logan, *Eyes on the Prize* interview, December 9, 1988, http://repository.wustl.edu/concern/videos/mc87pv33b.
43. Interview with Harry Belafonte, *Eyes on the Prize* interview, at 47:30, May 15, 1989, https://americanarchive.org/catalog/cpb-aacip-36800f8277a
44. David Garrow, *Bearing the Cross*, NY: HarperCollins, 2004 (1986), p 616

10

The Promised Land

On January 15, 1968, Martin Luther King Jr. celebrated his 39th and last birthday at his mother's home in Atlanta, as he always had done, with his favorite soul food: chitlins, pigs feet, and pecan pie. Two days later, he sat with his wife Coretta and his four little children and watched President Lyndon Johnson's State of the Union address. Johnson defended the Vietnam War at length and criticized protests in Black ghettoes: "The American people have had enough of rising crime and lawlessness in this country."[1] The president who had once been a close ally was now another enemy.

At the insistence of friends, King took a week of vacation in Jamaica, but it didn't help.

In the spring of 1968, he was back in Atlanta, having dinner alone with his mother and father. He always had been Daddy King's son in public, but in private he was his mother's child, and he felt he had to prepare her for his death. They had dinner, the usual sumptuous home-cooked meal that "Bunch" so loved to prepare for her family. It was a warm, clear evening, Daddy King later recalled, and they retired to the patio and watched the setting sun.

Daddy King was surprised by his son's bluntness, but he understood that Jr. wanted to be frank with his mother out of respect. "Mother," he said, "there are some things I want you to know. . . . There's a chance, Mother, that someone is going to kill me, and it could happen without any warning at all." Daddy King recalled, "ML said this quickly, and then stood up and walked to the far end of the patio. We sat silently."

He came back to his mother:

> But I don't want you to worry over any of this. I have to go on with my work, not matter what happens now, because my involvement is too complete to stop. Sometimes I do want to get away for a while, go

Soul on Fire. Nassir Ghaemi, Oxford University Press. © Oxford University Press 2026.
DOI: 10.1093/9780197657614.003.0011

> someplace with Coretta and the kids and be Reverend King and family, having a few quiet days like other Americans. But I know it's too late for any of that now. And if mine isn't to be a long life, Mother, Dad, well then I respect that, as you've always taught us to respect it as God's will.[2]

A few years earlier, in 1965, King had mused that maybe he could achieve his own personal "dream":

> At one time I dreamed of pastoring for a few years, and then of going to a university to teach theology. Perhaps, in five years or so, if the demands on me have lightened, I will have the chance to make that dream come true.[3]

As early as 1960, he had even inquired about buying a summer home in Maine to have a place to get away.[4] He never got away; he wasn't going to have the 5 years; time had run out on his personal dream.

It was late. The sun had long set, and he rose to leave. King Sr. later recalled that he and his wife were left with a deep aching feeling inside, not knowing what to say to each other.

* * *

King Jr. was an anxious man, according to some who knew the family well. He would have panic attacks at times; he smoked cigarettes, which are known to have an anxiety-reducing effect; he drank. He also had some physical manifestations of anxiety. He would get hiccups, according to Dr. Clifford Beal, a psychiatrist and family in-law.[5] And he had long had a tic, a movement, a twitch in his face. But now it was gone. Harry Belafonte described it thus: "Dr. King had a psychological problem in that he had a tic, a hiccup . . . he would suffer with it for a given period of time." Belafonte and others "talked about it and it was obviously psychological." Depression often causes anxiety, and anxiety can cause tics. Eventually, the tic disappeared and it was notable to Belafonte. He brought it up with King: "What happened?" King replied, "I've come to grips with death."[6]

"This may be our last movement,"[7] King told Bernard Lafayette, as he asked him to join the Southern Christian Leadership Conference (SCLC) to help organize what would be not just another march on Washington, DC, but a siege—the Poor People's Campaign. The dispossessed would camp out in the capital city for as long as it would take to force radical change.

Many of his allies worried. Old friends, and even his former PhD mentor from his Boston University days, wrote to him in opposition.[8] King had won some major victories, but his new ambitions seemed unwinnable. Could he manage a fight against the Vietnam War and another fight for radical economic change too? *The Washington Post* called King's Poor People's Campaign "an appeal to anarchy,"[9] which may not have been far from the truth. King didn't appear to have any clear idea of what this new march on Washington would do. A young Black Justice Department lawyer, Roger Wilkins (nephew of National Association for the Advancement of Colored People leader Roy Wilkins), was assigned by the Johnson administration to "host" King's march. Wilkins was an advocate of the civil rights movement and wanted to help King achieve his goals, but he believed that King's ideas were "vague." A multiracial group of demonstrators would come to the capital, many on mule trains, and that was about it. It was unclear what they wanted or what they would do.[10]

King's aides were lukewarm. James Bevel wanted to focus on the anti-Vietnam War movement; Jesse Jackson wanted to continue to expand the Chicago movement; Hosea Williams wanted to expand the voting rights and education activities in the South. Andrew Young watched the dissension and worried about where it would end:

> Martin felt that it was important to go and fail . . . even if we were run out of Washington like the [1932 World War I veteran] bonus marchers. . . . He talked seriously of mounting the kind of campaign [that] would possibly lead to our being in prison for a year or two. . . . He was consciously escalating the struggle. . . . We were going along but nobody was excited about a one- to four-year federal prison term. And we knew that that's the sort of thing that he was leading us into.[11]

A few years later, Vincent Harding had a discussion with Young, who said,

> In a way, it was probably best for us who worked with Martin that he was killed when he was, because he was moving into some radical directions that few of us had been prepared for. And I don't think that any of us would have been ready to take the risks of life, possessions, security, and status that such a move would have involved. I'm pretty sure I wouldn't have been willing.[12]

In his last SCLC retreat at Frogmore, South Carolina, in late November 1967, King had laid out the stakes: "This is a kind of last, desperate demand for the nation to respond to nonviolence. Now, they may not respond. I can't promise that. But I think we've got to go for broke this time."[13]

He went for broke with the Poor People's Campaign. And lost.[14]

* * *

Approximately 6 months earlier, in October 1967, his aides had convinced King to take a vacation, this time to Acapulco, to see if he could relax.[15] He checked into the Hotel El Presidente and, as usual, shared a room with his closest friend Ralph Abernathy. There followed an event that Abernathy omitted from his later frank memoir. On the first night there, King slept little. Around 3 a.m., as Abernathy told it later,

> "I awakened . . . [and] discovered that there was no Dr. King in the room and I was terribly frightened and I went out in the living area looking for him . . . and finally it came to me to look out on the balcony protruding in the Pacific Ocean.

There he found his friend and called out:

"Michael, what are you doing?"
"Thinking."
"What's the matter? What are you thinking about?"
"You tell me what I'm thinking about."
"I don't know."
"Can't you tell?"
"No, I can't think." Abernathy was frustrated.
"You see that rock out there?"
"Oh, sure, I see it."
"How long do you think it's been there?" King asked.
"I don't know. I guess centuries and centuries. I guess God put it there."
"I'm thinking about that rock. You can't tell me what I am thinking about looking at that rock?"
"No."

King started singing:

> Rock of Ages, cleft for me;
> Let me hide myself in Thee.
> Rock of Ages, cleft for me;
> Let me hide myself in Thee.
> Let the water and the blood
> From thy riven side which flowed
> Be of sin the double cure. . . .
> While I draw this fleeting breath,
> When mine eyes shall close in death,
> When I soar to worlds unknown

> And behold Thee on Thy judgment throne,
> Rock of Ages, cleft for me,
> Let me hide myself in Thee.[16]

Abernathy brought his friend inside the hotel room, and they went to sleep.

* * *

As King was preparing for the Poor People's Campaign, he received a call from his old friend James Lawson, the original teacher of nonviolence from the Nashville, Tennessee, sit-in days. Lawson was now a minister in Memphis, Tennessee, and he asked King to come to support a strike of Black garbagemen. King's staff and aides urged him against it. They didn't want him to get distracted from the Poor People's Campaign. King thought he could fly to Memphis, lead a march with Lawson and others, and then return to Washington to meet staff there preparing for the Poor People's Campaign. Memphis wasn't meant to be a major prolonged SCLC campaign led by King. King was intending to just lend his support, briefly, and then leave the Memphis strike in the hands of the local organizers there, such as Lawson.

King still had a few more months to live. And increasingly he dropped his trademark calmness and became impolitic.

In mid-March, on his first visit to Memphis that spring, he spoke to a mass meeting and referred to the Biblical story in which Jesus condemned a rich man who ignored the poor:

> And I come here to say that America too is going to hell if she doesn't use her wealth. If America does not use her vast resources and wealth to end poverty and make it possible for all of God's children to have the basic necessities of life, she too will go to hell.[17]

After King left, Lawson and other ministers prepared the way for a major march on March 28. King returned, but the march turned out to be a disaster. King was in the front of approximately 6,000 marchers, but at the back, young activists who were skeptical about nonviolence quickly became disruptive, and began rioting. King aborted the march, and was whisked away in a car.

King was distraught, realizing that he'd have to come back to prove that he could lead a peaceful, effective march.

Two days later, on Saturday March 30, 1968, King called a painful SCLC staff meeting during which he was angry and hostile, especially toward Jesse Jackson. King's anger stunned Jackson and Andrew Young and others present. They saw their leader suffering in a way they'd never seen before.

Young, Bevel, Jackson, and the rest of King's SCLC circle would go back to Memphis with him for another, better march.

That would be the last weekend of King Jr.'s life.

* * *

King flew to Washington, DC, the next day—March 31, 1968—to give his last Sunday sermon at the National Cathedral. His topic was "Remaining Awake Through a Great Revolution." He gave it slowly and in ringing cadences. There was no response from the audience; this was not the Black church experience, with responses such as "Yes, sir," "Make it plain," and "Amen" punctuating and giving color and emotion to King's preaching. The audience silently and politely listened as King defended his planned march on Washington and explained the expansion of his movement from racism to a fight against militarism and poverty. It listened as he directly upbraided his country for the evil war on Vietnam: "America has committed war crimes; it is the biggest criminal in the world." King was speaking in a Washington that only barely tolerated him.

The first few days of that last week, he was back in Atlanta. He didn't want to go to Memphis, but he had to be there on Thursday, April 4, when there was a court hearing about the march.

A few weeks earlier, he had sent Coretta flowers. They were red carnations, but she was surprised they were artificial. She asked him if that was a mistake. No, he replied, "I wanted to give you something that you could always keep."[18]

On Wednesday morning, Abernathy arrived at the King home at 7 a.m. for the ride to the airport. The kids were still sleeping; they weren't awakened. It was an ordinary good-bye.

At the airport, Andrew Young and Dorothy Cotton were waiting. The plane ended up being delayed because of a bomb threat.

They arrived in Memphis and that night, in the midst of a thunderstorm, he spoke one last time at a mass meeting in the Bishop Charles Mason Temple. He hadn't wanted to go; he wasn't feeling well. He sent Abernathy to speak, but Abernathy called him at the motel. The people weren't satisfied; they wanted King. Wearily, King dressed and went over. On his arrival, the crowd became jubilant.

King began by thanking Abernathy, who had introduced him effusively, as "the best friend that I have in the world." He went on to encourage the crowd and reminisced about his life. He recalled his 1958 stabbing and how that knife was stuck in his chest, inches from his aorta; how he had been told later that if he had sneezed, he would have died; and how that young White girl from New York wrote him a letter, grateful that he hadn't sneezed.

"And I want to say tonight . . . that I too am happy I didn't sneeze."

And he went on, reciting all the movements great accomplishments that he had witnessed and led:

> If I had sneezed (he said) I would have missed the freedom rides of 1961;
> If I had sneezed, I would have missed the Albany movement of 1962, when Blacks decided to straighten their backs up;
> If I had sneezed, I would have missed Birmingham, where we aroused the conscience of a nation . . . and Selma;
> If I had sneezed, I wouldn't have had the chance to tell America about a dream that I had had;
> If I had sneezed. . . .[19]

Now, he said, more work was ahead, and there would be more achievements, but he didn't think he would be there to see them. He described that on the flight from Atlanta that morning, there was a bomb scare; and after arriving in Memphis, he had received death threats. He realized that his life was in danger.

He talked about his death:

> We've got some difficult days ahead. But it doesn't matter to me now. Because I've been to the mountaintop . . . and I've seen the promised land. I may not get there with you; but we, as a people, will get to the promised land![20]

* * *

King had a late dinner at the house of Rev. Benjamin Hooks. Around 1 a.m., A. D. King arrived with his girlfriend and Georgia Davis Powers. The two women, who were close friends, had been vacationing in Florida when they heard about the riot in Memphis. They contacted A.D. to meet them, and they all drove together to Memphis.[21] They got rooms underneath King. When King returned from dinner, he joined A.D. and the two ladies, and then he spent the night with Powers. Dorothy Cotton was waiting in another room for King, but he never arrived. The next morning when King came to Cotton's room around 8 a.m., she threw a fit, they tussled, and she left for the airport, going back to Atlanta.[22]

He probably never slept that last night. After Cotton left, King went back to his room with Abernathy and rested in preparation for the day, as Andrew Young was in court seeking to lift the order prohibiting their march planned for April 8. King met briefly in the motel with some of the young "Invaders" and then had a catfish lunch with Abernathy. That would be his last meal.

Just one more campaign, he had thought. Just the Poor People's Campaign and then he could leave the arena for a while. Maybe if he survived, he could finally leave, take a year off and go to Africa; let Abernathy and Young run things for a while, as he recovered in Africa from a decade of nonstop activity.[23] The Poor People's Campaign would be the last one. But Memphis intervened. He had to stop there too; get it over with, like a dry run for the Poor People's Campaign. Then go to DC, and then, if he still lived, go to Africa.

Just one more campaign.

* * *

After lunch, King and A.D. made one last phone call home; it wasn't typical, but something made King feel that he wanted to speak with his mother—one last time.

At approximately 3 p.m., Ben Branch, a musician who headed a band from Chicago, the Operation Breadbasket Orchestra, gathered his group to practice in a room in the motel. Jesse Jackson and Rev. Samuel "Billy" Kyles, a local pastor, joined in singing.

About the same time, James Earl Ray checked into a rooming house across from the motel. His first room didn't have a view of the motel; he asked for another. He hid his Remington 30-mm rifle.

King waited all afternoon for word from Young at the court. Finally at approximately 4:30 p.m., Young came back; they had a pillow fight to relax. Then they got ready to go to dinner at Rev. Kyles' house.[24]

It was six o'clock in the afternoon, and King stood on the balcony of his motel.

Below the balcony stood James Bevel, looking up at his leader as King discussed that evening's plans for dinner. King had sent word to Kyles that he wanted a soul food dinner. King said he could get restaurant food anytime; he wanted soul food. He was looking forward to the roast and chitlins and turnip greens and cornbread that awaited him.[25]

Jesse Jackson stood nearby, as did Andrew Young, Hosea Williams, Bernard Lee, and Ben Branch.

Bevel watched King banter with the group below as he waited for Abernathy to come out of the motel room they shared. All his aides were looking at King as he talked, their backs to the assassin in the boarding house across the courtyard. Bevel was standing sideways.

King spoke to Branch and referred to one of his favorite gospel songs: "Ben, play Precious Lord tonight, and play it real good."

Abernathy was inside, splashing cologne on his face in preparation for the evening meal.

Branch called up to King. Get a coat, he said; it's a cool night.

King listened.

A shot rang out.

Bernard Lee had been in the Air Force. He knew it wasn't anything benign, like the backfire of a car. It was a rifle shot, probably a 30-mm rifle.[26]

A woman screamed.

Lee looked up and saw King's feet protruding over the balcony.

Bevel ducked for cover, then looked up at the boarding house right after hearing the shot. In a moment, he looked back, and King was sprawled on the ground.

"Wow, they can shoot all of us!" Bevel thought. The entire civil rights leadership of SCLC was standing in that courtyard, ready to be picked off one by one. For a moment, Bevel was convinced they'd all be killed.[27]

Andrew Young thought it was a firecracker. He looked up and didn't see King. Maybe he's clowning around again, he thought; faking like he'd been shot.[28]

But there were no further shots.

Jesse Jackson yelled out, "Somebody call an ambulance." Bevel ran off to do so. Lee, Jackson, Young, and Williams hurried up the stairs, where Abernathy was already cradling King's head. The right side of his face had been blown off.[29] Georgia Powers Davis ran up from her motel room on the ground floor. She saw that his necktie had been pierced cleanly in half just below the knot, with the knotted part pointing straight up.[30]

King probably never heard the shot.

He had a slight pulse and was unconscious in minutes, just before the ambulance arrived, his last vision likely being Ralph Abernathy's face, imploring him

> "Martin, it's Ralph. It'll be alright Martin. It'll be alright. Don't worry."
> "Oh, God. Ralph, it's over!" Andrew Young exclaimed.
> "Don't you say that," responded Abernathy.
> "Don't you say that, Andy!
> It will not be over.
> It will never be over!"[31]

His friends and aides were overcome; drenched in the Christian tradition, they knew a crucifixion when they saw one, and like the disciples of Jesus, they began to adore their master. As Young stated, they began to act "strange."

Jesse Jackson put his hands in the blood of the martyr and wiped it on his shirt. Abernathy got a jar and began to scrape blood into it, "crying it was Martin's precious blood. This blood was shed for us."[32]

Maybe, instead of Abernathy's voice, the dying King heard the lyrics he expected to hear that night:

Precious Lord,
Take my hand,
Lead me on,
Let me stand
I am tired,
I am weak,
I am worn,
Through the storm
Through the night
Lead me to the light
Take my hand
Precious Lord
Lead me home.

The disciples mourned in Memphis. King never made it out after all.

* * *

James Bevel, among the disciples, was the least demonstrative, but he was hurt as deeply as the rest: "Once upon a time Martin Luther King lived," Bevel thought to himself over and over again. "He doesn't live any more . . . doesn't live any more."[33]

Young looked down at his leader's body, with "such a clean wound that it literally severed his spinal cord. . . . It wasn't messy, just a very clean shot," and wondered to himself: "You're going to heaven and leaving us in hell. How are we going to get along without you? We were barely making it with you."[34]

Other leaders despaired of nonviolence. Floyd McKissick, the leader of the Congress on Racial Equality (CORE), which had been formed in the 1940s specifically to use Gandhian methods, concluded, "King was the last prince of nonviolence. Nonviolence is a dead philosophy. . . . the white people . . . killed nonviolence."[35]

Deenie Drew, a prominent civic figure in Black Birmingham, had been among King's earliest Alabama friends and still referred to him as "Mike." Years later, reflecting on King's deepening depression in his final year, Drew commented to an interviewer, "In his last year or so, I just feel that Mike had a death wish. . . . I had a feeling that he didn't know which way to turn."[36]

Certainly King wanted to live, if he could; but he was also willing to die, if needed. He had made this clear in many sermons over many years. Yet, one cannot know if his depression deepened to the point, as it does in approximately half of persons who are clinically depressed, where he had thoughts of not caring if he was alive or not. It's not technically suicidality, because one doesn't harm oneself. But sometimes depressed persons can reach the point where they don't care, and then they don't take precautions where they otherwise might.

Drew's speculation can't be proven or disproven. It stands as an unanswered question for history.

Dr. Vincent Harding, another old friend and colleague of King, active with him since the Montgomery days, would wonder about his friend's fate for the remaining four decades of Harding's life. In repeated speeches, given in many different settings in recent years, Harding pursued the same idea: Here we have a PhD in theology, from good economic means, who decides to risk his life every day for a hugely difficult cause, ending racism, and who "died among garbage men. . . . Some people thought he was crazy. King did not accept conventional wisdom. . . . But maybe the 'mad' men and women have something to tell us."[37]

In another setting, Harding expands on the theme:

> From my perspective, one reason we have to follow King out into those strange places that he goes is that the man shows that he is really sort of crazy by the stuff that he tries. . . . Where else can this Ph.D in philosophical theology end up, but going to the garbage workers? Crazy man. Everybody else knows what Ph.D.s are for, but he apparently didn't. He thought that they were for serving garbage men.[38]

When asked about the idea, this craziness, and whether he thought it reflected some mental abnormality in King, Harding replied,

> I was trying to evoke not so much a psychological state but a willingness to be and to do the unexpected, and to walk the uncharted and unpredictable path. And also partly joking about what it means to leave the South and go to Chicago in the winter. It's about being abnormal in the sense of doing what most people don't do. In today's terminology, it's trying to create a new normal.[39]

Floyd McKissick, a leader of CORE, shared Harding's insight: "You had to show courage. You had to be courageous sometimes to the point of stupidity, which most people [saw as] . . . it's crazy." McKissick said he was "characterized as one of those leaders who might have been irrational. My irrational was entirely logical in the framework of what was being done."[40]

Maybe it was helpful to be abnormal to see the need to create the "new normal."

* * *

Dr. Jerry Thomas Francisco, the official Medical Examiner of Memphis, had lying before him the body of a 39-year-old Black male, well preserved except for the fact that his jaw had been blown off and his neck partially severed.

Dr. Francisco was experienced, but he had never been called to the body of a famous person before. (Nine years later, he would be called to do an autopsy on another middle-aged man, 42 years old, who had suddenly died: Elvis Presley.)

Two assistants were on either side of him. A policeman stood behind them, grasping a shotgun. Another policeman stood on the other side of the door to the autopsy suite, also holding a shotgun.[41]

Dr. Francisco found an obvious old scar on the chest, right above the heart, from King's 1958 stabbing. He opened the corpse with a scalpel and went through each part of the body carefully. The doctor dictated aloud: "1. Remote scars as described 2. Pleural adhesions 3. Fatty change liver, moderate 4. Arteriosclerosis, moderate 5. Venous cut-downs 6. Tracheostomy." He observed that the patient's blood alcohol level was 0.01%, which is a residual level of prior drinking. Excessive alcohol use produces the fatty liver changes observed.

The rest of the examination of the body was normal. Of note, King's thyroid and adrenal glands were of normal size and normal microscopically, as was his prostate gland, with no evidence of inflammation, thus ruling out that prior urinary difficulties might have been due to benign prostatic hypertrophy, as opposed to sexually transmitted infections.

At last, Dr. Francisco turned to the paradoxically untouched skull of Martin Luther King. When King was shot, the bullet pierced his neck and cut his spinal cord. King's brain had escaped any gunshot damage and was fully present for observation. It was normal and untouched.

Dr. Francisco summarized:

> Gunshot wound to body and face with: fracture of mandible; laceration [of] vertebral artery, jugular vein, and subclavian artery, right; laceration of spinal cord (lower cervical, upper thoracic); intrapulmonary hematoma, apex, right upper lobe. . . . Death was the result of a gunshot wound to the chin and neck with a total transaction of the lower cervical and upper thoracic spinal cord and other structures in the neck. . . . The severing of the spinal cord at this level and to this extent was a wound that was fatal very shortly after its occurrence.[42]

Notes

1. Tavis Smiley, *Death of a King* (New York: Little, Brown, 2014), p. 148.

2. Martin Luther King Sr. with Clayton Riley, *Daddy King: An autobiography* (New York: Morrow,1980), pp. 186–187.
3. Alex Haley, "Playboy Interview: Martin Luther King," *Playboy*, January 1965.
4. King Center Archives, Box 87, Letter to Rev. John Ruth, June 19, 1960: My friend Herbert Oliver tells me that you are interested in selling your camp in Maine. For quite some time I have been interested in purchasing a summer home in that area of the country where I could bring my family and do some writing. Your camp sounds very interesting to me.
   C. Herbert Oliver was an activist in Birmingham, Alabama, and later moved to Brooklyn, New York, where he was a pastor. He died in 2021.
5. Interview with Dr. Clifford Beal, February 21, 2023. Dr. Beal said that King would have "bad anxiety, panic attacks, hiccups."
6. Harry Belafonte, *Eyes on the Prize* interview, May 15, 1989, question 34, https://americanarchive.org/catalog/cpb-aacip-36800f8277a.
7. Interview with Bernard Lafayette by James Findlay, day 4, p. 54, https://www.loc.gov/folklife/civilrights/survey/view_collection.php?coll_id=949.
8. Harold DeWolf, King's PhD advisor at Boston University, then dean of Wesley Theological Seminary in Washington, DC, met with Andrew Young and Wyatt Walker, King's top SCLC aides, about the plans for the Poor People's Campaign. DeWolf was very concerned and wrote King as follows: Dear Martin.... Are you taking into account the danger to all we treasure in the serious and prolonged disruption of major cities, especially Washington, if... [there is] a general disorder and lawlessness?... Have you considered the danger of provoking a Fascist-type revolution under military leaders... precipitating World War III?
   Letter dated December 11, 1967, King Center Archives, Folder 8:18.
9. David Garrow, *Bearing the Cross* (New York: HarperCollins, 2004 [1986]), p. 359.
10. Roger Wilkins, *Eyes on the Prize* interview, October 17, 1988, http://digital.wustl.edu/e/eii/eiiweb/wil5427.0886.174rogerwilkins.html.
11. Andrew Young, *Eyes on the Prize* interview, October 11, 1985, transcript p. 10, https://americanarchive.org/catalog/cpb-aacip_151-db7vm43n05.
12. Vincent Harding, *Martin Luther King: The Inconvenient Hero* (Maryknoll, NY: Orbis Books, 2008 [1996]), pp. 107–108. Harding originally published this quotation without identification. When I asked Harding about the identity of the person who made this statement, he told me "Andrew Young." Interview with Vincent Harding, December 28, 2012.
13. Garrow, *Bearing the Cross*, p. 582.
14. The Poor People's Campaign would march into Washington a few months after King's death. Roger Wilkins saw that King's friends were too overwhelmed by grief to function: Abernathy was the nominal leader but carried no weight with the marchers; Andrew Young was "sleepwalking"; only Jesse Jackson was active, trying to organize and motivate the demonstrators. The tents were set up, but they soon became filthy with human feces. Federal Bureau of Investigation (FBI) observers claimed that White women who joined the protestors were raped and noted in particular that James Bevel was having sexual relations with both Black and White women. FBI memos, July 17–18, 1968, Box 2.2, in Garrow archives.

    The FBI reports are corroborated by other supporters of the Poor People's Campaign. For instance, Michael Harrington describes it as follows:

    > The state of preparation for the poor people's march was very chaotic. That was typical of Dr. King. Careful organization and planning was not his strong suit. He was a genius at improvising. What he did understand was that his strength was in his appeal to masses of people.... Resurrection City was a mess. There was a great deal of violence inside Resurrection City. It was not the beloved community. The beloved community as we called it, really had come to an end. And I gave a talk there. And I was sitting down on the ground. People gathered around. And there was a Black man in the group listening to me who might have had some emotional problems. I think he probably did. And he decided that I was the representative of White racism in Resurrection City. And he began to attack me, and attack me, and attack me in a sort of a wild and even incoherent way.

Harrington grew fearful for his physical safety and took a plane to New York. He later reflected,

> [I] literally ran away from the meeting. I wanted to get as far away from this place as I could. . . . It dawned on me that . . . one of the most marvelous political movements in America, in the form which it took under Martin Luther King from 1955 to 1968, had come to an end. And that the beloved community was gone forever.
>
> Michael Harrington, *Eyes on the Prize* interview, October 11, 1998, question 9, http://digital.wustl.edu/e/eii/eiiweb/har5427.0719.063michaelharrington.html.

15. T. R. Reid, "King Hearings Begin on a Poignant Note," *The Washington Post*, August 15, 1978, https://www.washingtonpost.com/archive/politics/1978/08/15/king-hearings-begin-on-a-poignant-note/d0ea5740-5624-4eed-9036-b2ff0da9202f.
16. Testimony of Dr. Ralph D. Abernathy, August 14, 1978, hearings before the Select Committee on Assassinations, U.S. House of Representatives, 95th Congress, 2d session (Washington, DC: U.S. Government Printing Office, 1979), vol. I, pp. 33–34.
    A second description of this experience is found in Taylor Branch, interviews with Ralph David Abernathy, University of North Carolina at Chapel Hill, handwritten notes, November 19, 1984.
17. Clayborne Carson, ed., *The Autobiography of Martin Luther King Jr.* (New York: Grand Central Publishing, 1998), p. 354. See also https://www.commercialappeal.com/story/opinion/contributors/2018/03/15/opinion-kings-68-challenge-church-our-calling-memphis/423466002.
18. Coretta Scott King, *Coretta* (New York: Holt, 2017), Kindle edition, p. 155.
19. Garrow, *Bearing the Cross*, pp. 620–621.
20. https://www.youtube.com/watch?v=DKWCxKq0i1k.
21. Georgia Davis Powers, *I Shared the Dream* (Liberty Corner, NJ: New Horizon Press, 1995), Kindle edition, Chapter 19, "The Last Night"; Michael Fingers, "31 Hours, 28 Minutes: A Minute-by-Minute Account of Dr. Martin Luther King's Last Hours in Memphis," *Memphis*, April 2018, p. 78.
22. These events are documented in Abernathy's memoir, Davis Powers' memoir, and an interview with Dorothy Cotton. Abernathy did not identify the women at the time in 1989; Powers identified herself in 1995 to set the record straight, she said. Cotton identified herself in a recent interview. Ralph David Abernathy, *And the Walls Came Tumbling Down* (New York: Harper, 1989), pp. 434–436; Powers, *I Shared the Dream*, Kindle edition, Chapter 19, "The Last Night"; Jason Miller, interview with Dorothy Cotton, https://theconversation.com/the-civil-rights-activist-so-close-to-martin-luther-king-jr-she-was-thought-of-as-his-other-wife-118750.
23. Interview with Bernard Lee by Walter Burrell, June 23, 1977, transcript p. 219, in David Garrow papers, Pittsburgh, PA, Manuscript Collection 832.
24. Fingers, "31 hours, 28 minutes," pp. 72–81.
25. Interview with Rev. Harold Middlebrook by Joan Beifuss and Bill Thomas, July 18 and 21, 1968, in David Garrow papers, Pittsburgh, PA, Manuscript Collection 832, Box 1.9, transcript p. 39.
26. Interview with Bernard Lee by Walter Burrell, transcript p. 212, in David Garrow papers, Pittsburgh, PA, Manuscript Collection 832.
27. Interview with Rev. James Bevel by Katherine Shannon, July 6, 1968, The Civil Rights Documentation Project, transcript p. 15, in David Garrow papers, Pittsburgh, PA, Manuscript Collection 832, pp. 11–12:

> Everybody was pretty well looking at [King] because he was talking, which meant that everybody had their back turned to the assassin. . . . So when we heard the shots, my reaction was to look towards the building where the shots came from. And that was almost like a bat of the eye, because I didn't have my back to the assassin. My eyes could be on both. . . . So by the time I looked that way and I looked back, Dr. King was falling. It was like . . . a flash.
>
> My initial rection was, I guess that, "Wow, they can shoot all of us!" And what I was really waiting I guess to hear were the other shots, and wait for the pain, because I expected that if whoever shot King was fairly intelligent, they would have know that he

> wasn't doing the movement. It was his executive staff, and they should probably shoot all of us. So I was sort of waiting on that. That was so clear to most of us, that King articulated the movement, but he didn't create it. I thought that was pretty clear.

28. Andrew Young, *Eyes on the Prize* interview, October 11, 1985, transcript p. 16, https://americanarchive.org/catalog/cpb-aacip_151-db7vm43n05.
29. Interview with James Bevel by Katherine Shannon, The Civil Rights Documentation Project, Washington, DC, July 6, 1968, Garrow archive, p. 11.
30. Powers stated,

> Someone was pointing to the second floor. I looked up to my left and gasped. One of Dr. King's knees stuck straight up in the air and I could make out the bottom of one foot. People in the courtyard had scattered to take cover. Without pausing, I hurried up the stairs closest to my room. Reaching King's room, I stepped inside and saw Andy Young and Ralph Abernathy, their faces grim, feverishly telephoning for an ambulance. They hardly noticed me, and I went out on the balcony. Alone, I walked over and looked at Dr. King. He was lying in a pool of blood that was widening as I stood there staring. The bullet had pierced the right side of his neck. His tie had been severed about an inch from the knot. Both the knot and an inch of tie were sticking up. It is a picture permanently imprinted in my mind.
>
> Powers, *I Shared the Dream*, Kindle edition, Chapter 19, "The Last Night."

31. Flip Schulke and Penelope McPhee, *King Remembered* (New York: Pocket Books, 1986), p. 246.
32. Andrew Young, *Eyes on the Prize* interview, October 11, 1985, transcript p. 16, https://americanarchive.org/catalog/cpb-aacip_151-db7vm43n05. Abernathy would be grieving for a long time. On the occasion of King's 40th birthday, in a brief sermon he gave to King's family and friends at Ebenezer Baptist Church, Abernathy stated,

> I must close now Martin, for already the program has been too long. But honesty impels me to admit that nights are long, since you went away. I must repeat it for you, nights are long since you went away. I think of you Martin, both night and day. My buddy. My buddy. Your buddy misses you.
>
> In David Garrow papers, Pittsburgh, PA, Manuscript Collection 832.

33. Interview with Rev. James Bevel by Katherine Shannon, July 6, 1968, The Civil Rights Documentation Project, transcript p. 15, in David Garrow papers, Pittsburgh, PA, Manuscript Collection 832, p. 14.
34. https://theundefeated.com/features/andrew-young-on-mlk-assassination-youre-going-to-heaven-and-leaving-us-in-hell.
35. Schulke and McPhee, *King Remembered*, p. 253.
36. Garrow, *Bearing the Cross*, p. 602.
37. https://archive.goshen.edu/news/vincent-harding-king-for-the-21st-century-calls-us-to-walk-with-jesus-2/.
38. Vincent Harding, "Martin Luther King and the Future of America," *Cross Currents* 46, no. 3 (1996).
39. Interview with Vincent Harding, December 28, 2012.
40. Interview with Floyd McKissick by David Garrow, August 3, 1984, transcript p. 9, in David Garrow papers, Pittsburgh, PA, Manuscript Collection 832.One could add other examples. Fred Shuttlesworth was the leader of SCLC in Birmingham. Wyatt Tee Walker describes him:

> "We never could have been able to pull Birmingham off if it had not been for his Alabama Christian Movement for Human Rights. Some people said, "Fred's a little crazy." Well you need to be a little crazy to be in Birmingham. He was one of the bravest men I know. Now, some people say he was brave because he didn't have good sense. Fred had good sense, but he really had guts. He was one of the gutsiest men I know. He would try anything."

Interview with Wyatt Tee Walker by John Britton, October 11, 1967, transcript p. 82, in David Garrow papers, Pittsburgh, PA, Manuscript Collection 832.

41. MLK the Truth LLC, *The 13th Juror: The Official Transcript of the Martin Luther King Assassination Conspiracy Trial* (Google eBook, 2009), pp. 240–247.
42. Autopsy report by Dr. J. T. Francisco, Office of the Chief Medical Examiner, Tennessee Department of Public Health, dated April 11, 1968; accessed at https://www.autopsyfiles.org.

PART II

THE PSYCHOLOGY OF NONVIOLENCE

11

A Politics of Radical Empathy

> First, know thyself. . . . Secondly, accept thyself. . . . Third, trust thyself. . . . Fourth, deny thyself. . . . There is so much more to think about than ourselves.[1]

The central theme of this book is that understanding Martin Luther King Jr.'s mood states will give us a central insight into the core of his nonviolent resistance philosophy: His thinking was *a politics of radical empathy*. To be nonviolently resistant to injustice, you have to have radical empathy for everyone, including your opponents. This is the difference between his nonviolence and pacifism, as well as the reality of who he was and what he thought as opposed to today's sterilized version venerated in sculpture and holiday. King was no pacifist: He didn't oppose war per se. Like Gandhi, he stated that if you had to choose between accepting injustice peacefully or resisting injustice violently, then violent resistance is preferable. He believed that nonviolent resistance is even more effective and preferable than violent resistance to evil and certainly more so than passive acquiescence.

The perspective suggested here is that King's insight into and commitment to nonviolence grew out of a radical empathy for his opponents and that this empathy itself may have grown out of his experiences with depression. Furthermore, the reason why so many of us may not share this empathy is because we may not have had those depressive experiences. Radical empathy is not a natural trait of human nature, unless you're depressed. Otherwise, it has to be learned, and it is very difficult to learn. The rest of this chapter attempts to explains these concepts.

* * *

Love, *agape*, empathy—whether in English, Greek, or modern jargon, human life entails this basic principle: dependence of everyone on everyone else;

Soul on Fire. Nassir Ghaemi, Oxford University Press. © Oxford University Press 2026.
DOI: 10.1093/9780197657614.003.0013

the *existential equality of all persons*. When depressed, one knows the truth of empathy—about our fundamental similarities—more viscerally and painfully than normal people do. A few leaders, like King, who were intimately familiar with depression, made empathy the core of their political method. The politics of radical empathy, I believe, is the psychological underpinning of nonviolent resistance. Depression reveals the truth of empathy, and empathy, in turn, engenders unexpected powers of leadership.

The concept of empathy is relatively new, having been invented as a word and applied in psychology in 1903 by the German psychologist Theodor Lipps. He created the term *Einfühlung*, which means "feeling into," and this was translated into English in 1910 as empathy, which means "into suffering." The idea in German can mean "one feeling," reflecting not so much imagining oneself in another person's place but actually experiencing what the other person is experiencing. The German psychiatrist and philosopher Karl Jaspers first made empathy central to psychiatry in 1913, a revolutionary idea at the time.[2] His insight was ignored by psychoanalysis and behaviorism, the two strongest currents of 20th-century psychology, until a renaissance in recent years coming from sources in neuroscience.

Two features were identified in the brain: oxytocin receptors and mirror neurons. Oxytocin is a hormone that peaks during sexual activity and breastfeeding; it has been shown to enhance social affiliation. Animals with many oxytocin receptors are highly social and live in groups; those with few oxytocin receptors are loners. In humans, there are many oxytocin receptors in the brain, establishing a physiology for empathy. The second feature is mirror neurons: These are neurons in the brain that activate when we watch someone else doing something. So normally, if we move an arm or leg, the motor cortex of our brain will light up, but so will another part of the brain that doesn't have to do with movement—the insula. That's where these other neurons, now called mirror neurons, are located. They are so called because if we see someone else move an arm or leg, the mirror neurons in our brain activate, but our own motor cortex does not (because we are not moving ourselves). These neurons "mirror" the activity of another being. Similar research has since shown that some of the neurons which fire when one feels pain will also fire when one witnesses someone else in pain. Here is empathy itself, lighting up on a brain scan. Coining the term "mirror neuron system," researchers found that 10% of the human brain is wired to turn on as if it is doing what it is only observing.[3]

One-tenth of the brain is wired for empathy.

Besides being born with plenty of oxytocin receptors, how can one attain a high degree of empathy? One answer, I believe, is to be depressed. In one study, severely depressed patients had much higher scores on empathy scales than a college student control group; the more depressed patients were, the higher their empathy scores. This enhanced empathy was emotional, not cognitive; it reflected an actual sensation of sharing others' feelings, not merely an intellectual understanding of those feelings. This research suggests an important conclusion: When the depressive episode is over (and, short of suicide, all depressive periods end, usually within a year after they start), the intense experience of emotional identification with others might leave a lasting mental legacy. Emotional empathy, produced by the severe depressive episode, may prepare the mind for a long-term habit of appreciating others' points of view.

This is suggested by another study, in which patients with various psychiatric illnesses (depression, schizophrenia, and personality and anxiety disorders) completed an empathy scale and measures of current or past suicidal thoughts or attempts. Various scales have been developed to measure empathy; they involve self-description of how often one appears to understand the emotions or thoughts of others. A commonly used scale is the Interpersonal Reactivity Index, used in this study, which consists of 28 questions that measure four behaviors: "perspective taking" or "the tendency to spontaneously adopt the psychological view of others in everyday life"; "empathic concern" or "the tendency to experience feelings of sympathy or compassion for unfortunate others"; "personal distress" or the "tendency to experience distress or discomfort in response to extreme distress in others"; and "fantasy" or "the tendency to imaginatively transpose oneself into fictional situations." These patients were in standard outpatient treatment and had few, if any, symptoms of their disease at the time of the study. They then read a brief story about a woman who committed suicide by overdose. Researchers expected that subjects who were or had been suicidal would sympathize with the woman in the story, but in fact those who had never been suicidal were more sympathetic. The exceptions were depressed subjects with past suicidality; they were especially sympathetic to the story.[4]

This correlation between depression and empathy shouldn't surprise mental health professionals. Maybe nothing is more important than empathy in the daily work of the mental health specialist; nothing—not drugs, nor any specific psychotherapeutic technique. Subsequent studies have found that patients' ratings of their psychotherapists' empathy predict improvement for depression, even with treatments (e.g., cognitive–behavioral therapy) that do not emphasize empathy.[5]

Empathy seems central to the experience of depression and just as central to its treatment. You are wired to experience it in your brain and in your body, and it thereby becomes central to your mental life. This is how things are for most of us, and perhaps more so for those who experience depression.

The psychology of nonviolence as advocated by Dr. King is relevant especially today given the controversy around the Black Lives Matter (BLM) movement and the focus on structural racism, especially as it relates to police violence and racial bias in the U.S. legal system. The BLM movement may not succeed fully if it is not nonviolent fully, avoiding acts of vandalism or theft. And it will need to include the psychology of radical empathy to guide that nonviolent action. Structural racism will not be removed by public education or cultural peer pressure from one part of society toward another. Rather, King's politics of radical empathy may be the best method to bring those competing parts of society together behind a new anti-racist consensus.

* * *

As discussed more later, a potential risk is that the anti-racist movement of the 21st century will divide the country in identity politics, as opposed to the unifying effect of the civil rights movement of the 20th century. There are major cultural differences between the two movements that are worth exploring. King was educated and reared in the 1940s and 1950s, before the counterculture movement of the 1960s and 1970s. The latter movement, among other things, was heavily influenced by the philosophy of postmodernism, in contrast to the Enlightenment tradition in which King was reared. This distinction is important. The basic postmodernist view—most explicated in the 1960s and 1970s by French thinkers such as Michel Foucault—was that human knowledge is highly culture-bound. There are no absolute and essential Truths, with a capital T, but only socially constructed truths, with a lowercase t. What is called truth is a reflection of the dominant "discourse" of an ascendant social and political class. In the modern Western world, that class is the heterosexual White male power elite. Hence the emphasis on the classics of dead White men: Socrates, Plato, Aristotle, and so on. These social constructions can and should be changed by a new power structure built on those who have been left out: women, non-Whites, and non-heterosexuals. Hence the rise of women's studies, Black studies, Latino studies, and gender studies in the universities, overshadowing and sometimes replacing traditional disciplines such as history and sociology. Multiculturalism became the vogue, and any claim to absolute truth became suspect.

It is interesting to note that two fields in particular that have laid claim to absolute truths have become the target of the postmodernist ideology of the post-counterculture world of the 21st century: religion and science.

Religion is an obvious target. Friedrich Nietzsche is the primary philosopher of postmodernism, its first exponent, given credit for being so by Foucault and others. And Nietzsche famously declared God to be dead, based on this critique about the social construction of truth. Many modern leftist activists are inspired by Nietzsche and are comfortable with his critique of religion. King would not agree with them. He clearly and explicitly rejected Nietzsche's ideas, especially the concept that God is dead. King explicitly rejected the moral relativism of this way of thinking, a sibling to its epistemological relativism.

If there are no truths, only social constructions, then nothing is *really* true. If nothing is *really* true, then no one can really tell you that one thing is right or not. You are free to do what you want. All is permitted; nothing is forbidden.

Right next to God, Nietzsche buried science because science is the other field that claims absolute truth. The 21st century's postmodernist ideology can't accept absolute truth, so it not only must reject religion but also must reject science. This is ironic, as science and religion had been adversaries for a century before the rise of postmodernism. But in that Enlightenment era conflict, the issue was who had the Truth: science or religion, Darwin or the Archbishop. The 21st-century world questions Truth itself; science and religion both are rejected.

The rejection of science was present years ago with avowedly liberal educated elites refusing to provide vaccines to their children. They doubted the science. It has been followed by citizens refusing to wear masks and/or get vaccinated during a deadly worldwide pandemic. They have different rationales: White right-wing opponents distrust the government; non-White left-wing opponents distrust the medical Establishment; libertarians distrust everyone. Their rationales share one thing in common: a postmodernist distrust of science.

Science holds that certain things are true, no matter who runs society, no matter who controls power, and no matter any individual's personal opinion. Postmodernism can't accept this threat to its core belief. Hence, after the counterculture, the influence of science in society has weakened. Epidemic diseases are beginning to prove that these postmodernist ideas are not only wrong but also deadly.

* * *

There is much that the contemporary world can relearn from King in today's era of postmodernist ideology. The politics of identity groups is at odds with King's politics of radical empathy. A large part of the world will remain White, and male, and heterosexual. They need to be included in the fight against racism—not simply rejected as the enemy.

King's nonviolence wasn't idealistic: It wasn't based on a belief that people are inherently or mostly good, and if we treat each other well, all will be well in the world. It was based on the realistic observation that there has been consistent evil and war and violence throughout human history, in all cultures and ages, and that this violent evil is part of human nature, in all of us, in ourselves as well as our enemies. Given that we are all naturally violent, being nonviolent is both a necessity and a major struggle against our natural tendencies.

The most unnatural thing to do is to resist injustice nonviolently. All our instincts tell us either to passively accept injustice (our most common reaction) or to fight it violently. To resist while not injuring the enemy is very difficult to understand, much less to do.

King was realistic about this problem of human nature, but he also concluded that unless we made this superhuman effort to be nonviolent, the actual consequence of violent resistance, even to injustice, is always the continuation of violent struggle between enemies. The only realistic way to break the vicious cycle of human history is to end all violence, even in the most just causes, while at the same time resisting injustice so as to break the hold of violent evil (which is to say, normal) human nature.

This nonviolent resistance could only be appreciated once we realize that we are all the same; that we are all violent in our core; that in the most evil person there is some good, and in the most virtuous person there is some evil. We are all interconnected and interdependent, and I cannot be who I want to be unless you become who you want to be, and you cannot become who you want to be unless I become who I want to be.

These are paraphrases of stock King phrases in his speeches and sermons: this is his radical empathy, the basis of his nonviolent resistance politics. It means loving your enemies—even a Bull Connor; even, Gandhi said, a Hitler; even, a modern King might say, a Saddam Hussein or even an Osama bin Laden[6]—while at the same time nonviolently resisting the evil that those men promoted.

King may not have converted Bull Connor himself to nonracist views (although at one point, Connor's firemen refused to turn their hoses on nonviolent demonstrators), but King converted Connor's children and grandchildren. That's a secret to nonviolent resistance: King's goal was not just ending segregation legally (this was done in the courts, mainly by lawyers of the National Association for the Advancement of Colored People). King wanted to cure the *disease of racism*, as he put it; he wanted to change minds and hearts, not just laws. This approach also was highlighted in James Bevel's use of the phrase "political psychiatry." The White man was sick; nonviolence was the cure.[7]

In short, King had a psychological goal—changing racist feelings—and he used psychological means—*radical* empathy. We may realize better that this was his method, and why, by better appreciating how King himself might have developed this unusually radical empathy as part of his lifelong struggle with recurrent depression.

Notes

1. MLK BU Archives, *Ebony* column, August 8, 1958, Box 87.
2. Karl Jaspers, *General Psychopathology* (Baltimore, MD: Johns Hopkins University Press, 1997 [1913]).
3. Nassir Ghaemi, *A First-Rate Madness* (New York: Penguin, 2011).
4. Ibid.
5. Ibid.

6. Contrary to the direct claims of Clarence Jones. Clarence B. Jones and Joel Engel, *What Would Martin Say?* (New York: Harper, 2008).
7. Andrew Young also often explained some of the rationale for nonviolence in that manner, citing Bevel:

> James Bevel put our outrage into perspective when he said that we had to become "political psychiatrists" and view our oppressors as our patients. A psychiatrist doesn't get angry with his patients when they are violent towards him; the doctor must help his patients to realize that their violence grow out of sickness and insecurity. We must help them, not hate them.

Andrew Young, *A Way Out of No Way* (Nashville, TN: Nelson, 1994), p. 58.

There is a larger question of whether the metaphor of racism as a disease is apt. The only Black psychiatrist who has addressed this matter directly and at length is Alexander Thomas, and he criticizes this view on the grounds that a sickness is an abnormality that deviates from the more common norm, whereas racism is the norm in White America. Furthermore, Thomas argues, to view racism as a mental illness may work to absolve White Americans from taking responsibility for it. Alexander Thomas and Samuel Sillen, *Racism and Psychiatry* (Secaucus, NJ: Citadel Press, 1972), pp. 112–121.

My view is that the common frequency of racism demonstrates that it is built on core aspects of normal human psychology, namely limited empathy. Thus, I agree with Thomas that racism is normal, not abnormal. But I think the metaphor of racism as a disease is useful mainly because it then puts nonracists in the role of the doctor, which is to heal and treat, not to punish. The diagnosis, in short, may be wrong (racism is normal, not a disease), but the treatment may be correct (it cannot be punished away, but only healed).

12

A Psychology of Nonviolence

The radical empathy that underlies the psychology of nonviolence means that each person should seek common ground with another person, and each race, and each nation. It entails a radical monism about humanity.

It also requires more courage than a traditional reliance on using force, as Bernard Lafayette explains:

> The first principle of nonviolence is that you have to be courageous. It's not an absence of fear, but it's not being afraid of death, which is different than wanting to die. The question is if death is something you would give to achieve your goals.[1]

Martin Luther King Jr. taught that the attitude of nonviolent resistance must be "I will not fight, but I will not comply." And after achieving that state of mind, the next step would need to be taken: "I am not willing to kill, but I am willing to die."[2] Here is the extra courage of nonviolence. It is less courageous to grab a gun and hide and try to kill someone else before they kill you. It is more courageous to have no gun and be willing to die rather than to kill.

Among professional psychologists, few have thought about this topic more carefully than Dr. Charles Collyer of the University of Rhode Island. For years, Collyer taught courses and workshops on nonviolence, along with Lafayette, King's close aide. One of his insights is that the natural human state, the automatic response to injustice, is violence. Violent reactions are rapid and immediate, intuitive and emotional. Nonviolent action is slow; it has to be thought about and reasoned. It's more cognitive. Nonviolence has to be learned, whereas violence is instinctive.[3]

The psychology of nonviolence requires, then, as a primary step, the avoidance of immediate reaction, for the first reaction will be more likely to be violent. Second thoughts are more likely to be nonviolent.

Soul on Fire. Nassir Ghaemi, Oxford University Press. © Oxford University Press 2026.
DOI: 10.1093/9780197657614.003.0014

So when faced with an injustice, you must hold back initially, think first, then act. As Andrew Young often says, your mind is your best weapon. Use it instead of your hands.

Empathy then is central. You start thinking about things from your adversary's point of view. This doesn't change the fact that your adversary is unjust and has harmed you; nor that you dislike your adversary. But you're making a temporary retreat into your mind, before you decide what to do, to see if you can empathize in any way with your adversary. Is there any small part of your adversary that you can accept or agree with?

There always will be. Then you start with that part, you show your adversary that you agree and respect them on that matter. And then you move to tell them what you don't accept, and you resist it.

* * *

In the early 1920s, some National Association for the Advancement of Colored People (NAACP) activists were impressed by Gandhi and began to discuss the possibility of nonviolence in America. E. Franklin Frazier, a Morehouse College sociologist, published an attack on "non-resistance" in the NAACP journal, *The Crisis*, which W. E. B. DuBois edited. It was, in fact, an attack on what King would call "passive acquiescence," accepting the injustice of the status quo and saying you still loved White people, hoping to change their minds. A White Quaker suffragette wrote a critique, calling for a Negro Gandhi to arise, which DuBois didn't publish. DuBois showed the critique to Frazier, however, and in the next issue of *The Crisis*, DuBois quoted Frazier's reaction that if a Negro Gandhi arose in the South, "I fear we would witness an unprecedented massacre of defenseless black men and women in the name of Law and Order and there would scarcely be enough Christian sentiment in America to stay the flood of blood."[4] The options were either violent rebellion, which was doomed, or the very slow process of seeking purely legal change, which is the direction that DuBois' NAACP took.

When King took the lead of the Montgomery bus boycott in 1955, he changed the direction of the civil rights movement toward that nonviolent direct action which prior leaders had worried would fail and be bloody. The NAACP, then headed by Roy Wilkins, directly opposed mass direct action, even comparing it in private to Hitler's demagoguery.[5] King's approach was much more radical and was a major break with preceding civil rights leaders.

In fact, as Lonnie King, the leader of the Atlanta student sit-ins, would later reflect, all the movement activities from 1955 to 1968 led to approximately three dozen fatalities. With those sacrifices, a century of segregation and voting restrictions was ended. Violent action almost certainly would have led to hundreds, perhaps thousands, of deaths. Purely legal efforts almost certainly would have moved much more slowly, with decades more delay before real progress would have been achieved. Approximately three dozen sacrifices were needed, but not more.[6] And one of them had to be the leader of the movement.

That's part of the psychology of nonviolence, which makes it so difficult for a normal human being: One has to be willing to be killed rather than kill.

In the first months of the Montgomery bus boycott, DuBois, then 88 years old, reached out to the new Negro Gandhi he had foreseen and worried about. He didn't give him advice; he didn't express his doubts. He sent a poem of courage by telegram:

> Rev. Martin Luther King Jr., Dexter Avenue Baptist Church . . .
> Fear not O little flock the foe
> That madly seeks thine overthrow
> Dread not its rage and power
> What though thy courage often faints
> Its seeming power o'er God's saints
> Lasts but a little hour.[7]

* * *

One can think of democratic government itself as a form of nonviolence. Disagreements are solved with votes, and with one group accepting the view of another, even if it disagrees. A group doesn't say, "I lost the election, but I don't accept, so I'm going to war with you." This kind of reaction, seen in less democratic countries (and recently in the United States), grows out of a violent approach to change.

A nonviolent democratic attitude is limited to internal domestic debates, however. With regard to other countries, in foreign relations, there are no votes and no agreeing to disagree. Rather, a Western democracy will impose its will on other nations or groups with which it disagrees. In the colonial era, it was the Congo or India or the Philippines; in the Cold War era, it was Iran or Cuba or Chile; in the post–Cold War world, it is Afghanistan or Iraq or al-Qaeda.

Henry Kissinger famously defined this approach to foreign policy as the balance of power. Different groups of nations threaten each other to a point where everyone is afraid to fight. And that's called peace. This viewpoint is defined as being true to human nature because all people are violent and aggressive toward each other. In foreign relations, this approach leads to the balanced anarchism of constant low-level warfare, exploding occasionally into larger conflict. But the domestic history of Western democracies has shown that human nature doesn't entail this approach to political life. Nonviolent approaches are possible if people agree to them. Until now, this agreement has been limited to behavior within a nation. The question is whether it can be broadened to relations between nations.

The original insight behind the United Nations (UN) related to this argument. But the UN has failed to be functional in many cases, and it is hampered by insufficient commitment by its members to abjure violent action. When the United States invaded Iraq, for example, President George W. Bush ignored the opposition of the UN.

If nonviolence is to expand into all political relations, especially with other nations, as King wished, then it has to become a general philosophy of political life, not a tactic. It has a central personal aspect. Nonviolence isn't a social theory; it's a personal psychology, which can have social impact. It's not just altruistic; it's selfish too. As Bernard Lafayette stated, "The non-violent fight is about maintaining your self-respect, your dignity. And one of the reasons why we don't become violent with other people is because of what it does to us."[8]

In this aspect, it would follow again the evolution of democratic societies. In democracies, citizens shouldn't say, "I'll vote and if I lose, I'll violently attack my opponents." In other words, if the nonviolent approach (voting) fails, then violence is justified. Rather, the violent approach is rejected in principle, under any circumstances.

We have to see if this is possible in foreign relations. If one fails to convince another country or group to behave in a certain way, by nonviolent means (including economic sanctions), can a nation conclude that it will not go to war anyway?

It was difficult for Blacks and Whites in the United States to be nonviolent with each other, because they were different in many ways. It's even more difficult for different nations to be nonviolent with each other, especially if they are different races or religions or ideologies. Violence breeds on tribalism. Nonviolence, via empathy, grows when we focus on commonalities rather than differences.

* * *

The standard view is that some people are good and some are bad. In fact, everyone is partly good and partly bad. The first view makes it easy to become violent with opponents. The second view opens the way to a nonviolent relationship, beginning with some common ground. As Collyer states, "We are much more alike in this mixed bag sense than most of us think. The reason to care for other people is that they're not that different from me."[9]

There is a spiritual aspect to the nonviolent philosophy. It's important to acknowledge the historical fact that the demonstrators in the nonviolent movement in Birmingham, Alabama, for instance, were taught explicitly to use Christian principles. The "commitment card" that had to be signed and carried by demonstrators began as follows:

> I HEREBY PLEDGE MYSELF—MY PERSON AND MY BODY—TO THE NONVIOLENT MOVEMENT. THEREFORE I WILL KEEP THE FOLLOWING TEN COMMANDMENTS
>
> the first of which was
>
> MEDITATE daily on the teachings and life of Jesus.[10]

King tried to inculcate a personal psychology of nonviolence, which he based on the concept of agape—of understanding good will toward everyone. This idea has empathy at its core. It involves looking for good and seeking the positive. It is a positive state of mind. Hatred is too terrible a cross to bear, as King said: Hatred allows your enemy to take residence in your mind rent-free; it mangles the soul.

Nonviolence has to be a way of life for a person to be able to be nonviolent. It has to permeate a person's entire being. It is not only about avoiding physical fights but also about avoiding "verbal violence," as King put it, being polite and nonconfrontational. It was not just physical but also verbal, and even nonverbal—a calmness to your demeanor, a quiet to your tone of voice. As his closest aide Bernard Lee stated, "Nonviolence does not necessarily mean let someone slap you, but how you actually talk . . . just in the way you talk over the telephone."[11]

Nonviolence can't be a tactic because it can't be practiced if it's optional. It's always easier to be violent; it's safer. I can use a gun to protect myself; I can fight back. Violence can't be an option if nonviolence is to succeed, because the nonviolent activist has to take it to an extreme. The nonviolent activist will be tested continually by their opponent, provoked over and over again into violence, because then the activist can be defeated. The only way to be nonviolent is to refuse to see any other way out.

The debate had occurred in India too, when Gandhi first proposed a politics of radical empathy. Gandhi was viewed as a saint, and he clearly practiced his nonviolence as a part of his spiritual way of life and his religious commitment. But some of his followers only viewed it as a tactic, and the difference between these two approaches would unravel in the 1948 violent partition of India.[12]

King taught that you had to remove violent thoughts and words from inside you before you could be nonviolent physically toward others.

* * *

There's also a practical aspect to nonviolence. If you're in the minority, or if you're in the majority but are facing strong military repression, it's safer than violent resistance. King didn't deny the practical benefits of nonviolence. But he always tied it as well to its theoretical or spiritual basis. On the practical side, from his very first speech at Holt Street Baptist Church in Montgomery in 1955, King emphasized two aspects to nonviolent methods: "Not only are we using the tools of persuasion, but we've got to use the tools of coercion."[13] The nonviolent activist would prefer to persuade his opponent, and sometimes he would succeed: George Wallace went from being an ardent segregationist governor in Alabama in the 1950s and 1960s to being an active proponent of civil rights as governor in the 1990s. The method of nonviolence isn't dependent completely on persuasion, however. While Wallace was resisting desegregation, the nonviolent movement forced the governor to step aside, with the coercion of enforcement of federal laws by means of national troops.

Modern proponents of nonviolence, such as the Boston-based theoretician Gene Sharp, often emphasize these pragmatic and secular aspects of the approach.[14] Nonviolent methods are a different means to the same end as violent methods, in this way of thinking—an overthrow of a repressive government, for instance. This type of nonviolent method has been used in many areas of the world, including the "Arab Spring" of recent years in the Middle East, examined in a later chapter. Although King agreed with this approach, with nonviolence as essentially a kinder and gentler form of coercion, he thought the element of persuasion should not be dropped.

This persuasion might fail at a certain time; it might fail in changing the mind of one's individual opponent. It's very difficult for people to change their minds, especially about deeply rooted social or political beliefs. But the psychology of nonviolence seeks to change minds not just in the present but also in the future. In short, even if the individual racist won't change their mind, a nonviolent movement could have the effect that their children, or their grandchildren, would be less racist. A violent change of laws or government would not. Generational persuasion may occur, where individual persuasion does not.

Another aspect to the importance of a conceptual or personal commitment to nonviolence is that a purely pragmatic approach doesn't last. If one is nonviolent for purely practical reasons, then one will become violent when those practical reasons change. A longer term process of gradual reduction of violence won't happen because it will be easy to return to violent methods whenever one wishes to rationalize use of those methods. For example, the African National Congress (ANC) movement in South Africa was nonviolent initially in the 1950s. King was a major supporter. In the early 1960s, the ANC shifted to violent rebellion, and its leader, Nelson Mandela, was then imprisoned for three decades. Eventually, when the Cold War ended and U.S. support for South

Africa declined, Mandela was freed and the ANC reached power in the early 1990s. At that time, Mandela reverted to a nonviolent approach, avoiding violent retaliation against his prior enemies. It seems that Mandela was first nonviolent for practical reasons, then violent for practical reasons (Mandela said privately that he resumed armed rebellion because otherwise he would have lost the support of many of his followers), and then nonviolent again for practical reasons. One might agree with his judgments, but after him, South Africa has faced notable instability and violent conflict within and between ANC factions and other groups. A culture of nonviolence has not emerged.

Similarly, the nonviolent methods of the Arab movements of 2011 overthrew the dictatorships of Egypt, Tunisia, and Libya, but they were followed quickly by violent killings of leaders and a resumption of armed conflict between different factions.

Nonviolence can be used as a pragmatic method, but if so, it is little better than violent rebellion. In either case, short-term progress might be achieved against oppression, but long-term progress is lost.

Long-term movement toward peace and justice can be achieved only when all violent forms of action are rejected in principle. King and Gandhi offered religious and spiritual reasons for accepting nonviolence as a basic principle of life. Gene Sharp and others have used pragmatism as a secular rationale, but it fails for the reasons given. Along with the spiritual approach given by King and Gandhi, a psychological rationale is the best additional secular explanation for the need to be nonviolent in principle. Radical empathy for others is the basis of nonviolence. If we achieve it, then life in this world will become gentler and more just.

Notes

1. Interview with Bernard Lafayette, January 15, 2013.
2. Flip Schulke and Penelope McPhee, *King Remembered* (New York: Pocket Books, 1986), p. 83.
3. Charles E. Collyer and Ira G. Zepp, Jr., *Nonviolence: Origins and Outcomes*, 2nd ed. (Victoria, British Columbia, Canada: Trafford, 2006).
4. Frazier published his original commentary, "The Negro and Non-resistance," in the March 1924 issue of *The Crisis* 27: 213–214. The Quaker activist was Ellen Winsor, who wrote in her unpublished letter to DuBois,

   > Has not the Negro learnt to his sorrow that violent methods never win the desired goal? . . . Who knows but that a Gandhi will arise in this country to lead the people out of their misery and ignorance, not by the old way of brute force that breeds sorrow and wrong, but by the new methods of education based on economic justice leading straight to Freedom.

   She mentioned that Gandhi had "not one drop of white blood in his veins." DuBois replied kindly with a personal note; although he rejected publication of her letter, he commented, "I am, I must say, compelled to smile at the unanimity with which the great leader, Mr. Gandhi, is received by those people and races who have spilled the most blood." Quoted in Vijay Prasad, "Black Gandhi," *Social Scientist* 37 (2009): 3–20.

In the June 1924 issue of *The Crisis* (28: 58–59), DuBois published Frazier's response in full as part of DuBois' "Opinion" column. First, Frazier admits that he is not advocating "wholesale violence" but, rather, "violent defense in local and specific instances" to reduce attacks on Blacks. He commented on how after the Russo-Japanese war, Whites were more likely to respect Japanese individuals. Similarly, he argued, Whites would be less likely to slaughter Blacks in the South if they thought that Blacks might retaliate: "I am primarily interested in saving the Negro's self-respect. If the masses of Negroes can save their self-respect and remain free from hate, so much the better for their moral development." But often, nonresistance reflects cowardice, and violent retaliation reflects conformism. He wrote, "I believe it would be better for the Negro's soul to be seared with hate than dwarfed by self-abasement." In these comments, his perspectives are similar to those of Frantz Fanon. His essay was directed toward those who would be silent in the face of injustice. He wrote, "I do not oppose the efforts of those who endeavor to instill in the Negro a genuine belief in the brotherhood of man . . . but suppose there should arise a Gandhi to lead Negroes."

5. Referring to the NAACP and the Urban League, Levison said,

> They didn't believe in mass action. They felt that mass action—and Roy Wilkins stated this very frankly—only had the value of letting Blacks blow off steam but it accomplished nothing. He simply didn't believe in it. I remember one discussion . . . in the late 50s at which Norman Thomas [the socialist leader] was present. John Morsell [a sociologist and NAACP aide] said he and Roy had been talking about mass action and they came to the conclusion that mass action had been discredited by Hitler. . . . Norman Thomas exploded and said, you're exactly wrong. The day of mass action has just begun. And I would submit that history indicates that Norman Thomas was right. Because then the 60s followed.

   Interview with Stanley Levison by James M. Mosby Jr., February 14, 1970, transcript pp. 19–20. Ralph Bunche oral collection, RJB 539, Moorland–Spingarn Research Center archives, Howard University.

6. Interview with Lonnie King, August 13, 2013.
7. Telegram from W. E. B. DuBois to Martin Luther King Jr, March 1956. The poem has been corrected slightly grammatically. It is based on a medieval psalm by Jacob Fabricius, later the first stanza of the 1630 poem "Battle Hymn" by King Gustavus Adolphus. https://credo.library.umass.edu/view/full/mums312-b145-i418.

   King responded to DuBois with a form letter, apparently reflecting how busy he was in the middle of the bus boycott:

   Dear Friends:
   This is a note to express my deepest gratitude to you for your kind letter. Such letters from friends sympathetic with our momentous struggle for justice give us renewed vigor and courage to carry on.
   With every good wish, I am
   Cordially yours,
   [signed]
   M. L. King, Jr.
   President [Montgomery Improvement Association]
   MLK/ehr

   https://kinginstitute.stanford.edu/king-papers/documents/w-e-b-du-bois.
   This appears to have been the only direct communication between DuBois and King. A little over 1 month before his death, King lauded DuBois at an event on what would have been his 100 birthday in New York. "The Old Man," as he was known in the movement, had died 5 years earlier on the date of the March on Washington. DuBois had joined the American Communist Party at the end of his life and went into self-exile in Ghana, where he died. King appreciated DuBois' integrity and shared a similar leftward radical movement toward the end of his life. https://jacobinmag.com/2019/01/web-du-bois-martin-luther-king-speech.

8. Interview with Bernard Lafayette by James Findlay, Day 4, p. 39, 2002. https://webarchives.apps.uri.edu/xml/msg123.xml.
9. Interview with Charles Collyer, September 25, 2015.
10. The rest of the nine commandments were as follows:
    REMEMBER always that the nonviolent movement in Birmingham seeks justice and reconciliation—not victory.
    WALK and TALK in the manner of love, for God is love.
    PRAY daily to be used by God in order that all men might be free.
    SACRIFICE personal wishes in order that all men might be free.
    OBSERVE with both friend and foe the ordinary rules of courtesy.
    SEEK to perform regular service for others and for the world.
    REFRAIN from the violence of fist, tongue, or heart.
    STRIVE to be in good spiritual and bodily health.
    FOLLOW the directions of the movement and of the captain on a demonstration.
11. Interview with Bernard Lee by David Garrow, August 21, 1982, in David Garrow papers, Pittsburgh, PA, Manuscript Collection 832.
12. Among Gandhi's disciples, the American Richard Gregg came from a religious commitment and emphasized the need for a spiritual component to the commitment to nonviolence. In contrast, another of Gandhi's followers, Krishnalal Shridharani, took a purely tactical approach to nonviolence and proposed that it could be dropped for violent methods in the right circumstances. The two contrasting views are laid out in books they each wrote for Western audiences in the 1930s and 1940s: Richard Gregg, *The Power of Nonviolence* (New York: Cambridge University Press, 2018 [1934)]; Krishnalal Shridharani, *War Without Violence: A Study of Gandhi's Method and Its Accomplishments* (New York: Harcourt, Brace, 1939). When asked during the Montgomery bus boycott about major influences, King cited Gregg's book, which had been given to him by leaders of the Fellowship of Reconciliation, as one of five influential books (the others being books on Gandhi, Thoreau's *Civil Disobedience*, and the social Gospel work of Walter Rauschenbusch). King even wrote the foreword to a 1959 second edition of Gregg's book. Joseph Kip Kosek, "Richard Gregg, Mohandas Gandhi, and the Strategy of Nonviolence," *Journal of American History* 91 (2005): 1318–1348, https://kinginstitute.stanford.edu/king-papers/documents/foreword-power-nonviolence.
13. https://www.blackpast.org/african-american-history/1955-martin-luther-king-jr-montgomery-bus-boycott.
14. Gene Sharp, *The Politics of Nonviolent Action* (Manchester, NH: Porter Sargent Publishers, 2012 [1973]).

13

Love Your Enemies

Martin Luther King Jr.'s central commitment in his life was nonviolent resistance to injustice. The core of his efforts involved remaining faithful to nonviolence. He knew that his opponents were waiting for the day when he or his movement would sink into violence so that the repression could start, which would end the civil rights movement. His enemies long predicted that King himself, and the movement in the South, would become violent eventually.[1]

King successfully resisted this prediction all his life, leaving future generations an example that is difficult to understand, much less emulate.

How and why did King so treasure nonviolence as an approach to life?

This question, King would say, brings us to the central teaching of maladjustment that Jesus taught and that Gandhi and King codified in nonviolent resistance. To understand King the leader, based on appreciating King the man, we must translate our psychological insights about him into a better understanding of what he was trying to say—into an appreciation of the psychology of nonviolent resistance. King tried in many places, over and over again, to make that teaching clear. Perhaps now, after better understanding his personal psychology, we can understand what he meant.

We can start with his 1956–1957 *Ebony* columns, in which King responded to repeated questions about how to apply his nonviolent philosophy to everyday life. He defined nonviolence not as the avoidance of violence but, rather, as the willingness to suffer violence:

> To believe in nonviolence does not mean that violence will not be inflicted upon you. The believer of nonviolence is the person who will willingly allow himself to be the victim of violence, but he will never inflict it upon another. He lives by the conviction that through his suffering and cross bearing, the social situation may be redeemed.[2]

Soul on Fire. Nassir Ghaemi, Oxford University Press. © Oxford University Press 2026.
DOI: 10.1093/9780197657614.003.0015

Violence stems from fear, which is based on ignorance. We will be nonviolent, King taught, if we get to know each other as human beings, not in false stereotypes. A Black writer described disliking Jews. King warned him, "Men hate each other because they fear each other; they fear each other because they don't know each other; they don't know each other because they are so often separated from each other."[3]

To repeat, nonviolence is not a trait of weakness. It requires much more courage to accept violence and suffering than to resist violently. To another writer, he emphasized the strength needed to be nonviolent: "The man who does not hit back is the strong man. . . . It is ultimately the strong man who can do this. He who accepts violence without returning it is much stronger than he who inflicts it."[4]

* * *

In a word, nonviolence is about love, or empathy in psychological terms.

But not just any kind of love. The core of nonviolence is a radical love, a radical empathy, which means love for one's enemies, not one's friends. This is the psychological basis of nonviolence.

King's *Ebony* articles give examples, but he most fully explains his philosophy in his sermons, especially his masterpiece, "Loving Your Enemies," a favorite sermon of his that he repeated dozens of times in his life, which we'll analyze in the rest of this chapter. (This version is based on one of his early deliveries of this sermon, in 1957, at Dexter Avenue Baptist Church in Montgomery, Alabama.)

The Biblical source is well-known. King recites from the Gospel of Matthew:

> Ye have heard that it has been said, "Thou shall love thy neighbor, and hate thine enemy." But I say unto you, Love your enemies, bless them that curse you, do good to them that hate you, and pray for them that despitefully use you; that ye may be the children of your Father which is in heaven.

King notes that many view Jesus as "an impractical idealist," that the command to love your enemies is impossible to follow. King believes the opposite, that Jesus was a "practical realist" and that following this injunction is "an absolute necessity for the survival of civilization."

King divides the discussion into a How and a Why. How can you love your enemies? Is it even possible? And why? Why should you do such a counterintuitive thing?

There are three steps to the "how" of nonviolence, King teaches. First, you begin "by analyzing self." Sometimes, he notes, people don't like you, not for anything you've done or said, but just because they don't like you. Some people just hate for hating. But sometimes we provoke others, even unknowingly, to hate us. There is "something that we've done deep down in the past and we've forgotten about it" or "some personality attribute that we possess" that triggers "the tragic hate response in the other individual." We need to look inside first before we blame others for their hatred of us: "To begin loving others, we should criticize ourselves; we should see that we have our own faults and then we would be less inclined to fault others."

The next step a person should take is "to discover the element of good in his enemy." King repeats his analogy to schizophrenia and his other metaphor of an inner civil war within each human being. This is King's version of Freud's superego and id, of the Biblical conflict between angels and the devil, of good and evil. As a matter of human nature, this claim is a psychological fact, a statement of biology, a sign of Jesus' realism, as King would put it. As usual, James Bevel put it bluntly:

> The beginning of a movement is to begin to deal with yourself, to discover what a horrible son of a bitch you are. . . . My first job is to convince a community what they are, a bunch of no gooders. They say, "Oh no, I'm a nice Christian." Oh no, you are not. You are a scheming lying filthy man. Most people are afraid to be men. . . . What man's potential is to become—is the beginning of a movement.[5]

So we are partly good and partly evil: "Within the best of us, there is some evil, and within the worst of us, there is some good." There is no one who is all, completely absolutely evil, or good: "Discover the element of good in your enemy. And as you seek to hate him, find the center of goodness and place your attention there and you will take a new attitude."

This idea may seem simple, obvious, acceptable, but it may not appear so easy to accept it if we realize that it means that within Mother Theresa, there is some evil, and within Osama bin Laden, there is some good; or that within Albert Schweitzer, there is some evil, and within Adolf Hitler, there is some good. But that is exactly what King meant. (Gandhi had been explicit in this view regarding Hitler.)

So these are two initial steps to loving your enemies—two difficult steps. First, you have to analyze and accept your own faults and the evil within you. Second, you have to look for and identify and embrace the good within even your most evil enemy. Then there is a third and most practical step, easy to implement once you think of it: Don't hurt your enemy when you have the chance.

"Another way that you love your enemy is this: When the opportunity presents itself for you to defeat your enemy, that is the time which you must not do it." Nonviolence is about fighting evil acts or ideas, not evil persons:

> Love is creative, understanding goodwill for all men. It is the refusal to defeat any individual. When you rise to the level of love, of its great beauty and power, you seek only to defeat evil systems. Individuals who happen to be caught up in that system, you love.

This suggestion is the most practical, and the least obvious. If your enemy is within your grasp, and you can hurt him, badly, that is when you must refrain. When you have power, that is when you must show your love. This is an insight that Friedrich Nietzsche captured well: "Of all evil I deem you capable: Therefore I want good from you. Verily, I have often laughed at the weaklings who thought themselves good because they had no claws."[6] We really cannot be moral until we are powerful. The weak cannot show mercy and forgive. You have to be able to inflict damage so that abstention from doing so can be viewed as a moral act. If I'm too weak to hurt you, being peaceful means nothing. I have to be able to be violent, and then being nonviolent is a moral act.

This concept is missing in much current discussion of nonviolence. Many popular movements are viewed and praised as nonviolent when they are in rebellion, but once in power, they tend to use violent means, through military or police forces, to defeat their opponents. This approach—the exact opposite of King's concept of nonviolence—happened in India in the 1940s, and in recent years in the first Palestinian intifada, in the "Arab Spring" of 2010–2011, and in Myanmar in 2017.

* * *

In his sermons, King gives a classic analysis of love based on Greek philosophy, rooted in Plato, and derived from the famed liberal New York preacher Harry Emerson Fosdick.[7]

In Greek, there are three terms used for love: *philia*, *eros*, and *agape*. *Philia* means friendship; it means liking someone else because they are likable to you; something about them is agreeable to you. It is not what Jesus meant by loving your enemies. You can love your enemies and not *like* them as persons or in many of their features or actions. This conflation of loving and liking is a common error among those who don't understand the concept of loving your enemies. Jesus said "Love your enemy," not "Like your enemy." *Eros* means romantic or sexual love; this a love that is partly physical and sensual and biological. It's not what is meant by loving your enemy.

Agape is a love that is neither physical/sensual, like eros, nor personal, like philia; it is impersonal and more abstract. You love another person just because that person is a human being, not because of the person's personal qualities or because you are attracted to them. It is a "positive, redemptive good will toward all." This is what Jesus meant. You don't like your enemy; you're not romantically attached to them; but you love your enemy because that person is a human being, and you love all human beings. The best term, in my view, is empathy, as suggested by King's teaching that there is some good and evil in all persons. We can relate even to our worst enemy because we are a little bit like them.

"Agape love is the basis of nonviolence," says Bernard Lafayette. "You love expecting nothing in return."[8] Fosdick noted that love in the New Testament never is referred to as *eros*. *Philia* is used 25 times, but by far *agape* is meant most when referring to love, being used approximately 250 times in the New Testament.[9]

The idea of loving your enemies is summarized well in a piece of wisdom long taught by the greatest American psychiatrist, Harry Stack Sullivan: "In most general terms, we are all much more simply human than otherwise."[10]

The analysis above explains *how* to be nonviolent.

Next King explains *why*.

* * *

Why not just hate your enemies, as most of us do? The only logic to defend this natural human instinct rationally would be if by hating others, and violently opposing injustice, we could improve the world. But hatred of others only produces new evils or new injustices. This is "at the very center of Jesus' teaching," says King:

> Hate for hate only intensifies the existence of hate and evil in the universe. If I hit you and you hit me and I hit you back and you hit me back and go on, you see, that goes on ad infinitum . . . a descending spiral, ultimately ending in destruction for all and everybody.

This is indeed the history of the world from prehistory until today.

A second reason not to hate your enemy is a psychiatric one—hate "distorts the personality of the hater":

> There is nothing more tragic than to see an individual whose heart is filled with hate. He comes to the point that he becomes a pathological case. . . . For the person who hates, the good becomes bad and the bad becomes good. For the person who hates, the true becomes false and the false becomes true. That's what hate does. You can't see right.

King reveals the psychiatric sources for his reasoning:

> Psychologists and psychiatrists are telling us today that the more we hate, the more we develop guilt feelings and we begin to subconsciously

> repress or consciously suppress certain emotions, and they all stack up in our subconscious selves and make for tragic, neurotic responses.

A final reason to love your enemies is because it works; it is the most effective means of redeeming injustice and evil in the world. We noted previously that violence and hate only worsen evil in the world; love redeems evil. Hate can only defeat the enemy, who might rise up later in revenge. Love is "a power that eventually transforms individuals." Your enemy is not defeated but, rather, transformed into no longer being your enemy. This was the goal of King's movement. It wasn't just to end segregation as a legal structure; it was to end racism as a psychological way of being. You could only do so by changing people, not changing laws. King had moral, not just legal, goals.

So it is with all social change. Deposing a tyrant with hate and violence only replaces one tyranny with another. Injustice ends when no one experiences injustice. In an unjust world, the process begins by loving the unjust, while resisting the injustice.

* * *

In many sermons, over and over again, King identified three ways of responding to injustice: violent resistance, passive acquiescence, and nonviolent resistance. The first approach may sometimes succeed short term, but it often fails and, in the long term, increases injustice. The second is unacceptable morally, by accepting injustice, even though it is what most human beings do. The third, nonviolent resistance, is the only solution: It fights injustice and actually wins, not only for a little while, but even more so in the long term.

Bayard Rustin captured this concept in a slightly different but complementary way (in a 1960 draft speech for King as an encomium to A. Philip Randolph):

> [Nonviolence] rests upon two pillars. One . . . continuous militant resistance. The evil doer is subjected to pressure so that he never is permitted to rest. Second it projects good will against ill-will. . . . Continuous resistance in non-violent form breaks through the paralyzing peace which is peace for the master and misery for the mastered. Paradoxically, as it breaks the unjust social peace, it's weapon of good will and love builds the sacred base of real brotherhood.

There was a deeply religious character to this commitment. As James Bevel stated, "The movement was an act of God in history."[11]

This point was the last statement made to me by Rev. Michael Haynes. As I got up to leave from our interview, he said of his old Boston friend: "There's one last thing about King. This guy *means* it! 'Forgive your enemies.' I can hear him say it. The concept of love was very very deep in him."[12]

King's commitment to loving one's enemies was spiritually rooted but also psychologically based on the idea of radical empathy.

It is poorly understood, little enacted, and difficult to accept. But one road to accepting it might be to be a little depressed. As previously described, clinical studies have shown that depression enhances empathy and realism.[13]

A major way we humans are similar is that we all suffer. Depressed persons know this fact painfully, emotionally, personally, not just intellectually.

And yet, we often hate each other so much that we might even enjoy seeing or causing suffering: *Schadenfreude* is a nice German word that refers to this all-too-human flaw. But when you're depressed, in the darkness of deep suffering, you realize how suffering is central to being human and that we all suffer in some way, some time. Empathy, even love, may grow from that experience.

The diagnosis is the solution: Suffering leads us to empathize, and empathy reduces suffering. We are all very similar to each other. The depressed person sees this reality, while mentally healthy persons focus on the differences: different religions, political goals, competing projects.

Empathy is realistic; it reflects the nature of things. A little depression, of which King had plenty, reveals this truth.

These considerations suggest that one reason why the world has failed to be as nonviolent as it could be, why we have failed to follow King, is that too many of us view nonviolence as a philosophy, an intellectual exercise, or a cognitive decision. It may be that nonviolence doesn't work unless it's a feeling. There's no "philosophy" of nonviolence; it fails as a thought if the emotions don't serve it too. Nonviolence has to be personal, a psychological commitment, otherwise we can't live up to it socially. As a purely political tactic, it fails. Maybe that's what Gandhi meant when he said that you have to be the change you want to see in the world.

Notes

1. An example is a column by the conservative writer William F. Buckley titled "Buckley Predicts Negroes Will Use Violence in South," *San Jose Mercury News*, October 21, 1962, p. 25. In this article, Buckley criticizes King for meeting with the "confirmed, militant terrorist" Ahmed Ben Bella, newly elected president of free Algeria, during a visit by the latter to the United Nations in New York. Buckley concludes that King was signaling a willingness to use violent methods, as Ben Bella had done in the Algerian revolution.
2. King Center Archives, Box 87, October 9, 1958, *Ebony* magazine column.
3. King Center Archives, Box 87, April 6, 1958, *Ebony* magazine column.
4. King Center Archives, Box 87, October 21, 1957, *Ebony* magazine column.
5. Remarks of James Bevel, University of Tennessee at Chattanooga, April 2, 1965, p. 13, in David Garrow papers, Pittsburgh, PA, Manuscript Collection 832, Box 1.9.

6. Friedrich Nietzsche, *Thus Spoke Zarathustra* (Edinburgh, UK: TN Foulis, 1909 [1883]), Kindle edition, Part 2, Section 35. The translation provided is modernized from the original translation by Thomas Common.

   It also is a point made by Charles Collyer and Ira Zepp:

   > Paradoxically, it is desirable for a practitioner of nonviolence to be quite capable of violence. To abstain from violence only because one is too weak to use it, is not ideal. Better is to be capable of violence, but choose nonviolent options deliberately and consistently.

   They refer to training in martial arts for self-defense as an example of this approach to nonviolence. Charles E. Collyer and Ira G. Zepp, Jr., *Nonviolence: Origins and Outcomes*, 2nd ed. (Victoria, British Columbia, Canada: Trafford, 2006), p. 71.
7. Harry Emerson Fosdick, *On Being Fit to Live With* (New York: Harper, 1946), pp. 6–7.
8. Interview with Bernard Lafayette, January 15, 2013.
9. Fosdick, *On Being Fit to Live With*, pp. 6–7.
10. Harry Stack Sullivan, *Conceptions of Modern Psychiatry* (New York: Norton, 1953), p. 16.
11. James Bevel, *Eyes on the Prize* interview, November 13, 1985, transcript p. 29, at the 42 minute 15 second mark, https://americanarchive.org/catalog/cpb-aacip_151-gt5fb4x427.
12. Interview with Michael Haynes, April 15, 2013.
13. Nassir Ghaemi, *A First-Rate Madness* (New York: Penguin, 2011).

14

The Hero in History

What made Martin Luther King Jr. special?

The most common response is that he was a great orator. But there were many other civil rights leaders, such as Jesse Jackson and Bayard Rustin, who were great speakers. Another common response is that he was very well educated. But so were other civil rights leaders, such as W. E. B. DuBois and Roy Wilkins; many academics who were more educated than King never became civil rights leaders. Another perspective is that he was a very humble man, which was attractive to others. But there were other very humble civil rights leaders, such as John Lewis. Others will point to the broader concept of charisma, but King wasn't magnetically charismatic; he didn't stand out in a room or gladhand his way among strangers, like his father did. Or perhaps his lack of corruption would stand out; King insisted on living simply, renting a house most of his life and eventually buying a simple ranch home in a working-class Black Atlanta neighborhood.

An initial observation could be that, in some ways, King was not such a great a leader in his time. In retrospect, with memories that are selective and biased toward the positive, we may overestimate him. Or it could be that he even was overestimated while living. Some civil rights leaders, such as Thurgood Marshall, took this view, and some of King's friends, such as Stanley Levison, noted that King himself held this opinion. After receiving the Nobel Prize, King expressed the belief that he was getting too much credit, which belonged to others. He felt guilty about his fame. He knew he hadn't started the Montgomery bus boycott. It was started amidst a spontaneous movement of the people of Montgomery, Alabama. He didn't start many of the famous civil rights actions. The lunch sit-ins were spontaneous developments by students in North Carolina and other places. The Freedom Rides were begun by James Farmer and the Congress of Racial Equality. Even specific activities of the Southern Christian Leadership Conference (SCLC), such as the Birmingham demonstrations and the Selma movement, were planned and implemented by others within SCLC, such as James Bevel, rather than King. Andrew Young confirms this process: "The ideas and strategies came up to Martin

Soul on Fire. Nassir Ghaemi, Oxford University Press. © Oxford University Press 2026.
DOI: 10.1093/9780197657614.003.0016

from his staff, rather than from Martin down."[1] This claim was put forward most famously by Ella Baker, an early SCLC worker who left the organization because she believed that it was controlled excessively by King. Baker helped organize the Student Nonviolent Coordinating Committee (SNCC) instead and encouraged the young students to be active on their own, without reliance on King.

Among the major civil rights activists in the South, Baker stands out as the most prominent woman and also as the most skeptical about King's importance as a leader. These two factors might not be coincidental: She herself emphasized the sexism of the movement,[2] how in the Montgomery days there was no possibility that she could be a prominent leader given her gender. She also noted that she was old enough to be the mother of King and the other leaders. There were other factors: She came from New York, from the circle of Rustin and Levison, and was forthright and direct—a way of interaction that worked well in New York but not in the deep South. In any case, she left SCLC within a few years. In later interviews, she described not feeling "awe" for King; some of her ambivalence toward King may have related, she admitted, to the fact that King was in his early years of leadership in Montgomery. At that time, she said, King was demanding and difficult, and he didn't accept differing viewpoints. As she stated later, "Martin wasn't good at receiving critical questions. . . . After all, who was I? I was female; I was old. I didn't have a PhD."[3] She believed that he immediately wanted the movement to center around him as a leader—that his ego mattered. In later interviews after King's death, she avoided directly criticizing him, but she also didn't praise him much. When pressed about how she truly felt about him, she eventually made the following point: "To be very honest, the movement made Martin rather than Martin making the movement. This is not a discredit to him. This is, to me, as it should be."[4]

Baker's view was that the movement made King, that he was not its primary mover or focus, and that the civil rights process would have happened without King. This perspective has been expressed by many who followed Baker in their activism in SNCC, such as James Bevel, Diane Nash, and Robert Moses, and others too, such as the independent activist James Meredith. "King articulated the movement," Baker concluded. "He didn't create it."[5]

Another way of appreciating these questions is to think about the civil rights movement as really three movements, as Keith Miller puts it:[6] There was the movement that happened in real life; the movement as portrayed by the media; and the movement as remembered in the past, especially in the light of the King holiday. It's the second and third movements where King is portrayed as essential and central. But the actual movement as it happened, on a day-to-day basis over a decade in the South, existed outside of any single man, including King.

* * *

King himself recognized how the masses led the movement and drew him into it. Early during the Montgomery bus boycott, when King first met Stanley Levison, the two men were in a car, along with Coretta and others. The conversation moved to the fact that King had been subpoenaed in Montgomery and likely would be arrested when he returned. Coretta expressed concern for King's safety, and the car grew silent. King broke the tension with some self-reflection. As Levison recalled it later,

> [King] said, if anybody had asked me a year ago to head this movement, I tell you very honestly, that I would have run a mile to get away from it. I [had] no intention of being involved in this way. He said that as I became involved, and as people began to derive inspiration from their involvement, I realized that the choice leaves your own hands. The people expect you to give them leadership. You see them growing as they move into action, and then you know you no longer have choice. . . . You must stay in it.[7]

It was, Levison noted, "a profoundly moving impression" in their first conversation together.

A few months after King's killing, James Bevel pondered the meaning of the leader for the movement:

> The fact that King lived was just an incident. He was not the movement. He had not created the movement . . . he didn't make the movement. This is where White people are so stupid. . . . They think there are men who make the sun come up. The sun comes up on its own. Movements come on their own. Revolutions come on their own. So, if you kill the men who talk about the revolution, you're not killing the revolution. You see? . . . [King] was not the movement. He just talked the movement. He articulated it. He felt it. He saw it. He said the sun is coming up, so then, White America said, "We'll kill him to keep the sun from coming up." No![8]

Former student sit-in leader Diane Nash, Bevel's ex-wife, put it as follows:

> Taking nothing away from Martin, because I personally think he was a tremendous man, but it was truly a people's movement. And I think it's important to make that difference, because if people think that it was Martin Luther King's movement, then today . . . young people are more likely to say "Gosh, I wish we had a Martin Luther King here today to lead us."[9]

Their perspective is that the movement was a spontaneous mass movement, and King and the SCLC leadership in general took a lot of credit for things they didn't do.

Wiley Branton, a National Association for the Advancement of Colored People (NAACP) activist, tells a story about 1958, when he and Thurgood Marshall went before the Supreme Court in a special session about the Little Rock, Arkansas, school desegregation case. King wasn't involved at all in that legal case. Branton later recalled,

"King knew no more about the Little Rock case than what he read in the paper, like anybody else. . . ." After the Supreme Court ruling, Branton and Marshall hailed a cab back to their hotel in Washington. Their Black cab driver looked over his shoulder and commented to them, "Wasn't that a wonderful thing Dr. King did for us today?" Marshall laughed and turned to Branton: "Wiley, did you know that?"[10]

* * *

The question remains: What was the role of King as leader of the civil rights movement. How much did he matter, as opposed to other leaders or as opposed to the masses who engaged in political activism?

One approach would be to ask whether the civil rights movement would have happened without King. It clearly would have, because the Montgomery bus boycott prior to King's involvement, and the Freedom Rides, sit-ins, and the 1964 Mississippi summer project happened largely apart from his activism.[11] The legal activities of the NAACP in challenging segregation occurred without a role for King. The direct purpose of these activities was to end Southern segregation. But King had a larger goal: to end racism. Segregation might have ended violently, with a persistence of racial hatred, as happened during Reconstruction after the Civil War. King insisted on nonviolent methods, with the purpose of healing America's racial wounds, not just changing laws. The civil rights movement could have gone in a violent direction in Montgomery, and elsewhere, if King had not moved it firmly toward nonviolence. In his last years and after his death, the movement fell into violent methods, with riots and Black Panther rhetoric, and it petered out under the weight of easy repression and loss of public support.

In addition to the larger goal of ending racism nonviolently, King went further than desegregation and voting rights and sought major economic change in the entire country, as well as an end to the Vietnam War and other military actions. In these latter activities, King wasn't responding to any pressure among the Black masses, and he moved beyond where most of his peers in the civil rights leadership wanted to go.

In short, the movement began without King, and it would have gone somewhere without his leadership, but not where it went. King didn't create the movement, but he nurtured and fostered it into what it became.

The role of the leader is just this: not to create a mass movement but, rather, to keep it alive, to direct it toward constructive ends, and to become its symbol and its guide.

* * *

Two examples were provided previously. First was the initial mass meeting of the Montgomery boycott at the Holt Street Baptist Church. The crowd was malleable and would have followed any rabble-rouser into the streets. But King made his first political statement about using Christian nonviolent methods, and he calmed the crowd into continuing a disciplined boycott. The second example happened soon thereafter, when his house was bombed in Montgomery. A crowd had gathered with weapons and was confronting police; King insisted on Christian nonviolent methods, telling the crowd to disperse.

A number of other examples could be given, but one is emphasized here: the Atlanta movement. In 1961, young activists gathered at the Warren Memorial United Methodist Church in an effort to continue the sit-ins. The older civil rights leadership, including Martin Luther King Sr., opposed that strategy. They long had achieved good relations with Atlanta's White power elite, including the mayor, who opposed the sit-ins. King Sr. spoke against the young activists, urging patience. He was heckled and booed. Humiliated and embarrassed, King Sr. sat down. A key student leader, Lonnie King (no relation but a longtime congregant of King Sr.'s church), began to feel sorry for his old pastor. He later recalled,

> When they booed him [King Sr.], I went on the phone and called ML, I said, we need you to come over here; it's a mess and we need you to come. He said, I'm not feeling well, but I'll come over in a few minutes.

A little while later, King Jr. gave what Lonnie King would later say was the best speech of King Jr.'s life—better than "I Have a Dream," better than anything.[12]

He started slowly: "I'm surprised at you," King Jr. said to no one in particular. A full transcript has not been kept. But the content is reported to have included respect for the efforts of his elders over many decades of harsh segregation, admiration for the sit-in movement and the courage of the students who led it, and a wish to bring both groups together as opposed to "the cancer of disunity." He eventually got to the immediate topic of debate, commenting that Atlanta's White leaders had for the first time given "a written contract" to end segregation. "If this contract is broken, it will be a disaster and disgrace. If anyone breaks this contract, let it be the White man." He criticized the audience for "irrational emotionalism" but also chided the leadership represented by his father for a "tactical blunder."

The church was hushed. King Jr. had essentially supported the position of King Sr. But he had done so with a credibility, based on his own participation in the sit-ins and his prior leadership of direct action, that his father didn't possess. Without naming him directly, however, the son came to the father's defense:

> If I had been on that committee that met Monday afternoon, I wouldn't mind anybody saying, Martin Luther King Jr., you made a mistake. I wouldn't mind anybody saying, Martin Luther King Jr., you should have thought it over a little longer. I wouldn't have minded anybody saying to me, Martin Luther King Jr., maybe we made a tactical blunder. But I would have been terribly hurt if anybody said to me, Martin Luther King Jr., you sold us out! (Applause) I would have been hurt by that.[13]

King stopped. Another speaker rose and said, "If some of us stumbled, it made the rest of us stand up." And then he began singing the old spiritual, "I Know I Got Religion."

Recalled Lonnie King 50 years later,

> By the time ML was finished, he had calmed the water. Folks did not like the agreement, but they were willing to give it a chance, because this young man had come back from Montgomery, and asked them to give it a chance.[14]

In these kinds of settings, a demagogue would have been supported by the masses of the civil rights movement, and violent and harsh methods would have been easy to use. King's leadership kept the movement disciplined and directed toward its goal of ending racism.

A central feature of King's leadership was that he wasn't afraid to be unpopular. And the more sincere he was, the more popular he became. As he stated in a 1958 *Ebony* column, responding to letters from readers, in this case a publicity director of a Tennessee civic organization,

> Too many public figures spend time attempting to win the admiration of certain groups of individuals by smooth words and perfunctory back slaps. Often these methods lead to the opposite effect. . . . You can never please all of the people.[15]

The concept of nonviolence was not necessary for the civil rights movement at all. This fact reflects a central difference between SNCC leaders and King.

Most young SNCC activists were pragmatic: For them, nonviolence was only a tactic, to be used when helpful, to be stopped when not. Emphasizing this practical rationale, Bayard Rustin later would recall, "There's no way for a minority to fight the majority. As I used to say to the fellows: 'Anybody in this room who has got a tank in his garage, raise his hand.'"[16] Nelson Mandela's African National Congress took the same approach in South Africa. It was nonviolent in the 1950s and then switched to armed rebellion in the 1960s. Mandela only returned to nonviolence following 30 years of imprisonment.

King went much further (like Gandhi): For him, nonviolence was a moral principle, not a tactic; it was a way of life, not a political strategy. Short-term failure didn't invalidate nonviolence, for it was the only route to long-term success. Segregation could have ended violently or nonviolently. But racism could only be improved nonviolently because a violent movement would only produce anger and defensive reactions in the White population. So nonviolence was central to King's leadership, making the civil rights movement go far beyond short-term legal and political goals to long-term psychological and moral goals.

The leader was indispensable for that civil rights movement, the one that was committed to nonviolent change, and which didn't stop with segregation or voting rights. King's movement had its share of short-term successes, as is well-known; he also experienced, in his last years, painful short-term failures. He failed to achieve the major economic changes he wanted, nor did he end the Vietnam War. The SNCC activists deserted nonviolence as a tactic when it failed in those goals in the 1960s, but Black nationalist violence failed even more drastically in the 1970s.

By then, the leader was dead, and no other leader was able to keep the movement united and focused on long-term nonviolent change. In his memoirs written just before his death, Stokely Carmichael recalled his impression of the reaction of Black America when King was killed: "This time you went too far, killing this good, decent man, this man of peace. When you killed Dr. King, you killed nonviolence."[17]

The movement, nonviolent or violent, was over. This demise of the civil rights movement demonstrated King's indispensability.

* * *

What made him special?

It wasn't the oratory; others had it. It wasn't the education; others had PhDs. It wasn't the courage; others had it. It wasn't any tactical skill or political power; others had those abilities. It wasn't just his religious commitment. Or just his personal morality.

King had all the strengths mentioned above, and some weaknesses. What made him special, in addition, could be the manic traits that were part of his personality—his cyclothymic temperament—which spurred his incredible energy, resilience, productiveness, grit, and refusal to submit. One also can see repeated depressive experiences as informing his exquisite empathy toward his enemies, his opponents, and his graciousness toward his friends. These personality traits and mood states—along with the spirituality he inherited and imbibed from his family and grew, his profound study of philosophy, and his intuitive connection to the African American experience—produced a special mix that he accepted as his lot, for better and for worse.

There was something special about him after all.

* * *

The conventional wisdom among many social activists is that the best means to advance a movement is grassroots organizing. Certainly grassroots organizing is important, but it is not the most important aspect of social activism. Equally important is the task of organizing the movement's leadership. Or more succinctly, based on the reasons given above, it is just as important to find a great leader for the movement.

So where do we get the leader?

My view is that leaders are born, not made. The term "natural" leader is accurate. Contrary to all the seminars and books in the business world on how to become a leader, you cannot become a leader. You are one; the only question is whether you have followers or not. Hitler was the same person when he sat alone in a jail cell in Munich after the failed putsch of 1923 as when he stood in front of tens of thousands in huge rallies a decade later. Winston Churchill was the same person who sat on the back benches in 1935, ignored by his party and his people, as when he took the leadership of government from the King 5 years later, with his country on the brink of invasion. King was the same person attending funerals and visiting parishioners in Montgomery hospitals in 1954 as when 2 years later he would stand in front of mass rallies leading the bus boycott.

The leader is always the same; it's the followers that change. The leader exists naturally; the leader isn't made. It's the followers who need to be made. The movement needs to be created with grassroots organizing; that's true. The followers are made. But they are made to find a leader. It's like a key with its two interlocking pieces. The followers are useless without a leader, and the leader is unknown without the followers.

* * *

What does it mean to say that leaders are born, not made? My view is that a central feature is that the leader has core natural leadership qualities: realism, empathy, creativity, and resilience.[18] The first two traits naturally flow from the experience of depression, whereas the second two flow from mania. In short, the natural leader is manic–depressive. Even that is not enough; it is necessary but not sufficient.

The manic–depressive leader cannot be too ill. Sometimes with severe manic–depressive illness, in the most extreme episodes, a person can experience delusions or hallucinations. Obviously, in such states, one is not realistic; rather, the opposite is the case—one is out of touch with reality completely. One is not empathic; rather one is in one's own world.

So manic–depressive illness is helpful, but only if it is on the mild to moderate side, not if it is too severe.

Even then the leadership skills provided naturally by manic depression can be used for good or ill. The leader is charismatic, but that leader can be charismatic like Churchill or like King, or like Hitler. Charisma is value-free; it can be used to entice followers to virtue or to vice.

So manic–depressive leaders need some cultural education; they should be guided to spiritually wise goals. Love needs to be taught to the leader when the leader is young, not hate; care for all of humanity, not just some of them; awareness of the rights of one's opponents, not just one's friends. These are, of course, certain humanistic and democratic values. Not all might agree with them; for instance, for White racial partisans, their philosophy excludes the rights of others. So it was with Nazism. What is suggested here is how a leader can lead others toward a more democratic and humane world. There are assumptions in that goal.

Leadership is, in that sense, value-neutral. Effective leadership may seem "good" to one group or "bad" to another, depending on those groups' social or political goals. A charismatic leader might attract half of a nation in a direction that's completely rejected by the other half. One-half views the person as a good leader; the other views the person as a terrible one. In fact, the leader is effective, for good or ill.

So the manic–depressive leader, directed toward humane goals, needs some spiritual training. By spiritual, I mean an awareness of the larger universe, a direction toward a meaning in life beyond the self and one's own material interest. Of course, this kind of spiritual training can happen in the context of religious formation. It may be no accident that some of the greatest modern leaders, from the perspective of a democratic humanism, were religious figures: Gandhi and King stand out. In fact, the only ones who were committed to a nonviolent method were those two, and they were both highly devoted to their religions as the basis for their nonviolent approach. It does not bode well for the classic

Western secular ideology of separation of religion and politics to make this observation: Our greatest nonviolent political leaders in the modern world were religious leaders.

Perhaps we shouldn't separate church and state, or mosque and state, after all.

* * *

The following features can be identified using the example of King in particular, but also Gandhi: The leader has a mild to moderate version of manic–depressive illness, and the leader has a strong spiritual formation within a religious tradition. The next observation is that the leader is within the liberal wing of that tradition, with humanistic and democratic values. This third point is important. King once called himself a liberal evangelical; he was trained in Northern educational settings in which the main kind of Christianity he was taught was a liberal rationalist Protestantism. Based on the ideas of some 19th-century German theologians who advocated the "social Gospel," and influenced by the rationalist philosophies of thinkers such as Georg Hegel, King's teachers affected him. He accepted the idea that religion was not just a matter of emotion but also had to be in accord with reason and connected to the most profound philosophical insights of human civilization. He accepted the social Gospel, that Christ came to help the poor in this world, not just the next.

Yet King also had been raised in the Southern Black Baptist church, which had a strong evangelical aspect. Parishioners believed in a personal relationship with God, and they had a strong emotional bond with their church.

King mixed the two religious strands: He advocated the social Gospel and taught a rational approach to religion, understanding the advantages and disadvantages of living in accord with its spiritual teachings. Yet he accepted also the inherently emotional nature of the personal connection to God that was at the core of his religious experience. That was his "evangelical liberalism."[19]

Readers will observe that evangelism these days at least has a very illiberal bent to it. It is politically and socially conservative; it is not connected to the social Gospel, at least not in a political sense, such as advocating socialist economic programs, as King did, to help the poor. Evangelism can be liberal, not just conservative.

The same could be said, to put it briefly, about Gandhi. He is worshipped in India today, especially by the Hindu parties that currently rule. Yet those parties discriminate against Muslims and strongly adhere to inhumane Hindu practices, such as discrimination against the lowest caste of "Untouchables." Gandhi rejected both of these attitudes; he was a liberal Hindu, much different than the conservative Hindus who rule India today.

For those who advocate separation of church and state as a necessity for democracy, they are advocating, in fact, based on other assumptions. Their problem really isn't religion and politics; it's *conservative* religion and politics. The same advocates of democracy tend to idolize King and Gandhi, despite their mixing of *liberal* religion and politics.

The ingredients of the great nonviolent leader now can be summarized in three parts: manic–depressive illness; a spiritual religious upbringing; and a liberal approach to religion. A final step might be to add an education in the Western humanities and/or Eastern philosophies, including mysticism. King's graduate studies were mostly in philosophy, not theology proper. Gandhi was educated as a lawyer and fully familiar with the Western approach to advocating for legal rights. King had a personal mystical experience in his kitchen in Montgomery at the height of the bus boycott; Gandhi was an avid practitioner of the Hindu tradition of meditation and seeking an unconscious connection to the universe. These further personal aspects to King and Gandhi emphasize the central importance of the spiritual component to their nonviolent leadership.

Ella Baker might have claimed otherwise, but the denouement of the civil rights era after King's assassination shows that the movement didn't outlive its leader. The leader hadn't created the movement, but maybe he re-created it in his own image, and, in the end, it couldn't survive without him.

Notes

1. https://www.washingtonpost.com/archive/entertainment/books/1996/11/03/to-be-young-gifted-and-black/f6d1b08c-272a-42ec-95af-3f8c4935O118.
2. We can cite in support of Baker a later comment by Bernard Lee: "Martin, you have to understand, was absolutely a male chauvinist. He believed that the wife should stay home and take care of the babies while he'd be out there in the streets." Lee was referring to how Coretta Scott King wanted to be more active in some of the movement's activities, but her husband wanted her to stay at home mostly. Interview with Bernard Lee by Walter Burrell, transcript p. 212, in David Garrow papers, Pittsburgh, PA, Manuscript Collection 832.
3. Oral History Interview with Ella Baker by Eugene Walker, September 4, 1974. Interview G-0007, Southern Oral History Program Collection, http://docsouth.unc.edu/sohp/G-0007/excerpts/excerpt_8082.html.
4. Interview with Ella Baker by John Britton, June 19, 1968, Howard University Archives, pp. 38–39.
5. Interview with Ella Baker by Clayborne Carson, May 5, 1972, p. 11, in David Garrow papers, Pittsburgh, PA, Manuscript Collection 832, Box 1.9.
6. Interview with Keith Miller, April 27, 2014.
7. Interview with Stanley Levison by James M. Mosby Jr., February 14, 1970, Ralph Bunche Oral Collection, RJB 539, Moorland–Spingarn Research Center archives, Howard University.
8. Interview with Rev. James Bevel by Katherine Shannon, July 6, 1968, The Civil Rights Documentation Project, transcript p. 15, in David Garrow papers, Pittsburgh, PA, Manuscript Collection 832.
9. Interview with Diane Nash by David Garrow, July 17, 1983, in David Garrow papers, Pittsburgh, PA, Manuscript Collection 832, File 1.9.

10. Interview with Ella Baker by David Garrow, March 8, 1984, transcript p. 18, in David Garrow papers, Pittsburgh, PA, Manuscript Collection 832, File 1.9.
11. As Andrew Young stated,

    > Martin was learning from a Rosa Parks. He didn't have to teach Rosa Parks anything. Martin's responsibility in the movement was to interpret Rosa Parks, to interpret the student sit-ins, to interpret the children in Birmingham to the majority of the world.

    Eyes on the Prize interview, October 11, 1985, p. 18, http://repository.wustl.edu/concern/videos/sf268667q.
12. Interview with Lonnie King, August 13, 2013.
13. Lionel Newsom and William Gordon, "A Stormy Rally in Atlanta," *Today's Speech* 11, no. 2 (1963): 18–21.
14. Interview with Lonnie King, August 13, 2013.
15. King Center Archives, Box 87, June 7, 1958, *Ebony* magazine.
16. Bayard Rustin, *Eyes on the Prize* interview, 1979 (exact date not given), question 52, http://digital.wustl.edu/cgi/t/text/text-idx?c=eop;cc=eop;q1=rustin;rgn=div2;view=text;idno=rus0015.0145.091;node=rus0015.0145.091%3A1.53.
17. Kwame Ture and Ekwueme Michael Thelwell, *Ready for Revolution: The Life and Struggles of Stokely Carmichael (Kwame Ture)* (New York: Scribner, 2003), p. 658.
18. Nassir Ghaemi, *A First-Rate Madness* (New York: Penguin, 2011).
19. Kenneth L. Smith and Ira G. Zepp, Jr., *Search for the Beloved Community: The Thinking of Martin Luther King Jr* (Valley Forge PA: Judson Press, 1998). Smith was one of King's professors at Crozer Theological Seminary, and they remained lifelong friends. Zepp was among King's White religious allies and marched with him in Selma. This book describes King's religious thinking from the inside, by those who knew him early in the course of his education and remained in touch with him throughout his life. They cite a letter from King to one of his Crozer teachers, George Washington Davis, who influenced King in his thinking. Davis had published an article titled "In Praise of Liberalism" in *Theology Today* in 1948. A few years after King went to Boston University for his graduate studies under Dr. Harold De Wolf, he wrote to his mentor Davis:

    > Dr. DeWolf refers to himself as an evangelical liberal and, as I remember, this about the position you hold. So you see that it was not difficult for me to emerge from your classroom to Dr. DeWolf's. I find the atmosphere in both classrooms saturated with a warm evangelical liberalism. (pp. 16–17)

15

Nonviolence in a Postmodern World

More than half a century after the civil rights movement of the 1960s, those who live in the 21st century struggle to understand what that movement meant and what lessons it can teach people in the present and the future.

The era of the 1960s was important for larger social changes besides the civil rights movement focused on race. Reverend James Lawson, one of Martin Luther King Jr.'s earliest activist friends, doesn't like the phrase "civil rights" movement; that's a legal term which dates back to the Civil War. It meant giving Black Americans certain legal rights. The movement aimed at more than merely legal redress. Lawson prefers to call it the "freedom movement"[1] because that was its larger goal: an expansion of the ideal of freedom in American society—personal freedom, racial freedom, political freedom, economic freedom.

That was the direction King went in the final years of his life. There is a clear radicalization in his evolution: from a moderate persona at the start in the 1950s to a mainstream activist in the early 1960s, the years of his greatest popularity, to a radical anti-war socialist in his final years. In this evolution, King went in a leftist direction. He wasn't as far away from some of his Black nationalist critics, such as the Student Nonviolent Coordinating Committee (SNCC) and the Black Panthers, as it might have seemed.

Everyone of whatever persuasion gave King one supreme quality: integrity. All knew that he wasn't in the movement for himself; it wasn't for power, prestige, political office, or perks. He could have become a college president or theology dean in a cushy campus anytime he wanted. King's motives never were questionable. And for that reason, James Bevel respected him, even though he sometimes thought King was too hesitant or slow. For that reason, the Black Panthers and Stokely Carmichael and other young radicals respected him.[2]

As Carmichael stated years later,

> No one who truly understands the struggle can in any way fault King. King really comes out almost perfect, perfection. Of course his political

Soul on Fire. Nassir Ghaemi, Oxford University Press. © Oxford University Press 2026.
DOI: 10.1093/9780197657614.003.0017

> errors are to be understood. But I mean in terms of his commitment, in terms of his total love. In terms of his total dedication to the struggle, one can find no shortcomings here.[3]

As long as King was alive, he was, in a way, the lid on a boiling pot of increasingly radical Black resentment. When he was killed, the pot boiled over.

Perhaps the metaphor isn't right, though; for King himself was boiling over in his final years. He had realized that the civil rights movement had not been enough. Securing the end to legal desegregation wasn't enough. Larger changes were needed in American society to end racism. And these larger changes included changing the entire military and economic structure—a true revolution. These ideas made him an enemy to President Lyndon Johnson and to the mainstream of the American public. He became too radical.

In these ideas, he was ahead of his time, and not only closer to the Black Panthers and to his earlier nemesis Malcolm X but also even a presentiment of a movement that half a century later would be called anti-racism.[4]

* * *

Between then and now, there has been a major cultural change, mentioned earlier. It has been called the "counterculture," but a more specific description is a transition from traditional Western Enlightenment beliefs to what has been called "postmodernism." This transition is something that King experienced, and also resisted to some extent, but which he, like most in his generation, likely didn't fully appreciate.

The movement of the 1960s wasn't just about ending racial discrimination, sexual inequality, or resisting an unjust war in Vietnam. Those social and political goals were the expression of a deeper change. The generation of the 1960s consisted of the famed baby boomers, born after World War II in the 1940s and 1950s to a parental generation that had experienced the worst economic depression in American history and the most terrible war in modern history. The parents had gone through Hell; the children were raised in Heaven but had to come to terms with the near-destruction of Western civilization just before their arrival. All the while, the nuclear bomb loomed, the Cold War was underway, and there was the sense—made real during the 1962 Cuban missile crisis—that the whole world could end in an explosion at any moment.

This world was post-Holocaust, post destruction of Germany as a central source of European culture, post-Hiroshima, and engaged in a constant Cold War struggle between two empires. Born into this world, a new generation had lost faith in the beliefs of the old world.

The Founding Fathers' pieties no longer rang true. All men were created equal; and if you just created a government with enough checks and balances, everyone would get equal rights and peace and justice would prevail. With freedom of speech and freedom of religion, society would prosper with new knowledge fostered by science, and life would become gentler and kinder.

The Great Depression had proven that such a society could starve most of its members. The First and Second World Wars proved that nations professing those principles for their own people could destroy each other. The use of chemical weapons and then nuclear weapons showed that science was not benign; in fact, it could destroy the entire world.

Those beliefs of the American Revolution were held widely in the 18th century; they also were the beliefs of the founders of English democracy (e.g., John Locke and John Stuart Mill) and of French democracy (e.g., Jean-Jacques Rousseau and Voltaire), and they were the core of European culture as it evolved after the Middle Ages, in the Renaissance and Enlightenment eras of the 16th to 18th centuries. Those beliefs were behind the rapid industrialization of the West in the 19th century and the rise of modern capitalism.

The 20th century proved to be an era of violence and conflict greater than the world had ever known. The principles of science and progress of the prior centuries were put to the test, and they seemed to have failed.

* * *

"Postmodernism" is a recognition of this failure. And the "counterculture" of the 1960s was an application of this recognition to modern Western culture. The past half-century has witnessed the gradual settling of the ideas of the counterculture into the bosom of Western culture, such that now it is not "counter" anything. Now Western culture is postmodernist; the counterculture is the culture. Today's zeitgeist is not the same as it was even two generations ago.

Another way of appreciating this massive cultural change is to see it reflected in attitudes such as criticism of the "dead White men" whose ideas were viewed as central to Western culture: Start with Socrates, Plato, and Aristotle—move on to Seneca, Augustine, and Aquinas—and keep on going to all the Enlightenment philosophers and their American and French revolutionary disciples. Those were all the dead White men who created the world that nearly imploded in the 20th century.

That's the world of the Enlightenment. They thought that Science, with a capital S, could replace religion; that Truth, with a capital T, could be known by Science; and that human beings then would have Freedom, with a capital F, a kind of joyous anarchy when the needs of each would be met by the abilities of all.

It all ended in the gas chambers, and in the huge crater of Hiroshima.

The following generations—bred on mostly German and French thinkers such as Friedrich Nietzsche, Martin Heidegger, and Michel Foucault—turned it all around. There is no single Truth, only small truths that are relative to time and place. There is no God, only small gods that we worship and discard according to cultural needs. There is no Science, only the beliefs of scientists masquerading as knowledge. Knowledge is power, but in a harmful way: If you have the power, you can enforce your views as knowledge.

We see the cultural effects of this radical cultural change. The hegemony of the mainly White, mainly male Western establishment has ended. The "Founding Fathers" might have believed in absolute truths: All "men" are created equal; free speech is good; religious freedom is needed. But today's postmodern world says it's all relative.

You are identified by your identity. You can't be just a man. You are a man of a certain race or ethnicity; or you're a woman of a certain race or ethnicity.

Racial mixing is now routine. So you're not even really just Black or White or another ethnicity. You are half and half, or some other combination.

When King was arguing for integration, some of his most strident opponents claimed that integration really was about racial mixing. Southern racists especially were concerned about sexual activity between Black men and White women. Such claims usually were the pretext for most lynchings in the early 20th century. King actively argued against racial mixing, saying that Blacks didn't intend to mix with Whites through sexual activity; they just wanted social rights, such as integration in the workplace or in housing.

Perhaps King was trying to mollify his enemies. In fact, as described previously, he had a serious White girlfriend in seminary and had considered marrying her. Maybe he knew that his enemies were right: Integration would lead to racial mixing. Today, it's clear that was the case, but this racial mixing has happened in the context of the larger cultural change. It not only is accepted but also, in many quarters, is celebrated, partly because it's challenging another cultural category: race.

In today's culture, race is not a pure category; it's biological basis is rejected. Race is a social construct, which means it's an attitude that is dependent on what society wants to believe. It's relative to society, not an absolute "thing" out there in the world. The same holds for gender. Gender is a social construct, changing in different societies during different eras.

In fact, everything is a social construct; that is the core idea that postmodernism uses to replace the core beliefs of the Enlightenment. "Social constructionism" is the label for this view that all beliefs are relative to the social demands and power groupings in a specific culture at a specific time. Those demands and power groups will change over time, and then the culture's beliefs change.

Long held in fields such as anthropology, this social constructionism now has been extended to all fields of knowledge, the social sciences, and even the natural sciences (especially psychiatry).

* * *

Social constructionism teaches, then, that we shouldn't be tied to race and gender. We shouldn't try to force everyone into the categories of Black or White, male or female. Spectra exist; all sorts of variations are possible; and each person is free, and each society is free, to advocate for whatever variation they like.

This description is not meant to be implicitly critical but, rather, merely descriptive. The point that deserves to be made here is that King explicitly rejected all kinds of relativism, and he would have rejected social constructionism, applied as broadly and extremely as it is today.

The impact of this postmodernist belief system on the construct of race in particular is relevant to understanding how our society today and in the future can incorporate the experience of the 1960s civil rights movement.

The contemporary debate about race has shifted to the concept of "anti-racism." The basic idea behind this cliché is that we must go beyond viewing racism as a problem of an individual's beliefs or feelings and see it as built into the structure of society. "Institutional," "structural," and "systemic" racism are the phrases that capture this notion. It may be that we can become individually less and less racist so that the average White person may harbor few, if any, discriminatory feelings toward the Black race, for instance. Yet still, because Whites on average are wealthier than Blacks, and live in safer neighborhoods, and attend better schools, Whites are more likely to enter prestigious universities, which then privileges them in the job market and in lifelong achievement. The idea is to view racism as part of this structure of society, and not just as an individual matter. It is both.

Furthermore, as spelled out first in the early 1980s by the Southern White feminist writer Blanche Boyd, the concept of anti-racism brings attention to racism in all its forms, not just the most obvious.[5] In the South, racism was explicit, overt, and personal. In the North, racism was implicit, covert, and institutionalized. Many Americans wanted to pretend that racism had ended when individual Whites did not believe consciously that Blacks were inferior or bad in some way, or when individual Whites no longer personally discriminated against individual Blacks. Boyd's observation was that such conscious changes, although progress, were superficial. Just below the surface, if triggered by an event such as a mugging or political conflict, many of those apparently nonracist Whites would jump to racist instincts, such as being afraid of Blacks or harboring suspicion about Blacks.

It is very likely that King would have agreed with many of these perspectives. He had observed how racism in the North was less personal but just as deep as in the South. The violent reception he received from angry Whites when he marched in Chicago was disturbing to him. He was struck in the head by a rock and fell to one knee; he later told reporters, "I've been in many demonstrations all across the South, but I can say that I have never seen, even in Mississippi and Alabama, mobs as hostile and as hate-filled as I'm seeing in Chicago."[6]

Beyond seeing racism under the surface in the North just as it existed above ground in the South, King had moved away from viewing racism as a problem of individual Whites to a problem of the larger American society, less as a problem of the South but also of the North. By the mid-1960s, when the Vietnam War had commenced, he viewed racism as tied to militarism. The United States was racist in its foreign policy as it sought to subjugate non-White peoples in other lands—not just Vietnam but, in prior years, Cuba and many parts of Latin America, Iran, the Congo, South Africa, and the Philippines. This militarism led to excessive government spending on racist wars, with the ensuing claim that there were not enough funds to help poor Black and Hispanic and even White people inside the United States.

And this militarism was tied to capitalism. An important reason we fought in Vietnam and Korea, and overthrew popular anti-American governments (in places such as the Congo, Iran, Chile, Cuba, Guatemala, and the Dominican Republic), was that those regimes negatively affected American business interests. The American military was used to help American companies make profits. Capitalism drove imperialism, and both were based on racist attitudes.

King called himself a democratic socialist and advocated at the end of his life for a guaranteed minimum wage for all Americans, not as a means-tested welfare program but, rather, as a right for all.

He spoke thus to the journalist David Halberstam in the summer of 1967:

> For years, I labored with the idea of reforming the existing institutions of society, a little change here, a little change there. Now I feel quite differently. I think you have to have a reconstruction of the entire society, a revolution of values.[7]

And he made the link to implicit racism, not just its overt manifestations, as Halberstam notes: "After Chicago he decided that only a small part of white America was truly committed to the Negro cause, mostly kids on the campuses. 'Most Americans,' he would say, 'are unconscious racists.'"[8]

Exactly one year before his murder, on April 4, 1967, King gave his famous speech at Riverside Church, where he first clearly denounced the Vietnam War. He spoke of "exposing the evils that are deeply rooted in whole structure of our society. It reveals systemic rather than superficial flaws and suggests that radical reconstruction of society itself is the real issue to be faced."[9]

In his final Southern Christian Leadership Conference (SCLC) retreat in Frogmore, South Carolina, in late November 1967, King repeated his final perspective: "Let us . . . not think of our movement as one that seeks to integrate the Negro into all the existing values of American society." King wanted to change those values. Andrew Young expressed it as follows: "Even if you're a winner in a rat race, you're still a rat."[10]

* * *

King had begun to go in that direction after the Meredith March and Carmichael's separation of SNCC from him with the Black Power slogan. A few months later, at the SCLC retreat in Frogmore, King tried to explain the change in his strategy to his closest supporters.[11]

After Birmingham and Selma and all the other civil rights actions of the 1960s, King noted that the gains in civil rights were met with two reactions: "White backlash and Black Power." White backlash was the resistance to further change by extending civil rights to addressing poverty in general, and especially in Northern Black ghettoes. Black Power reflected the despair of the masses of Blacks who saw how difficult it was proving to achieve major social change by nonviolent means. King accepted the idea of Black Power if it meant healthy self-esteem, but not if it meant violence or Black separatism. King believed White backlash was more of a problem, because it reflected resistance to larger change. Desegregation had cost America nothing, "not a single penny," but "we are now making demands that will cost the nation something."

As noted previously, King went on to state clearly in private at the SCLC retreat what he avoided saying in public: "There must be a better distribution of wealth, and maybe America must move toward a Democratic Socialism." He then went on to give a lengthy discussion of Karl Marx and Marxism, both erudite and funny at the same time, to make the key point that his hearers should put aside claims that he is a communist because his socialism was morally based on the Christian concept of justice:[12]

> When we talk about this redistribution, and when you read about me being a Communist you really know where I stand. I am simply saying that . . . God never intended for some of his children to live in inordinate superfluous wealth while others live in abject, deadening poverty.

It's worth noting that King's attraction to socialism was long-standing and can be found in his college notes as far back as his seminary years.[13] In the McCarthy decade of the 1950s, he likely suppressed those views, especially because J. Edgar Hoover's Federal Bureau of Investigation (FBI) consistently accused him of communist sympathies. By the late 1960s, King might have felt more able to express his Christian socialist sympathies.

He restated his commitment to nonviolence, to Love, as the only way truly to achieve justice and reduction of evil in the world, and ended thus:

> We must question the values upon which our society thrives. There [are] still three basic evils in America: the evil of racism, the evil of excessive materialism, the evil of militarism. And we must come to see, and we must not be intimidated on this point, that these three are inseparable triplets. . . . Many of our problems . . . are odd because we live in a sick nation that will brutalize unjustifiably millions of boys and girls, men and women in Viet Nam. . . . We have some difficult days.

King's private Frogmore speech is little discussed, and it bears a full reading.[14] Here we see King grappling with the legacy of Malcolm X and the challenge of younger Blacks attracted to Malcolm's past militancy. King tried to show that he too was a militant leader, while remaining clear about his nonviolent methods. For the remaining years of his life, he would find that he was viewed as too conservative by the young radicals and too radical by former movement allies and White liberals. Like his hero Gandhi, King was going his own way. He was a great leader; the question was whether he would continue to have followers.

* * *

That King was radical and very unpopular with the wider American populace, with 75% of the public disapproving of him.[15]

It was that King whom his close friends, such as Vincent Harding, despaired about. It was that King whom Harding thought was an "inconvenient hero"[16] who had to be killed so that, once killed, he could be safely idolized. It was that King who had to be converted into a bland holiday, put at the service of the very capitalist structure he distrusted. He became commercial, as Stokely Carmichael put it.[17]

There are dissenting voices. King's close aide and lawyer, Clarence Jones, who to this day idealizes King as almost superhuman in his qualities,[18] wrote at book-length about how he thinks King is misunderstood in the opposite direction.[19] In Jones' view, King would have opposed affirmative action, because he emphasized the need for individual responsibility; King would have opposed illegal immigration, because he didn't believe in breaking the law for economic or financial gain, as opposed to real political repression; King would have supported Israel in its fight against Palestinians, because he was fervent in his fight against anti-Semitism and because Palestinians were more violent than Israelis; and King would have supported the post-September 11, 2001, invasion of Afghanistan (and possibly Iraq), because the Islamic world needed to be held accountable for its enabling of violent extremism.

Before we deride these views as more Clarence Jones than Martin Luther King Jr., it's important to acknowledge that Jones was very close to King. Perhaps his own views have evolved in a more conservative direction than might have been the case with King; perhaps not. It's important to recall that James Bevel became a supporter of the proto-fascist Lyndon LaRouche group and that Bevel, Hosea Williams, and Ralph Abernathy supported Ronald Reagan in the 1980 election.

Certainly, Jones may be right about King's sympathy for Israel, but one might doubt some of Jones' assertions, especially the claim about affirmative action, given King's clear socialist critique of systemic racism in his final years. Reading Jones' denunciation of Islam as "less a religion than a cult of death,"[20] it is difficult to imagine such a discriminatory opinion from a man whose attitudes, as Jones acknowledges, had moved increasingly closer to those of Malcolm X.

* * *

The turning point was the Selma campaign.

In the prior year of 1964, King had won the Nobel Peace Prize, and *TIME* magazine had named him Man of the Year. In Gallup polls, he was listed as the fourth most admired person in America (after Lyndon Johnson, Winston Churchill, and Dwight Eisenhower). In 2 years, when King started to oppose the Vietnam War, two-thirds of Americans disapproved of him, and by his death, King had a 75% disapproval rating. Immediately after his murder, America began a process of atonement. By 1999, King was back on the Gallup list, now the second most admired person in America, after Mother Theresa, and just ahead of John F. Kennedy and Albert Einstein.[21]

The hero was convenient once he was dead.

Selma in 1965 turned out to be both the high tide of the traditional civil rights movement and the beginning of an end to its limited legal goals. It ended in actuality with the close of the Meredith March in 1966, when Carmichael finally broke with King and called for Black Power. That event in turn led to King's final radicalization.

Ironically, the advisor who saw what was happening most clearly, and who worried most about its outcome, was the former communist Stanley Levison, the figure whom the FBI chief J. Edgar Hoover viewed as the power behind King's throne. Despite repeated harassment about Levison from the FBI, King never cut off his political confidante. Clarence Jones, who also was very close to Levison, has been adamant that the two were inseparable in their political thinking and that King "totally trusted" Levison: "They agreed almost 100 percent philosophically on secular matters."[22]

In a private letter from early 1965,[23] soon after the Voting Rights Act had been introduced, Levison saw that the Movement was entering a new, and even more difficult, phase. The immediate occasion for the letter was opposition King was receiving, from both White liberal and some Black groups, to his attempt to begin to organize Blacks to vote *in the North,* not just the South:

> Dear Martin,
> Selma and Montgomery made you one of the most powerful figures in the country, a leader now not merely of Negroes but of millions of Whites in motion [underlining in original]. . . . You are one of the exceptional figures who attained the heights of popular confidence and trust without having obligations to any political party or other dominant interests. Seldom in American history has anyone come up by this path. . . .You are free of the taint of political ambition, wealth, power or the pursuit of vanity. Your image has more purity than any American has attained in decades.

Levison was not flattering for the sake of flattery. Levison's encomium here was a mere statement of fact, an important preamble to why King's future looked bleak compared to his past.

In his letter, Levison asked what had led to King's success:

> How is this explained? It is due to the deeply impressive power of non-violent action to summon courage and determination from Negroes. Someone asked a Negro if he thought they would win, and he responded, "We won when we started." This is profound.

And then the problem: "Whenever one attains a commanding position of power, he also evokes fear. . . . What are they afraid of?" Levison goes on to say that some people fear that King will move to attack "sacred structures of economic interest"; here, we hear the old communist speaking: Capitalism is at the root of American society, including racism, and capitalism itself might be put at risk by King's movement. Levison is correct: This probably was the fear of many in White America, most of whom were conservative—Richard Nixon's silent majority. Others, Levison added, merely fear "that with your unique independence and influence you can err in judgment," producing a "major irreversible error" despite good intentions. This second fear reflected the ambivalence of King's moderate allies in the civil rights movement, especially the leadership of the National Association for the Advancement of Colored People and Black politicians. Indeed, 2 years later, when King finally spoke against the Vietnam

War, *every* major civil rights organization publicly disagreed with him, arguing that he was opining outside his field of specialization.

Levison moved to his main purpose in writing King, an insight that would be sadly proven true by the final 3 years of King's life:

> There is another deeper lesson. . . . The coalition of Selma and Montgomery, with its supporting multi-millions, . . . is a coalition around a fairly narrow objective. . . . It is militant only against shocking violence and gross injustice [underlining in original]. It is not for deep radical change. . . . America today is not ready for a radical restructuring of its economy and social order. . . . This is a subject for careful study because the movement can head into a cul-de-sac if it can see no real progress without radical alteration of the nation.

Levison foresaw the future. This is exactly what happened.

* * *

It never was fully clear what "Black Power" meant. To Stokely Carmichael and the Black Panthers, it seemed to mean something similar to what some now term "anti-racism," but with a revolutionary slant. "When you talk of Black Power, you talk of building a movement that will smash everything Western civilization has created," Carmichael said.[24] This extreme view seemed to be the assumption of many.[25] Or it could be put it in a more moderate way, as Carmichael did in a 1967 book with Charles Hamilton:

> It is a call for black people in this country to unite, to recognize their heritage, to build a sense of community. It is a call for black people to begin to define their own goals, to lead their own organizations . . . to resist the racist institutions and values of this society.[26]

This approach sounds similar to the anti-racist perspective of attacking institutional, not just personal, racism.

In practice, however, Black Power seemed to mean literally putting Black leaders in positions of political power.

King wasn't opposed to Black political power. He even participated in it during his life. Cleveland in 1967 was a case in point. During violent summer riots the prior year, King frequently had come to quell violence. Afterwards, SCLC engaged in voter registration efforts for the 1967 election, which held the possibility of electing the first Black mayor in a major American city, Carl Stokes. In Cleveland, Blacks could actually vote for a Black mayor to see if Black Power could lead to real change.

Although leading Black ministers had invited King to Cleveland, Stokes told King that he wasn't needed and in fact might harm Stokes' chances for election. He later recalled the conversation: "I explained to Dr. King that I had carefully put this whole campaign together. I had worked to get actual White votes. I couldn't afford to do anything to aggravate the White voter." Then Stokes told King, "You're going to create problems that we do not have now and may not be able to handle. I would rather that you not stay." King had already decided: "I will have to stay, but I promise there will be nothing inflammatory."[27]

Nonetheless, King was having an impact. That summer, there were riots in Detroit and in Newark, New Jersey, but not in Cleveland, where King rode around town on a flatbed truck exhorting people to remain nonviolent.

In October 1967, largely due to King's efforts, thousands of new Black voters had registered over the summer, and Stokes won the Democratic nomination. Cleveland was a Democratic town, but many Whites feared a Black mayor. In the November general election, facing the Republican grandson of President William Howard Taft, Stokes eked out a victory with a margin of less than 1% of the total.

At Stokes' headquarters, as votes were counted late into the night and victory finally was declared, King reacted with much satisfaction. "He was very, very happy," Louis Stokes, the brother of the candidate, later recalled. Carl Stokes got ready to give his victory speech. As he turned to enter the hotel reception area where he would speak, joined by many supporters on the podium, Stokes turned to his brother. "Lou, would you stay upstairs with Dr. King while we go down?" Andrew Young and Jesse Jackson were disappointed. They had expected Stokes to call them down for the victory speech; but as they watched the television, they suddenly saw Stokes giving his victory speech without them. King tried to explain it away. "Look, he's got to run this town," King commented to Young; Stokes didn't want to seem beholden to King. But Jackson sensed King's disappointment: "He would have savored the victory, but he wasn't allowed to."[28]

King made his last public appearance in Cleveland a month later. Carl Stokes was reelected once and then retired. In late 1968, Louis Stokes was elected Ohio's first Black congressman. One of his first acts in Congress was to introduce a bill for a holiday for King; 14 years later, it passed, the same year that Harold Washington was elected the first Black mayor of Chicago.

* * *

King didn't live to see it, but Black Power, in its democratic form, succeeded. In the 1960s, there were only approximately 500 Black elected officials in the United States. By the 1980s, there were 10 times that number or more. Key figures in the civil rights movement, in both SCLC and SNCC, had become mayors, state legislators, and congressmen: Andrew Young, John Lewis, Marion Barry, Walter Fauntroy, John Wilson, Ronald Dellums, and others. Jesse Jackson ran credible campaigns for president and became an influential figure in the Democratic Party. His campaign manager, Ron Brown, became Secretary of Commerce. Colin Powell became America's top general, and Condoleezza Rice became National Security Advisor. The presidency itself eventually was won by Barack Obama.

Black Power had been achieved, if it meant election of Black leaders to key positions of power within the structure of American society. And yet, as many noted, all this political power had not translated to major tangible economic progress or improved social quality of life. Black ghettoes persisted and grew larger; crime increased; drug abuse rose; prisons filled; public schools continued to be poor quality. Police too often killed, rather than protected, Black men. The odds for the average poor Black child to rise up in society remained low.

Black Power had changed little in a racist society.

American society in the early 21st century had progressed in terms of legal segregation compared to the 20th century. But the larger structural changes that King had identified were not achieved, just as Stanley Levison had predicted. American society wasn't ready for radical change. Black Power was allowed if Black politicians wanted to replace White politicians, while leaving the basic structure of society intact.

Anti-racism speaks of changing that structure. But it continues to speak of "power" because it believes in nothing but power, and nothing outside power. There is no absolute basis on which all can agree to build a society. Whites have their power structure; Blacks and other non-Whites need to change that structure to get power for themselves. Interest groups fight each other, without any common interest. So Whites begin to fight back, with the rise of "White nationalist" groups that are racist overtly, and largely White right-wing populist movements premised on defending the current power structure. They want to make America great again, implying that the past, which clearly was more racist than the present, was better. One side sees the nation as founded on genocide against non-White Native Americans, then built on the slave labor of non-White Africans, and then grown on the imperial exploitation of non-White Latin Americans and Asians. The other side just sees the greatest nation in the world.

Two competing visions fail to coincide in a postmodern world in which truth is viewed as the power of one's group interest. There is no common ground.

* * *

King wasn't postmodern; and his God wasn't a social construction. His God was a real Being, who would fight to help the poor, not defend the rich; He would end racism against any minority, whether Black or immigrant or Muslim. This God was rational too, the God of Jefferson whom you could understand if you reasoned objectively about existence.[29] The knowledge of science lived alongside this God, for its truths were absolute too. If vaccines worked, they worked, no matter how one felt about them. If psychiatric illnesses were diseases of the body, they were diseases, not just social constructions.

It wasn't up to humans to decide; Nature, and Nature's God, decided.

King didn't like Nietzsche, or the idea that God was dead.[30] If the postmodern world indeed had killed God, and buried Science next to Him, what was left? The conflict of racism versus anti-racism might not be solvable. Valuing another dead White male, the German philosopher Georg Hegel, King often spoke of the need for a synthesis between two antitheses. But a synthesis implies an eventual common ground. It implies going beyond postmodern impulses to something that is real, and not purely constructed out of power preferences.

Or perhaps we can understand the application of Hegel's thinking better with other terms. Hegel rarely used the concepts of thesis, antithesis, and synthesis; in fact, he criticized any such formula.[31] Instead, Hegel analyzed the "dialectic" of all knowledge and reality by emphasizing that paradox was at the heart of reality. Things could turn into their opposites, or take on aspects of their opposites. Nothing was simple or straightforward or pure. One worldview would be overcome by another, but the second would be transformed in the process into something different too. In fact, most appropriate to the Black American experience, Hegel's key metaphor was between a Master and a Slave. The Master seemed in charge, but he was affected harmfully by having to suppress the Slave. The Slave, meanwhile, could transform the experience of his labor into creative action. The free man, in Hegel's conception, is neither master nor slave but, rather, the outcome of their conflict.[32] The dialectical process is this overcoming ("aufheben"), which is central to everything.

The postmodern ideology of today views all claims to knowledge as partial, and all concepts as relative social constructions. Nothing is absolute; nothing is real; all is relative to humankind. This perspective harkens back to the pre-Socratic era of sophism, that man is the measure of all things. Hegel clearly was different, a clear believer in Absolute Truth, but a sophisticated thinker who realized that such Truth was the outcome of a historical process of paradox and conflict of opposites. His student Martin Luther King Jr. realized that human existence was paradoxical, conflictual, and a struggle. But, like Hegel, King believed in an absolute Truth above and beyond it all, toward which human history evolved. Call it Freedom, Truth, God, the Promised Land. They all deserve capital letters, which our postmodernist zeitgeist denies them.

* * *

It's worth emphasizing why King's slogan wasn't Black Power, and what it was. He had a slogan, which he tried to get Stokely Carmichael to accept instead of Black Power: It was "Freedom Now." The difference is immense, and in part it is the difference between his more traditional commitment to Enlightenment values of freedom and equality, as opposed to today's postmodern focus on the social construction of all values and beliefs, and their basis in power. King wanted more freedom—freedom that was denied to Blacks by segregation, but also denied to them by capitalism-based poverty and by imperialism-based war. He wanted that Freedom now, not in a very gradual long-term approach, but in a concerted active approach that tried to achieve as much as possible as soon as possible. Freedom isn't about power. Caesar can have his power, as long as I'm free. In fact, I might become Caesar and reduce the freedom of others. Power just isn't relevant. Or maybe it is relevant but only as a means, not an end.

Today, even King has become a plaything of power-based interest groups. For some, he's a progressive activist against the status quo. For others, he's a proponent of law and order against violence. Both groups fail to realize that his absolute commitment to freedom and equality requires giving up an emphasis on power. It requires radical empathy for one's opponent.

King's friend, Vincent Harding, realized that the poet got it right, a year after King's murder:

> Now that he is safely dead,
> let us praise him.
> Build monuments to his glory,
> sing hosannas to his name.
> Dead men make such convenient heroes.
> They cannot rise to challenge the images we would fashion from their lives.
> And besides,
> it is easier to build monuments
> than to make a better world.[33]

Notes

1. Interview with Rev. James Lawson, January 25, 2021.
2. Carmichael stated,

> Well, anyone who doesn't know Dr. Martin Luther King, knows that he loves humanity. So, ah, having the opportunity and the honor of knowing Dr. King could only fire more my enthusiasm for him for the love of the people he had because unlike others who don't him, that know he loves the people, I had a chance to work with him and actually see this love manifest itself. So, ah, I've always had the greatest, ah, love and respect for King, if for no other reason, because he loved our people. And because

he loved our people he would not compromise or he would never in any way become corrupted. This I knew.

Stokely Carmichael, *Eyes on the Prize* interview, November 8, 1988, question 40, http://digital.wustl.edu/e/eii/eiiweb/car5427.0967.029stokleycarmichael.html.

3. Stokely Carmichael, *Eyes on the Prize* interview, November 7, 1988, question 71, http://repository.wustl.edu/concern/videos/j38608711.
4. The first use I could find of the term "anti-racism" is a 1975 article by the Marxist scholar Herbert Aptheker: "The History of Anti-Racism in the United States," *The Black Scholar* 6, no. 5 (1975): 16–22. Perhaps the first use of the concept as it is used today was made by the Southern White lesbian feminist writer Blanche Boyd in her 1981 book titled *The Redneck Way of Knowledge* (New York: Vintage, 2011 [1981]).
5. Boyd, *The Redneck Way of Knowledge*.
6. https://time.com/5096937/martin-luther-king-jr-picture-chicago.
7. David Halberstam, "When 'Civil Rights' and 'Peace' Join Forces," in *Martin Luther King Jr.: A Profile*, ed. C. Eric Lincoln (New York: Hill & Wang, 1984 [1970]), pp. 201–202.
8. Ibid., p. 202.
9. Vincent Harding, *Martin Luther King: The Inconvenient Hero* (Maryknoll, NY: Orbis Books, 2008 [1996]), quoted on p. 20.
10. King cited in David Garrow, *Bearing the Cross* (New York: HarperCollins, 2004 [1986]), p. 582. Andrew Young, originally interviewed by T. H. Baker, June 18, 1970, Atlanta, LBJ archives, quoted in Garrow, *Bearing the Cross*, p. 582.
11. Address at SCLC staff retreat, Frogmore, SC, November 14, 1966. King Center Archives, Box 119.
12. King stated,

> Now I will tell you what I think about Karl Marx right quick. As I have ready him thoroughly from *Das Kaptial* [sic] which he wrote with Engles [sic] down to the *Communist Manifesto*, and I can tell you very quickly what I think about him. You know, interestingly enough I read the philosopher Hegel before I read Karl Marx, and Marx read Hegel. But I have learned some from Hegel, and that is to look at reality from a dialectical point of view. Now Marx learned that, but he didn't carry it far enough. So I look at Marx always with a yes and a no. And there was some things that Karl Marx did that were very good. Some very good things. If you read him, you can see that this man had a great passion for social justice. You know Karl Marx was born a Jew, had a rabbinic background. And somewhere in those early days, I think Karl Marx probably turned to [the] testaments and read Amos saying, "let justice roll down like waters and righteousness like a mighty stream." When he was six years old, he converted to Christianity, and so he had a little Christian background, too. And somewhere along the way he must have read where Jesus said, "If you do it unto the least of these, you do it unto me." Now Karl Marx got messed up first because he didn't stick with that Jesus he read about. But secondly because he didn't even stick with Hegel. He read Hegel and he took his dialectic. And he read another German philosopher by the name of Feuerbach, and he took his materialism and he worked out a system called dialectical materialism. And working that out, he didn't see the spiritual undergirding of reality. And so it led him to an ethical relativism. It led him to the conclusion that the end justifies the means. It led him to the conclusion that you could use any means to get that end—just get to that end. So if it means cutting off individual liberties, that's all right . . . [in] the dictatorship of the proletarian [sic]. The great weakness of Karl Marx is right here, that he didn't realize that means and end must cohere. Now the way I look at it is this. Capitalism fails to realize that life is social. Marxism fails to realize that life is individual. Truth is found neither in the rugged individualism of Capitalism nor in the impersonal collectivism of Communism. The kingdom of God is found in a synthesis that combines the truths of these two opposites. Now this is where I leave brother Marx and move on toward the kingdom.

Address at SCLC staff retreat, Frogmore, SC, November 14, 1966, King Center Archives, Box 119.

13. In the King archives at Boston University, there is a random note separate from class notes, in handwritten pencil:

> What will the new movement be called in America? I must admit that I don't know. It might well be called Christian socialism, communism, or socialist democracy. But what does it matter anyway, "a rose called by a different name smell [sic] just as sweet." The point is that we will have a definite change.

MLK BU Archives, Box 1, Folder 3: Crozer Term II—November 30, 1948–February 16, 1949.

14. Perhaps its most extensive discussion is in Adam Fairclough, "Was Martin Luther King a Marxist?" in *Martin Luther King Jr.: A Profile*, ed. C. Eric Lincoln (New York: Hill & Wang, 1984 [1970]), pp. 228–242.
15. https://www.usatoday.com/story/opinion/2018/04/04/martin-luther-king-jr-50-years-assassination-donald-trump-disapproval-column/482242002.
16. Harding, *Martin Luther King: The Inconvenient Hero*. Harding wrote of the King national holiday, "The dominant image has been that of the great orator at the Mall, the dreamer of interracial harmony, the stirring and mildly challenging preacher" (p. 1). But, "Who stands with a hero who insists on living for the broken and exploited, who refuses to deny nightmares, who will not let dreams die, and is not afraid to go on exploring, stumbling, trembling, wherever visions lead him?" (p. 21).
17. Stokely Carmichael, *Eyes on the Prize* interview, November 7, 1988, question 41, http://repository.wustl.edu/concern/videos/j38608711: "King is just becoming commercial, and most people don't know him. . . . If you know King, I have a dream is one of his most vulgar speeches."
18. Clarence Jones stated,

> He was not only a gifted orator, but had a near photographic memory. He was encyclopedic in his knowledge of the political classics of John Stuart Mills, Locke, Thomas Hobbs, Voltaire, Hegel, Schopenhauer, Darwin, Karl Marx, the New and Old Testament of the Bible, the Talmud, the Greek classics, and several works of William Shakespeare. In 12 years and 4 months, from 1956 until April 4th, 1968, with the exception of President Abraham Lincoln and The Emancipation Proclamation of 1863, Dr. King may have done more for racial, social, political justice and equality, than any other single event or person in the previous 400 years of history of the United States. He never made ANY decision with respect to the exercise or non-exercise of his leadership based on any consideration whatsoever as to whether such exercise or non-exercise would result in ANY financial benefit inuring to him, directly or indirectly. Who today is most like Dr. King? No one. Who today is most like Galileo, Michelangelo, Copernicus, William Shakespeare, Beethoven, Mozart, Bach or Aristotle?

Email from Clarence Jones to author, May 21, 2013.

19. Clarence B. Jones and Joel Engel, *What Would Martin Say?* (New York: Harper, 2008).
20. Ibid., p. 175.
21. https://news.gallup.com/poll/20920/martin-luther-king-jr-revered-more-after-death-than-before.aspx; https://www.usatoday.com/story/opinion/2018/04/04/martin-luther-king-jr-50-years-assassination-donald-trump-disapproval-column/482242002.
22. Email from Clarence Jones to author, May 21, 2013.
23. King Center Archives, dated April 7, 1965.
24. https://www.nytimes.com/1998/11/16/us/stokely-carmichael-rights-leader-who-coined-black-power-dies-at-57.html.
25. The young White Northern minister intern Gurdon Brewster tells an anecdote of a man who had been a parishioner of King's Ebenezer Baptist Church for some years and became a convert to Black Power. When Brewster walked by him near the church, as the man was seated, Brewster described the following: "I could see the outline of a gun held in a holster against his skin. 'I'm Black Power now,' he said. 'Nobody messes with me.'" Gurdon Brewster, *No Turning Back: My Summer with Daddy King* (Maryknoll, NY: Orbis Books, 2007), p. 226.
26. Kwame Ture and Charles V. Hamilton, *Black Power: The Politics of Liberation in America* (New York: Vintage Books, 1992 [1967]), p. 44.

27. https://clevelandmagazine.com/in-the-cle/the-read/articles/kings-speech.
28. Ibid.
29. In his Crozer Theological Seminary notes, in a course on "Practice Preaching" by Robert Keighton, King writes in the margin of lecture notes on William James' *Varieties of Religious Experience*, "Good book to read," and next to it underlined and in all caps, "The Science of Religious Experience." MLK BU Archives, Folder 4, Term III February 22—May 6, 1949.
30. King wrote thus in *Stride Toward Freedom*:

    Perhaps my faith in love was temporarily shaken by the philosophy of Nietzsche. I had been reading parts of the *Genealogy of Morals* and the whole of *The Will to Power*. Nietzsche's glorification of power—in his theory all life expressed the will to power—was an outgrowth of his contempt for ordinary morals. He attacked the whole of the Hebraic–Christian morality—with its virtues of piety and humility, its other worldliness and its attitude toward suffering—as the glorification of weakness, as making virtues out of necessity and impotence.

    https://kinginstitute.stanford.edu/king-papers/documents/my-pilgrimage-nonviolence

31. Gustav E. Muller, "The Hegel Legend of 'Thesis, Antithesis, Synthesis,'" *Journal of the History of Ideas* 19, no. 3 (1958): 411–414. Muller demonstrates that this common misinterpretation is a repetition of the perspective of Karl Marx, in his elaboration of Hegelian ideas.
32. The Master and Slave dialectic is central to Hegel's introduction to *Phenomenology of Spirit*. https://en.wikipedia.org/wiki/Master%E2%80%93slave_dialectic.
33. "A Dead Man's Dream," by Carl Wendell Hines Jr., 1965, quoted in Harding, *Martin Luther King: The Inconvenient Hero*, p. 3. Originally published in Ira G. Zepp, Jr., and Melvyn Palmer, eds., *Drum Major for a Dream: Poetic Tributes to Martin Luther King Jr.* (Thompson, CT: InterCulture Associates, 1977), p. 23. Reprinted 2002, Writers Workshop. In fact, Hines wrote this poem in homage to Malcolm X after his assassination, but it was taken up by Harding and others as appropriate to Dr. King. https://afamwilsonnc.com/2017/01/16/now-that-he-is-safely-dead.

16

Nonviolent Intifada

The civil rights movement in the United States was preceded by Gandhi's movement in India, and it has been followed by the growth of interest in nonviolent social change throughout the world, especially in the 1990s at the end of the Cold War. King joins Gandhi as inspiration for the growth of nonviolent ideas politically, and some even have concluded that political violence has decreased drastically and is destined to disappear.[1] Belief in this kind of progress often is based on limited knowledge about the psychology of nonviolence. Readers of this book might appreciate that nonviolent resistance means much more than not using weapons; it means a change in one's attitude toward one's opponents. This kind of change is abnormal, unnatural, and difficult for mentally healthy persons. Depressive persons seem to be able to empathize with their opponents more easily.

Nonviolent change is more about changing one's own mind than unarmed political action.

Whether King's example and philosophy can serve the world today and in the future is an open question. One place we can look to test this question, perhaps its most difficult test, would be in relation to the endemic political violence of the Middle East. One reason to look there is that the Middle East lies outside the cultural and religious context of both King (Western Christianity with African roots) and Gandhi (Indian Hinduism). If King's philosophy is universal, it would have its greatest test in the Muslim Middle East. Also, violence as a means of engaging in politics has been central to Middle Eastern history dating back two millennia. In contrast, the evolution of political democracy in Western culture has led to nonviolent political change for half a century or more in most Western countries. India too has an old tradition of pacifism, along with more standard violent practices.

The political setting of the Cold War, which was the context of most of King's life, has disappeared, leading to a decline in tyranny-based Cold War policies in much of the world (e.g., Latin America, South Africa, and Southeast Asia). But

Soul on Fire. Nassir Ghaemi, Oxford University Press. © Oxford University Press 2026.
DOI: 10.1093/9780197657614.003.0018

political conflict in the Middle East has increased, not declined, with decades of intense terrorism and multiple wars internally and with Western nations.

If nonviolent action can change societies for the better, its greatest test would be in the Middle East.

It might be argued that nonviolent change has been shown to be effective in the Middle East already, especially in the "Arab Spring" of 2010–2012. In that period, peaceful protests erupted in Tunisia, leading to the end of a long-standing dictatorship. This was followed by massive protests in Egypt, leading to the fall of decades-long one-man rule. Then came Libya, where popular protests overthrew the 45-year rule of Muammar Qaddafi. A rebellion arose against the Syrian authoritarian government, and protests occurred in multiple other Arab countries.

Many in the West applauded these changes as movement toward democracy and as nonviolent movements of change. The mistake in these assumptions was apparent from the beginning, and in the end. The Egyptian demonstrators engaged in repeated rape of innocent women who walked anywhere near them. An election led to a president from the socially conservative Muslim Brotherhood, which led to a military coup d'etat. One-man rule was replaced eventually with one-man rule; it was just a different man. The Libyan rebellion led to the brutal killing of Qaddafi by a mob, and it has been followed by violent anarchy. Tunisia has been stably unstable, with increased political violence.

In short, the apparently nonviolent movements of these Arab countries engaged in violent acts and led to either more violence or a return to the status quo ante.

The Arab Spring was not a nonviolent movement, and certainly not a successful one. Can nonviolent change happen in the Middle East. Can King's ideas be spread elsewhere? The psychology of nonviolence may provide the answer, and it may best be understood by considering the only political movement in the modern Middle East that explicitly upheld nonviolent methods—the First Palestinian Intifada of 1997–2000, led by Mubarak Awad.

* * *

There is a small village in the West Bank, a little north of Ramallah, named Qattana. In 1986, Israel decided to dedicate a street to Martin Luther King Jr. in West Jerusalem. To beautify the street, its organizers wanted to plant olive trees there. Ever since the 1967 war, it had been standard practice to uproot olive trees from villages in the West Bank to make room for Israeli settlements. Palestinians were attached to olive trees, which tended to live for centuries and were symbolic of their connection to the land. For King's park, Israeli authorities decided to bring in olive trees that had been taken away from the destroyed West Bank village of Qattana.[2]

Mubarak Awad, a young psychologist and political activist who was committed to nonviolent principles, flew to the United States. He wrote letters to and then met with Coretta Scott King and explained what was happening. "She said many of my friends told me not to support the Palestinians."[3] Mubarak asked if they were Jews; many were, King said. Awad came home disappointed. From then on, when describing the leaders of nonviolence, he referred to Gandhi, not King.

The Arab–Israeli conflict is at the core of much of the violence in the Middle East, and King never took a definitive position on it. The 1967 war, in which Israel occupied the West Bank and Sinai, occurred in the midst of King's major political activity, yet he avoided talking about it. In a few public talks to Jewish groups, he praised Israel and supported its rights while at the same time referring to the rights of Palestinians. King's main followers, such as Andrew Young and Jesse Jackson, later were viewed as more sympathetic to the Palestinian cause than to the standard pro-Israel viewpoint of the mainstream American Jewish community. Young had to resign as United Nations ambassador for meeting with Palestine Liberation Organization (PLO) representatives in 1979. Jackson's 1984 presidential campaign sunk after private comments with offensive terminology about Jews were reported. But not all of King's circle had these views. Stanley Levison was a major funder and supporter of the American Jewish Congress, a strongly pro-Israel group, and Bayard Rustin was and remained into the 1980s a supporter of Israel and an opponent of Palestinian self-rule.

King seemed to be somewhere in the middle, sensitive to Palestinian rights but also supportive of Israel. He also was very close to Levison, who was a major fundraiser for the Southern Christian Leadership Conference (SCLC). Key American Jewish leaders, such as Rabbi Abraham Heschl, supported King personally and financially. Heschl grew to be quite close to King and marched with him in Selma. A strong opponent of the Vietnam War, like King, Heschl supported Israel's war with Arab nations. King never made a statement supporting or opposing the Arab–Israeli war.

King's views on Israel and Palestine conflicted with those of Gandhi, who opposed the creation of Israel and supported Palestinians' right to remain in their land.

* * *

Mubarak Awad is Christian himself, but his approach to nonviolent methods isn't rooted primarily in religious sources. He realizes that Gandhi as a Hindu and King as a Christian would have limited influence with the majority Muslim population of Palestine. In this sense, Awad's approach is more similar to that of the Student Nonviolent Coordinating Committee, which took a political and nonreligious approach to nonviolent methods. But Awad shares with King and the SCLC the commitment to nonviolence as a way of life, and not merely as a tactic. As Awad states, nonviolence "needs to seep from the mind to the heart." It involves three parts of reconciliation, forgiveness, and not being angry. All three parts are difficult, especially in Israel and Palestine. Forgiving the other side is very difficult, he notes. Not being angry is tough. And then reconciling isn't even a goal for many. So we have to begin with ourselves, Awad believes: The nonviolent person should begin by getting rid of anger as much as possible. "My wife hates that I don't angry or upset, no matter what," he comments wryly. "The expectation from others is that you have to get angry. But anybody who makes you angry controls you. I don't want to be controlled by anybody."[4]

Awad put his principles into practice during the First Intifada of the late 1980s. The PLO had been engaged in armed revolt against Israel for two decades, ever since losing the 1967 war. Such efforts, including violent terrorism, had backfired. Not only had they not regained any lost territory but also they were forced out of their exile in Lebanon and decamped in humiliation to Tunisia. At that point, when PLO leaders such as Yasser Arafat were far away from their political base, new leaders began to emerge in the West Bank. Among them, Awad advocated a new approach: Give up armed conflict, and begin nonviolent resistance, like Gandhi (and King). Awad had concluded that the PLO "was always a failure in armed struggle. We killed so many young Palestinians just to please the leaders that we are fighting."[5] It was time for a change.

Awad met with a key leader of the PLO, Khalil al-Wazir, whose nom de guerre was Abu Jihad (Father of Jihad, which often is interpreted as holy war, although it also means to struggle). Abu Jihad, who was assassinated by Israeli operatives in Tunisia in 1988, became a convert, accepting the nonviolent approach completely. So did Salah Khalaf (Abu Iyad), head of PLO intelligence and second in command to Arafat. Together, they convinced Arafat to give it a try, with a reluctant Arafat taking the pragmatic approach that he had nothing to lose. In November 1988, 7 months after Abu Jihad's murder and 5 months after Awad's deportation, the PLO officially repudiated the policy of armed struggle. A month later, it rejected political terrorism.

What followed was a period of the greatest success in half a century of Palestinian activism. The nonviolent Intifada already had started in the West Bank in 1987, under Awad's leadership, and it continued into 1993 as official PLO policy.

Awad's approach was psychological: "Occupation is based on fear. We switched that completely, with a psychological change in people's mentality that they are free even under occupation."

Like King's movement in the South, Awad's Palestinians received training in nonviolent methods and thinking:

> We train Palestinians that you should not be afraid of Israelis; they are already afraid of you. . . . Go to villages and tell them that three Israeli jeeps should not be able to control this village. In every village, raise the Palestinian flag and burn tires and block the roads. Do it in every village. We did that and it became one of the most exciting things in the First Intifada.[6]

Like Bevel, Awad emphasized activity by adolescents and young adults, and made imprisonment a badge of honor:

> The Israelis arrested youth and we told them to stay in prison. Let the Israelis pay for you. If the Israelis didn't come, we called the news media. Even the fear of going to jail was removed. Then the Israelis became occupiers; it became a burden on them to control the villages.

Awad taught his people about the moral core of their struggle: "Nonviolence is something we are doing for the sake of Palestine. We will not shoot back, because we are not killers." And after decades of military success, Israel was confused with the new Palestinian movement: "The Israelis preferred that Palestinians used arms and bombs, because they can defeat them quickly that way, but nonviolence took them by surprise: When they say, 'There is a curfew, go home,' we don't."[7]

This nonviolent resistance had an impact on Israeli soldiers. Said one paratrooper, "I feel humiliated in front of the person I must beat up. These are not the values I was raised on. I feel the victim getting stronger, while I become weaker."[8]

The Israeli government imprisoned Awad and others, but it realized that imprisonment didn't stop the movement. The government couldn't kill Awad easily, because he openly rejected violence. Finally, the government decided to deport him to the United States, where he has lived for more than 30 years.

* * *

For Awad, the Israeli occupation was analogous to segregation or slavery; it was like the apartheid of South Africa, and it has similar racist undertones:

> Israelis are White Europeans who came at the end of the era of colonization. That didn't work well in the mentality of Arab people. It's a White colonization against the brown Arabs. They took the land; they didn't buy it, exactly like thieves.[9]

Hence, Palestinians felt a sympathy for King, despite his pro-Jewish sympathies, and also for other Black activists. Among the latter, Nelson Mandela returned their sympathy most strongly, unlike King, always maintaining a strong policy in favor of the PLO and Palestinian rights.

The nonviolent movement of the First Intifada led to increased international sympathy for Palestinians and eventually to an agreement for partial self-rule in the 1993 Oslo peace accord, mediated by U.S. President Bill Clinton, between Israeli leader Yitzhak Rabin and the PLO's Arafat. For his efforts, Rabin was assassinated by an Israeli 2 years later. After Rabin, Israel took a right-wing turn and never returned to work on expanding the Oslo peace process. Finally, in 2000, with Clinton gone, Rabin long dead, and Israeli right-wing leader Ariel Sharon in power, Palestinians broke out into the Second Intifada, but this time they gave up their prior nonviolent methods, as Awad watched helplessly from the United States. Palestinians began with stones and moved on to gunfire and suicide bombings; Israel used its powerful army. Over 4 years, approximately 4,000 Palestinians and Israelis were killed, and the movement ended in 2005 with no progress in the conflict.

Looking back, Awad views the successes of the First Intifada as short-lived because the PLO leaders used nonviolence only as a tactic, without really believing in it, since they had failed in armed struggle; they gave it up later when they thought violent methods could work again. It was easier to blame the Israelis than to take the most courageous risk of unarmed resistance. Says Awad, "In one of my speeches, I told Palestinians that we are under occupation because we choose to be under occupation. If you can't accept death, then it's your choice to be occupied. That didn't go well."[10]

The experience of the First Intifada, the only explicitly nonviolent persistent political movement in the Middle East, gives room for hope but also concern. The hope lies in the fact that a nonviolent movement took root among mostly Muslim Palestinians. The concern involves how it didn't last. One observation is that ongoing and charismatic nonviolent leadership, such as that provided by King in the United States and by Awad in Palestine, is needed for a nonviolent movement to persist.

In Palestine, change may happen eventually, either by violent or nonviolent means. The difference will not be in the fact of change but, rather, how long it lasts and whether hearts and minds also change in future generations. As Awad states, "The Palestinian Israeli conflict is going to be resolved, but we have to figure out how to do it with the least amount of deaths."[11] The lesson of King's movement was that nonviolence was needed not only to end segregation but also to begin the process of curing the disease of racism. It's one thing to change laws, to draw new borders, to create governments; it's another for Blacks and Whites, Jews and Arabs/Muslims, to respect and value each other.

Notes

1. https://en.wikipedia.org/wiki/The_Better_Angels_of_Our_Nature.
2. Mieke Bal, Jonathan Crewe, and Leo Spitzer, eds., *Acts of Memory: Cultural Recall in the Present* (Hanover, NH: Dartmouth University Press, 1998), p. 156.
3. Mubarak Awad interview, March 15, 2013.
4. Ibid.
5. Ibid.
6. Ibid.
7. Ibid.
8. Earl Raymond Thorpe, *The Other Truth About the Middle East Conflict* (Morrisville, NC: Lulu Enterprises, 2006), p. 155.
9. Mubarak Awad interview, March 15, 2013.
10. Ibid.
11. Ibid.

17

Where Does the Anger Go?

On Sunday, August 20, 1967, *The New York Times* published a long article by psychiatrist Alvin Poussaint titled, "A Negro Psychiatrist Explains the Negro Psyche."[1] Approximately 2 weeks later, Martin Luther King Jr. was scheduled to give a plenary address at the annual convention of the American Psychological Association, on the topic of how individual psychological maladjustment was needed to correct social evils. Poussaint had been active in the civil rights movement, marching behind King in the Meredith march the prior year. The two men knew each other well. Poussaint had just left the South to take up an academic career in Boston, where he would prosper for half a century at Harvard University.

In the article, Poussaint had raised some key psychological issues about the nonviolent basis of the civil rights movement. After it was published, King contacted the doctor and told him that he liked the article.[2] The two men had little chance to pursue the topic, however, because King's life would end within the year. But the questions Poussaint raised deserve closer scrutiny, in part also because they seemed to resonate with King.

There is an old cliché in the psychiatric community, derived from Sigmund Freud in his classic article on depression, "Mourning and Melancholia."[3] Depression, he said, is anger turned inwards. We can grieve too much when someone close to us dies, such as a parent, Freud wrote. Normal grief is brief and logical; depression is like an abnormal grief, long and illogical. That's because we have some unresolved feelings toward the dead person; perhaps we harbored feelings of anger toward a parent, resentment for childhood wrongs. We can't express that anger explicitly; it makes us too guilty. So we turn the anger inward, we direct it at ourselves, and then we become depressed. We blame ourselves illogically, we demean ourselves, turning those angry unconscious feelings away from their true target—a parent.

Depression happens, in short, because we aren't angry enough in the real world, toward others; we then turn our anger on ourselves.

Soul on Fire. Nassir Ghaemi, Oxford University Press. © Oxford University Press 2026.
DOI: 10.1093/9780197657614.003.0019

Poussaint saw that this Freudian theory of depression posed a problem for King's nonviolent philosophy. In the marches of the movement, civil rights activists were yelled at, jeered at, and spat upon by angry White onlookers. Policemen sometimes cursed them with racial epithets; other times the marchers were physically attacked by their White opponents or the police. Dogs were released, fire hoses sprayed water, and sometimes guns were shot.

And all the while, the teaching of the movement leadership was that the activists shouldn't respond in kind. They shouldn't yell back, or argue, or fight back, or even defend themselves physically. In short, they couldn't express any anger, verbal or physical.

Despite often receiving formal training in nonviolent resistance, and despite many activists being fully committed to Christian teachings of nonviolence, Poussaint observed that they still were human beings. They got angry. Anyone would. But they couldn't express their anger toward their opponents.

So, Poussaint wondered, where did the anger go?

* * *

Poussaint had marched with the marchers. He was field director for the Medical Committee for Human Rights, a group of medical volunteers who accompanied the civil rights marches. Poussaint carried his medical black bag, ready to treat any activists hurt by the physical attacks that were all too common. Trained in psychiatry, Poussaint also was there to tend to the mental needs of marchers. More often than not, he found that there was more mental than physical damage:

> I used to sit there and wonder, "Now, what do they really do with their rage?" Well, after a period of time it became apparent that they were directing it mostly at each other and the White civil-rights workers. Violent verbal and sometimes physical fights often occurred among the workers on the civil-right projects throughout the South. While they were talking about being nonviolent and "loving" the sheriff that just hit them over the head, they rampaged around the project houses beating up each other. I frequently had to calm Negro civil-right workers with large doses of tranquilizers [antipsychotic medications] for what I can describe clinically only as acute attacks of rage.[4]

Forbidden from responding to their White attackers, the marchers turned on each other. They were angry, agitated; they had to get it out.

Poussaint was describing the Meredith march of 1966 in particular, during which Stokely Carmichael of the Student Nonviolent Coordinating Committee

(SNCC) called for "Black Power." That event was the beginning of the end of the nonviolent movement.[5]

Poussaint viewed the turn to Black Power as a psychological event:

> The workers who shouted it the loudest were those with the oldest battle scars from the terror, demoralization, and castration which they experienced through continual direct confrontation with Southern White racism. Furthermore, some of the most bellicose chanters of the slogan had been, just a few years before, exemplars of nonviolent, loving passive resistance in their struggle against White supremacy. These workers appeared to be seeking a sense of inner psychological emancipation from racism through self-assertion and release of aggressive, angry feelings.

In other words, nonviolent struggle might achieve social progress but at the price of personal psychological harm. Violent struggle may fail, or even cause social harm, but it had important personal psychological benefits.

It was difficult to love in the midst of so much hatred. Poussaint described a civil rights activist in Mississippi who said, after a sit-in demonstration, "White racism has made me hate White people and hate myself and my brothers. I ain't about to stop hating White folks, but I'm not gonna let that self-hatred stuff mess me any more!"

Poussaint observed that "nonassertiveness" was a "learned adaptation" through centuries of slavery, the only way to survive in a setting of pure despotism. The Black church reinforced this approach to survival through its highly pacifist interpretation of Christianity. But if you can't assert yourself, there will be "devastating" effects in your psyche, Poussaint wrote. Blacks became afraid to assert themselves in any aspect of society: business, school, work. Hence, they failed to achieve. Others suffered anxiety and depression.

Poussaint described a young Black man who came for treatment for anxiety. He had been raised mainly in White environments and was engaged to a White woman, whose parents disowned her. He had a reputation for being very calm and understanding when Whites showed any subtle or not-so-subtle signs of racism. He denied any conscious anger toward them and held to a philosophy of seeking to understand and value everyone, regardless of race. As his psychotherapy proceeded, he began to express deeply held anger toward a lifetime of racist experiences. His anxiety transmuted into rage. Or, put otherwise, his unconscious rage had been the cause of his conscious anxiety. He left his fiancée, moved away, and became a "Black nationalist."

Poussaint saw other channels for the repressed rage. You could seem "cool" or put your energies into music or sports. Or you could identify with the oppressor, becoming as "White" as you could in your manners and interests. Or you could do the opposite: supporting outspoken Black leaders such as Malcolm X, because you had no means to speak out in your own life. Or you could become a chronically sullen person, with "a chip on the shoulder." Or you could turn to drug abuse and alcoholism.

These social ills stemmed, in part, from the psychology of self-hatred, Poussaint wrote. They would be solved more easily when Blacks had more self-love than self-hatred inside of them. They would need to be much more assertive, short of violence, but nonetheless assertive. They would have to lose their fear, which as James Meredith said at the end of his 1966 march, would leave White America with two choices: "to kill them or let them be free." Poussaint called for "constructive aggressiveness" in the civil rights struggle, for the benefit of both Whites and Blacks. Blacks needed it for their mental health; Whites needed it to prevent a race war. Or as Poussaint closed, speaking to American society, "Stop oppressing the Black man, or be prepared to meet his expressed rage."

Another psychiatrist, also a revolutionary, had made similar observations a few years before Poussaint.

* * *

Frantz Fanon was a psychiatrist from Martinique, trained in France, who became a leading figure in the Algerian Revolution of the late 1950s and early 1960s, before his death from cancer at age 36 years in 1961. He became an icon of the Black nationalist movement of the later 1960s, especially the Black Panthers, who made him famous as a proponent of violence in the struggles of colonial peoples against White racism, explained in his classic book, *The Wretched of the Earth.*[6] There, the storyline goes, Fanon argued that the colonialist oppression of non-White peoples produced a deformation of the personality of the African and the Caribbean Black. These deformed Blacks could only cleanse themselves and their messed up personalities in a violent reaction against the White colonialists. Violent revolution not only was justified on the usual political and economic and social grounds but also was justified in the interests of the individual psychological health of oppressed persons.

Fanon's book ends with an appendix of a number of psychiatric case histories of patients whom Fanon treated. Today, the cases would be described as representing post-traumatic stress disorder (PTSD). What is interesting is that PTSD occurred not only in the Algerian victims of French police or military repression but also in the White policemen themselves. Colonialism caused psychological damage for everyone, Algerians and Frenchmen.

The Wretched of the Earth was a hit in the early 1960s, just before Fanon's premature death. But he had also written in 1952 a book in French, later published in English in 1967: *Black Skin, White Masks.*[7] In it, we see a different Fanon, or perhaps a different side to him—one in which he is not an exhorter of revolution but, rather, a clinician of pain. This Fanon hardly even mentions violence, much less defends it. He rather seeks to empathize, and to do so with everybody. Fanon quotes the famous observation of W. E. B. Dubois about "double-consciousness":

> The world yields [the American Black] no true self consciousness, but only lets him see himself through the revelation of the other world. It is a peculiar sensation, this double-consciousness, this sense of always looking at one's self through the eyes of others, of measuring one's soul by the tape of a world that looks on in amused contempt and pity. One ever feels this two-ness—an American, a Negro; two souls, two thoughts, two unreconciled strivings; two warring ideals in one dark body.[8]

Fanon adds, "White civilization and European culture have forced an existential deviation on the Negro . . . what is often called the Black soul is the White man's artifact."[9]

DuBois famously began his greatest work, *The Souls of Black Folk,* by calling out the implicit racism that faces anyone who isn't White in a White world: How does it feel to be a problem?[10] This is the racial, indeed existential, dilemma: One's mere existence is a problem, not anything one says or does.

Your mere existence—you—are a problem.

* * *

Fanon starts where psychoanalysis starts: with the family. He notes that a normal White adult is raised in a family in which he receives a normal amount of attention and care and love. He then enters a society in which he and his parents and siblings and his family's experiences are validated by everything he sees around him: everything—his religion, his politics, his habits, his virtues and vices—they are all validated as normal and acceptable. He is normal.

Not a single Black man or woman, or for that matter, not a single immigrant or immigrant's child, has any chance at that kind of normality. All Blacks are fated to abnormality. No matter how well sheltered or cultured the upbringing of a non-White, he will enter a foreign world, one that does not recognize him, and in which he does not see himself.

He then has two choices: Either he rejects himself and accepts the world, or he rejects the world and becomes angry or depressed. Fanon wants to break this cycle:

> I have only one solution: to rise above this absurd drama that others have staged around me, to reject the two terms that are equally unacceptable,

> and through one human being, to reach out for the universal. When the Negro dives—in other words, goes under—something remarkable happens.

As a psychoanalyst, Fanon wants to help his patient become conscious of some of his racial inferiority feelings and to empower him to change the social structure that causes those feelings: "The Black man should no longer be confronted by the dilemma, turn White or disappear."

Fanon's view is that there is a complex dialectic here between what society does to the individual and what the individual allows society to do to him: "I have ceaselessly striven to show the Negro that in a sense he makes himself abnormal; to show the White man that he is at once the perpetrator and the victim of a delusion."

Fanon is not seeking to elevate Blackness or to simply blame Whiteness, nor does he think that there is any possibility of being color-blind. We are not wed to the past, he argues forcefully, but we are who we are, and our society is built on the past, with its prejudices as well as its glories. There is no way to escape the reality of the deformative effects of racism on all people. The first step is to acknowledge it; the next is to fight it.

Fanon relates how in Algeria he would be stopped by the French police, who would mistake him for an Arab. After realizing their error, they would apologize profusely and would assure him that Arabs were unreliable, unlike Negroes. Fanon was "astonished to learn that North Africans despise men of color" and that he had difficulty establishing good relations with them. "The Frenchman does not like the Jew, who does not like the Arab, who does not like the Negro."[11] And the cycle of racism goes on.

* * *

The Black man wants to be like the White man, he writes, and the White man wants only to be human. Let them both be human, he argues. Fanon's goal is an "authentic disalienation" of humanity. Simply attacking the enemy will not do:

> I find myself suddenly in the world and I recognize that I have one right alone: That of demanding human behavior from the other. One duty alone: That of not renouncing my freedom through my choices. . . . Superiority? Inferiority? Why not the quite simple attempt to touch the other, to feel the other, to explain the other to myself?[12]

This Fanon of *Black Skin, White Masks* seems like a different person than the Fanon who extols violence as a means for psychological redemption in *The*

Wretched of the Earth. Indeed, perhaps Fanon's tenure in Algeria radicalized him, for not only is the tone of these two works different but also, even within *Wretched of the Earth*, Fanon's style as political theorist is radically different from that of his chapter written as a clinical psychiatrist. That book begins famously with the blazing chapter "Concerning Violence." The first sentence states, "Decolonization is always a violent phenomenon," and he doesn't look back. This is followed by other theoretical chapters on spontaneity, national consciousness, and culture, the chapters that so entranced many radicals decades ago. Yet curiously little attention has been given to the final full chapter of the book, "Colonial War and Mental Disorders," a compilation and discussion of real psychiatric cases treated by Fanon in Algeria. Here, not only does he feel initially a need to apologize for including this chapter in the book but also his tone is quite different, more subdued, more anguished, as in *Black Skin, White Masks*.

* * *

Fanon argued that the essence of colonialism was to be a "fertile purveyor" of psychiatric diseases:

> Because it is a systematic negation of the other person and a furious determination to deny the other person all attributes of humanity, colonialism forces the people it dominates to ask themselves the question constantly:
>
> "In reality, who am I?"[13]

Fanon then described four basic categories of cases:

1. So-called reactive psychoses, such as mania and psychotic depression in the setting of killing and mayhem
2. Psychiatric cases that are the effects of "total war," such as the taxi driver who becomes impotent after his wife is raped or the European torturer who ties up and beats his wife on the slightest provocation
3. The effects of torture, such as paranoia, phobias, and depersonalization
4. Psychosomatic disorders, such as gastric and other ailments that occur after torture and brainwashing in particular

Fanon the psychiatrist used drugs, such as high doses of antipsychotics or sedatives, a quite progressive approach in that era. But he was, at root, an existential psychiatrist: He saw his patients as people, first and foremost, caught up in a crazy world.

* * *

In the following, Fanon interviews two Algerian boys who killed their European friend:

> Why did you kill him?
> Because he trusted us to go up on the hill.
> Did he do anything to you?
> No.
> So why did you kill him?
> Because they kill us.
> But did he ever hurt you in particular?
> No. In your opinion (one child says to Fanon) what should we have done?
> I don't know (Fanon replies), but you are a child and what is happening concerns grown up people.
> But they kill children too.
> That is no reason for killing your friend.
> Well kill him I did, now you can do what you like.[14]

* * *

Fanon, the psychiatrist, treats Algerians and Europeans alike. Although he takes sides in the war, he doesn't judge individuals while he treats them, and he never condones personal violence. Yet as soon as the psychiatric chapter is over, we meet again Fanon the political theorist, in his fiery conclusion, famously writing, "Come, then, comrades; it would be as well at once to decide to change our ways. . . . Leave this Europe where they are never done talking of Man but murder men wherever they see them."[15]

Poussaint was going where Fanon went: The civil rights movement and freedom movements in other countries were not purely social processes. They weren't just about changing laws or governments. They were about changing personalities; changing the way people see themselves; and changing how people, White and non-White, interact with each other.

The question was: Which approach is best—violence or nonviolence?

Usually this question is asked and answered only from a social, cultural, or political perspective; or it might be addressed from religious or spiritual perspectives. Fanon and Poussaint are asking it from a psychological perspective. What is the answer for the human personality?

King made it clear, as discussed in prior chapters, that nonviolence was much better for the human psyche than violence. But in his article, *based on his experience with King's civil rights disciples themselves*, Poussaint was throwing doubt on this idea. Fanon made the same observation and seemed to struggle with the solution too.

If you can't hate your enemies, do you end up hating yourself?

* * *

There may be a way out of this dilemma, and the way out might begin by recognizing that the way in was wrong. Freud's hypothesis never has been proven, and there is evidence against it. It's a speculation, not a fact. There are other perspectives. Instead of viewing depression as the effect of anger, one could view anger as the effect of depression. Many psychotherapists notice that the most common emotion that people express when they come to counseling is anger. They are angry at their spouse, their boss, their children, the world. Anger is very common.

In the course of psychotherapy, if you try to get behind the anger, you find many other things: sadness, anxiety, fear, denial. But especially sadness. Decades after Freud, other psychoanalysts[16] made this observation and explained depression as a primary emotion, not the effect of anger or other feelings but, rather, a principal emotion that is among the first that a human experiences. They spoke of the "depressive position,"[17] which the infant experiences early in life when faced with the mother's inevitable inability to always meet its demands immediately. The baby is hungry, it cries; the mother brings the breast, the baby is satisfied. But sometimes there is a delay, or the breast doesn't come. Even with a short delay, the baby cries; it's sad. This sadness is normal and common, and not just in infancy. Adults feel sadness because they experience loss: Parents die, children die, people become ill, jobs are lost, relationships end. Each experience produces sadness, just as in the infant. There's no anger turned inward; there's just sadness.

Anger, instead, is the effect of sadness. It's the "projection" of how I feel to you. I deny my sadness by becoming angry at you. I'm not sad, because I'm hurt in some way; you're the cause of my unhappiness, so I become angry at you.

Anger is a projection, an attempt at denial, in this view; the real cause, the underlying feeling, is sadness or depression. If this perspective is right, it might solve the problem of Fanon versus King; it might explain what Poussaint observed in Mississippi. Depression increases empathy for others, as we've explained previously. If this is so, a nonviolent attitude can grow organically out of the experience of depression, as described previously. You empathize with your opponent, so you don't hurt that person. But then you have to be aware of and accept the depressive experience; you have to allow yourself to be sad. You might even become clinically depressed. If you don't experience the depression, if you can't accept the pain of sadness, you can resist it by projecting your sadness to your opponent and seeing them as its cause. In that case, you become violent; it makes sense to harm your opponent. Or, in the case of Poussaint's observation, if you can't become violent toward your enemies, you become violent toward your friends. And yet, as Fanon observed, that violence doesn't appear to be curative. The French policemen suffer as much as the Algerians they kill or torture. One might add that the history of postcolonial Africa doesn't suggest any major psychological growth. Algeria is free; so is Libya, and Sudan, and a host of African countries. And yet violence flows, both with crime as with political and military conflict between ethnic groups and political parties.

* * *

Like many in the Black radical movement, Stokely Carmichael viewed Africa as the solution. If it could be freed from White domination, then Africans would rule with wisdom. Carmichael moved to Guinea and changed his name to Kwame Ture (honoring his two heroes, whom he got to know well, Kwame Nkrumah and Sekou Toure, leading revolutionaries who became presidents of Ghana and Guinea, respectively). A few months before his death of cancer in 1998, in his last interview, Stokely Carmichael/Kwame Ture admitted the problem: "Leaders in Africa are so corrupt that we are certain if we put dogs in uniform, and put guns on their shoulders, we'd be hard put to distinguish them."[18]

If Fanon hoped that the violent overthrow of European rule would make the African man and woman more free psychologically, calmer, less anxious, less depressed, less angry, and less violent, that outcome hasn't happened.

Maybe the problem was that it was too easy to blame the European colonists. You could be angry with the Whites and the Europeans; you could even kick them out of your country. But then you were still sad because of the tragedy of living in poverty and corruption. So you had to blame someone else, but this time only people of your own skin color remained.

What if the anger was replaced by sadness? What if you realized that you should be sad with the state of your world? What a tragedy. It's worthy of sadness, of depression. But I won't blame someone else; I won't pin it solely on my oppressor, because there's enough blame to go around to everyone. Then, perhaps, anger could be replaced by sadness, and projection by empathy, and violence by nonviolence.

The same problem holds for White people. They get angry at non-Whites because Whites don't want to be sad. They don't want to accept the tragedy of our world. America was founded on the genocide of an entire race, who are now living in an Africa-like level of poverty on reservations. What a tragedy. This genocide was followed by 300 years of slavery and another century of proto-slavery segregation. What a tragedy.

Instead of accepting the tragedy, and being sad about it, Whites often are defensive. The sadness is turned into anger. White parents argue against teaching about the central role of genocide and slavery in the history of the country; instead, let's just praise the Founding Fathers, and democracy, and freedom.

Sadness becomes anger, which justifies violence and rejection of the opponent.

A similar phenomenon happened in post-Nazism Germany. After World War II, a great silence descended on the German populace. A wall of denial was built.[19] Silence was the solution to the problem of acknowledging their genocide. What a tragedy.

Germany should have been deeply sad. Knowing it couldn't be angry, it couldn't blame someone else any more, the German nation became quiet. True, it made reparations to Israel, but the issue raised here is psychological, not social or economic. What do you do when your parents committed evil acts? You should feel great sadness, great remorse. But you can't tolerate the sadness.

So where does the depression go?

* * *

One way of understanding King's call to nonviolence is to view it as a call to accept the experience of depression. It's a call to accept the tragedies of the world and to take responsibility through a feeling of sorrow. This depressive politics would not blame others. It's not about blaming Whites or Germans; it's about not blaming anyone at all; it's about everyone taking responsibility. No one is responsible for the harms done by their parents or grandparents or ancestors. But they shouldn't deny those harms. And they shouldn't be silent about them. And the descendants of the oppressed aren't better than the descendants of the oppressors. The tragedies of the past affect everyone equally in the present.

If the goal is forgiveness, there has to be apology. And if there is to be apology, there has to be rejection of denial. Terrible events occurred; our ancestors caused those events, or were complicit in them; maybe even we were complicit. I accept my role; I accept my ancestors' roles. I do not deny them. I apologize on their behalf for what they did, not what I did. And the descendants of the oppressed, or the oppressed themselves, can then forgive and say, let us live forward as brothers and sisters.

This process was attempted in South Africa at the end of apartheid, and in some Latin American countries such as Chile, after the end of Cold War–era autocracies. But these efforts are incomplete as long as any party denies any aspect of what happened or tries to defend a past that is indefensible in the present. King realized that segregation was just a modern continuation of slavery, and changing laws wasn't enough. A changing of hearts was needed, and the philosophy of nonviolence was an attempt to change those hearts.

That attempt would run counter to human nature because it would generate strong feelings of sadness, which are difficult to tolerate, and usually are resisted by denial and projection into anger. That's what happened: Sadness became anger; nonviolence became violence; and the civil rights movement ended.

The question isn't then: Where does the anger go? The question is: How much sorrow can we tolerate?[20]

Notes

1. https://www.nytimes.com/1967/08/20/archives/a-negro-psychiatrist-explains-the-negro-psyche-the-negro-psyche.html.
2. Interview with Alvin Poussaint, May 15, 2013.
3. Sigmund Freud, "Trauer und Melancholie," *Internationale Zeitschrift für Psychoanalyse* 4 (1916–1917g [1915]): 277–287; "Mourning and Melancholia," in *The Standard Edition of the Complete Psychological Works of Sigmund Freud*, ed. James Strachey (New York: Vintage, 1999), Vol. 14, pp. 243–258. As Paul Roazen has shown, Freud wrote his paper in reaction to a presentation on depression by Viktor Tausk a few months earlier. When Freud published it, he did not credit Tausk's presentation. Tausk likely had manic–depressive illness and committed suicide within a few years. Paul Roazen, *Brother Animal: The Story of Freud and Tausk* (New York: Knopf, 1969), pp. 191–192.
4. https://www.nytimes.com/1967/08/20/archives/a-negro-psychiatrist-explains-the-negro-psyche-the-negro-psyche.html.
5. Carmichael would be followed by H. Rap Brown as leader of the SNCC, and by 1968 the SNCC allied with the Black Panther Party, which made explicit calls for an armed revolution. SNCC dissolved soon thereafter.
6. https://en.wikipedia.org/wiki/The_Wretched_of_the_Earth.
7. https://en.wikipedia.org/wiki/Black_Skin,_White_Masks.
8. Originally published in *The Atlantic*, "Strivings of the Negro People," August 1897, https://www.theatlantic.com/magazine/archive/1897/08/strivings-of-the-negro-people/305446. See also https://plato.stanford.edu/entries/double-consciousness.
9. Frantz Fanon, *Black Skin, White Masks* (New York: Grove Press, 1967), p. 16.
10. W. E. B. DuBois, *The Souls of Black Folk* (New York: Oxford University Press, 2009 [1903]), p. 7:

    > Between me and the other world there is ever an unasked question: unasked by some through feelings of delicacy; by others through the difficulty of rightly framing it. All, nevertheless, flutter round it. They approach me in a half-hesitant sort of way, eye me curiously or compassionately, and then, instead of saying directly, How does it feel to be a problem? they say, I know an excellent colored man in my town; or, I fought at Mechanicsville; or, Do not these Southern outrages make your blood boil? At these I smile, or am interested, or reduce the boiling to a simmer, as the occasion may require. To the real question, How does it feel to be a problem? I answer seldom a word.

11. Fanon, *Black Skin, White Masks*, p. 103.
12. Ibid., pp. 229–231.
13. Frantz Fanon, *The Wretched of the Earth* (New York: Grove Press, 1968), pp. 249–250.
14. Ibid., pp. 270–272.
15. Ibid., p. 311.
16. The leading thinker in this group is the mid-20th-century British pediatrician and psychoanalyst Donald Winnicott. The overall thinking is part of the "object relations theory" approach to psychoanalysis, which has been mainstream in psychoanalytic psychotherapy for the past half century. https://en.wikipedia.org/wiki/Donald_Winnicott.

17. https://www.oxfordclinicalpsych.com/view/10.1093/med:psych/9780190271367.001.0001/med-9780190271367-chapter-39.
18. Paula Span, "The Undying Revolutionary: As Stokely Carmichael, He Fought for Black Power. Now Kwame Ture's Fighting for His Life," *The Washington Post*, April 8, 1988, https://www.washingtonpost.com/archive/lifestyle/1998/04/08/the-undying-revolutionary-as-stokely-carmichael-he-fought-for-black-power-now-kwame-tures-fighting-for-his-life/4adb14ec-0db8-4668-8af6-84f877b3c61a.
19. Karl Jaspers, *On the Question of German Guilt* (New York: Fordham University Press, 2001 [1947]). See also https://www.britannica.com/biography/Karl-Jaspers/Postwar-development-of-thought#ref93349.
20. This emphasis on sadness as part of normal development may link to the fact that most human beings can understand and appreciate clinical depression. There's less stigma with depression and anxiety than with other psychiatric states because we all experience sadness and anxiety as a normal personality trait, like height and weight, with most of us having some anxiety all the time normally. But mania seems abnormal, and unconnected to normal human experience. That stigma against mania is based on a misunderstanding, however, because mania reflects two other normal experiences: happiness and anger. When people are manic, they are happy (or irritable) in their moods. We all experience happiness, as well as sadness, so mania shouldn't seem so foreign to us. Psychiatrist Hagop Akiskal was asked what is the difference between hypomnia (mild manic episodes) and normal happiness. Akiskal replied that hypomania is recurrent; happiness is not. There's more than a little wisdom there. Happiness is a stable state of mind; it's not joy or euphoria; as a mood state, it's more akin to satisfaction and a calm tranquility of mind. If someone is happy, then they're happy most of the time. But hypomania, by definition, is brief and recurrent; it lasts days to weeks and then goes away, and then it comes back again months or years later.

18

"The Loneliest Minority of All"

Martin Luther King Jr. wasn't the only civil rights leader with depression or manic traits. In this chapter, preliminary evidence for likely mood illness is presented for a number of other civil rights figures, both prominent leaders and lesser known activists.

The point of this chapter is not to prove that each person listed here had manic–depressive illness; skeptics will not be convinced. Of the leaders discussed here, some cases are more definitive than others: Some are known publicly to have been diagnosed with psychiatric illness by physicians who treated them; approximately half committed suicide. No claim is made that any possible diagnoses are definitive but, rather, the reader is asked to consider their possibility, and the more than chance likelihood that so many prominent civil rights leaders appear to have had likely or possible psychiatric conditions.

The goal of the chapter, at minimum, is to show that psychiatric illness is not incompatible with contributing in a positive way to a very beneficial social movement.

Malcolm X

In March 1964, in one of King's many visits to Washington, DC, on behalf of the civil rights bill, he ran into a tall, lightly colored, auburn-haired Black man in the halls of Congress; Malcolm X had come to listen to the Senate debate on the civil rights bill. It was the only time they would meet in person (although, unknown to King, Malcolm sometimes would stand unobtrusively in the audience when King spoke, such as at the famous March on Washington, and again a year later when King spoke in Harlem after returning from Europe on his Nobel Prize trip).[1] A classic picture of the two on that occasion shows a hearty handshake with broad smiles, as if they were old allies.

Soul on Fire. Nassir Ghaemi, Oxford University Press. © Oxford University Press 2026.
DOI: 10.1093/9780197657614.003.0020

Malcolm had become infamous in the United States as the chief spokesman for the Nation of Islam. Malcolm and the Nation of Islam were separatist, not integrationist; supported violent self-defense "by any means necessary," not nonviolence; and were anti-White (often referring to White people as "devils"). Nonetheless, the angry rhetoric of Malcolm X struck sympathetic chords in the Northern ghettoes; Malcolm connected because he was one of them.

Raised initially in Michigan, Malcolm Little had suffered many losses as a child. His father, who was an activist for Black rights and a follower of the separatist leader Marcus Garvey, was run over by a train while laying on the tracks. Whether he was killed by White racists, as Malcolm thought, or died by suicide is not established. His mother became chronically psychotic and was institutionalized in a mental hospital. Mental illness would run in the family; years later, one of Malcolm's brothers also became chronically psychotic and homeless. After his mother's institutionalization, the many Little children were dispersed in the family. Malcolm landed with an aunt in Boston, where he grew up as a teenager and young adult. Malcolm became a petty criminal and ended up in the Massachusetts prison system, where he converted to Islam after some of his siblings did so back in Michigan. He then became a fanatically committed follower of Elijah Muhammad.[2]

There are some interesting similarities between the personalities of Malcolm X and King, some of which might be related to the impact of varieties of manic–depressive illness. For instance, Malcolm, like King, was famous for his sense of humor.[3] "Every time I hear Martin, he's got a dream," Malcolm would joke.[4]

Like King, he was assassinated at age 39 years and had clear awareness that death was near in his final months. A few days before he was killed, Professor C. Eric Lincoln, an old friend, invited him to speak on the following Tuesday to students at Brown University. Malcolm answered that he would do so if he was not dead by then. "Come on, Malcolm, cut the bullshit," Lincoln replied. Malcolm was serious. "Tell your kids I'll be up there on Tuesday if I'm alive."[5] That Sunday, February 21, 1965, with his wife and children watching in the front row, as he had requested in an unusual move, he was murdered.

In the months prior to his death, he appears to have been clinically depressed, like King had been.[6] Otherwise, like King, he was a high-energy, active man, with little need for sleep, usually only needing about 4 hours nightly.[7] His energy and drive helped fuel his undeniable charisma. He had other manic traits that were constant and part of his personality, like King.

He was very talkative. Said Benjamin Karim, a close aide, "He was chattery. One minute he'd be talking about temple business and the next he would again be telling us . . . that he had decided to name the child after the King of the Huns."

He had constant and rapid thoughts, again described by Karim: "Malcolm had no time for nothing. I don't think Malcolm's mind ever stopped . . . his mind was running on another, totally different track, and his hands were rarely quiet." He would constantly doodle, often on napkins at the temple restaurant, and then he would take his napkins with him because "he didn't want anyone trying to psychoanalyze him."

He was constantly moving, "pacing . . . tapping his fingers and feet."[8]

On at least one occasion, while in jail, Malcolm experienced auditory hallucinations.[9]

Put together, these were all manic symptoms, which, when constant, represent manic traits as part of a mood temperament. There isn't good evidence that Malcolm, unlike King, had common or frequent depressive symptoms or brief depressive episodes throughout his life, and thus the most likely diagnosis of these constant manic traits for Malcolm would be hyperthymic temperament (see Appendix 1).

Further evidence for a likely hyperthymic temperament is found in Malcolm's family genetics for severe mental illness, much stronger than in the case of King. As noted previously, Malcolm's mother became chronically delusional and lived most of her life in a state mental hospital. In his *Autobiography*,[10] Malcolm X attributes her psychosis to the stress of the murder of her husband.[11] Since then, other possible explanations, including mental illness, tend to be ignored by biographers or academics. Malcolm's younger brother, Reginald, to whom he was very close and who helped convert Malcolm to Islam, later had a falling out with the Nation of Islam. After his isolation, Reginald also became chronically psychotic and spent the rest of his life in a state mental hospital, just like his mother.[12] Malcolm's grandson and namesake, Malcolm Shabazz, was highly impulsive, causing a fire when he was a teenager that led to the death of his grandmother, Betty Shabazz, Malcolm's wife. The younger Malcolm later was murdered in Mexico at age 28 years, reportedly after a dispute about a large bar tab and female companions.[13]

In short, Malcolm X likely had lifelong hyperthymic temperament, and probable clinical depression just before his assassination at age 39 years. King had lifelong cyclothymic temperament, and likely clinical depression just before his assassination at age 39 years.

The two men were quite similar psychiatrically, if not politically. But they grew to be similar politically too.

Up to that chance 1964 meeting, Malcolm X and King had been on opposite sides of history. King studiously avoided running into Malcolm, despite King's many visits to Malcolm's home turf of New York City, where Malcolm was the main minister for the large Nation of Islam mosque there. In March 1964, Malcolm X was in the midst of a major transition. Only 3 weeks earlier, Malcolm had publicly left the Nation of Islam and had begun the slow process that, years later, King would see as movement toward King's own positions. As they shook hands at the behest of photographers, King was surrounded by his entourage of Ralph Abernathy and Bernard Lee; still, King seemed more uneasy than Malcolm, who no longer belonged to any organization. Malcolm had much more reason to be uncomfortable; he wasn't *TIME*'s Man of the Year; he was a marked man, targeted, unlike King, not by current enemies but, rather, by old friends.

During the Selma movement of February 1965, Malcolm X made his first and only personal visit to the South during an active civil rights campaign. While King was in jail, Malcolm met with Coretta Scott King and sent a message of support to her husband. He still didn't support nonviolence as a sole method, but he didn't oppose King's use of it. "Whatever means will get results in Selma is the means that should be used," he told a reporter. "Dr. King and his followers are very intelligently trying to impress the people of this area that they should give the Black man the right to vote."[14] He spoke briefly at a local church despite misgivings of King's circle. He emphasized the need to resist, not to acquiesce to, continued White domination. A few weeks later, he was dead.

Bayard Rustin

When King Jr. was coming of age in college and seminary, another Black man, struggling with Christianity and racism and a desire to change the world, found himself on a dark Los Angeles street in the middle of the night. Bayard Rustin was 17 years older than King, raised by Quaker grandparents in Pennsylvania and a resident of New York City from age 25 years until his death 50 years later in 1987. Rustin was thin, with a square afro that over the years would be white at the tips and black at the bottom. He wore square glasses that gave him an academic air, and he moved quickly and nervously.

In 1936, he had joined the Young Communist League, attracted by the fact that communists were one of the few radical groups that viewed racism as a major enemy. A few years later, he shifted to the Socialist Party and became close to A. Philip Randolph, a Black trade union leader and socialist activist. He also became a close friend and disciple of A. J. Muste, a former Trotskyist sympathizer turned socialist; Muste was the leader of the most prominent American pacifist organization, the Fellowship of Reconciliation (FOR). In 1942, working with FOR members, Rustin helped found the first Black pacifist organization, the Congress of Racial Equality (CORE), and then Rustin and CORE leaders organized the first freedom bus ride into the South, which led to Rustin's arrest and beating. Rustin then refused to serve in World War II and spent 2 years in jail (1944–1946). He was jailed numerous other times while demonstrating in favor of India's independence and colonial revolts in Africa.[15]

By the time King was just getting ready to strike out into the world, Rustin had already spent more than a decade struggling for a nonviolent end to racism. But Rustin had an open secret: He was, and would remain for five decades, the only openly gay Black civil rights leader. He also was reckless in his homosexuality; for instance, he had a routine of trolling Times Square to meet up with other gay (preferably young, White, and thin) men.[16]

On the night of January 21, 1953, Rustin was lecturing in Los Angeles for the Quaker-based American Friends Service Committee. He had given a talk at the Pasadena Athletic Club based on his recent visit to Africa, and then stayed awake late into the night. At 2.30 a.m., he tracked down a car with two White men in it and offered them oral sex; they agreed. He went into the front seat with one man and then into the back seat with the other; then the Pasadena police arrived. Rustin was arrested for public "lewdness and vagrancy." The *Pasadena Independent* ran the news the next day: "Arrest Negro Lecturer for Morals Accusation." Rustin pleaded guilty to a misdemeanor charge of a "lewd and lascivious act" and was sentenced to 60 days in jail.[17]

Three years later, Rustin would be the first national civil rights leader to rush to Montgomery, Alabama, to get to know the new young minister who was leading a bus boycott.

On numerous occasions over two decades, Muste told Rustin to stop his reckless behavior or else he would be fired from FOR. Being gay wasn't the problem for the liberal Muste or most FOR leaders; being reckless was the problem. Such activity, viewed as immoral by most Americans, would damage the political efforts of FOR to influence American society. Rustin agreed in principle, but he wouldn't or couldn't stop his behavior.[18] He did agree to Muste's request to get psychiatric treatment, and he engaged in psychotherapy with an open-minded psychiatrist, Dr. Robert Ascher, who, contrary to the mainstream view in psychiatry back then, validated Rustin's sexual orientation and tried to help him manage how he expressed it. Unlike King, Rustin accepted psychiatric help and was open about it, even introducing Ascher to a biographer and waiving medical confidentiality so that his psychiatric state could be understood accurately by others.[19]

The story of Rustin is amazing in many ways. Only now is it beginning to be told in full, with all its paradoxes. Rustin was openly homosexual at a time when the world was very homophobic, even within radical circles such as the pacifists and socialists who were his friends. But beyond his homosexuality and his affinity for socialism, both of which were radical enough at the time, Rustin's personality and his psychiatric condition were unusual.

Rustin was a great civil rights leader in his own right. Long before the Kings were known to anyone but their families, Coretta Scott first heard about nonviolence as a political strategy in a speech given by Rustin at her Alabama high school. Rustin inspired Coretta, so that when she later met King Jr., they already were thinking along similar lines. In the late 1940s, Rustin organized the first Freedom Rides in the South, the "journey of reconciliation." Almost two decades before the next generation would succeed with the same tactic, Rustin organized young activists to board buses from the North to the South to advocate for their desegregation. Rustin and others were arrested; the project was abandoned.

Rustin thought he might be the Black Gandhi; he was going to be Martin Luther King Jr. before Martin Luther King Jr. existed.

At his peak, his charisma rivaled that of King and Malcolm X. In the 1940s, when King was still a teenager and Malcolm X was in jail for petty crime, Rustin was traveling the country wowing pacifist audiences, as a biographer summarizes:

> *Electric. Charismatic. Prophetic. Magnetic* [italics in original]. The words occur again and again as his associates recalled those early encounters with him. . . . He was "one of the more dynamic pacifist speakers. He was just very very charismatic, his personality as just electric." . . . He "magnetized and charmed" . . . [he was] "a prophetic type" . . . "a sensation. . . . There was a magic about Bayard. . . . He sang like an angel."[20]

He was musically talented, being an excellent singer and accomplished on the guitar. He released an album of Black spirituals on which he was the main singer.[21]

But his sexual recklessness proved to be an obstacle that he couldn't overcome. It is ironic that King also was sexually reckless, but their differing sexual orientations led to differing reactions. Rustin was arrested, and he was ostracized by many in the civil rights leadership; King's behavior, in contrast, was denied or tolerated.

As noted previously, Rustin was an accomplished orator. He could mesmerize audiences and was very quick intellectually. He held his own in a famed public debate with Malcolm X in 1962,[22] whereas King did quite poorly in a 1960 televised public debate with the Southern conservative White columnist James J. Kilpatrick.[23]

Rustin often wore fancy hats and spoke with a slight British accent, which he sometimes exaggerated on purpose.[24]

In all these traits, there is evidence for some manic traits as part of his personality, or hyperthymic temperament, especially related to sexual impulsivity, extraversion, and social flamboyance. Whether he also had other manic traits or periods of severe depression is not clear.

After being the main organizer for the 1963 March on Washington, Rustin remained a New York advisor to King. In the ensuing final years of King's life, the previously radical Rustin became increasingly more moderate, whereas the previously moderate King became increasingly more radical. Rustin parted with King on the Vietnam War because Rustin believed that opposition to Lyndon Johnson's foreign policy would damage the president's support for the domestic civil rights movement. So it was. Johnson became increasingly critical of King and more influenced by the Federal Bureau of Investigation's (FBI) campaign against King. Rustin also became more pro-Israel after the 1967 war, whereas King tried to balance his support for Israel with his sympathy for Palestinian rights. Eventually, in the 1970s and into the 1980s, Rustin became more conservative politically; he had evolved into a traditional liberal Democrat with hawkish foreign policy views. One place where he stayed radical was in his advocacy for gay rights. On that issue, he was ahead of his time, and far ahead of most of the civil rights leadership.

James Meredith

James Meredith was a independent activist whose actions included desegregating the University of Mississippi and the 1966 March Against Fear when he was shot, followed by the "Meredith march" by all major civil rights groups, which would prove to be the last unified civil rights march of the 1960s.

Bill Minor, a journalist from the *New Orleans Times-Picayune* who covered Meredith's 1962 registration at Ole Miss, concluded that something was wrong with the young Black man. Minor wrote later,

> After an hour or more of talking with Meredith back in 1961, I was convinced that he was at least, extremely naïve, beset with a messianic complex. He insisted he was not on a messianic mission. . . . I thought he was crazy to believe he would be admitted as the first Black student at the University of Mississippi without causing an uproar.[25]

Fifty years, later, Meredith mused,

> There's nothing more powerful than someone that everyone can say is crazy, but everybody knows they're not. Fear is a two-way street. . . . Nothing is more powerful than a person being in a situation where everyone thinks they ought to be fearful, and they do not show any fear.

Meredith was waging a war, like King, not against the laws of segregation but, rather, against the psychology of racism that underpinned those laws. Fear was the basis of racism, Meredith thought, fear of the other: Whites feared Blacks, Blacks feared Whites. Meredith was going to show that he feared no one.

In 2008, Meredith reminisced about how close Minor had gotten:

> Bill Minor . . . [was] the first person to interview me. He figured me out right away, but then he backed off on it. . . . What he decided on, which was the best choice for me, was to tell everybody that ever came to Mississippi to interview me that I was crazy.[26]

Almost five decades later, Meredith revealed the truth about who he was to journalists from his local Jackson, Mississippi, newspaper:

> I have never felt that I was a prophet, that I had a divine responsibility to tell the world what God intended for them to know. But today is the first time I'm admitting it. A lot of people have sensed it.

He was always on a mission, Meredith admitted, a mission from God, like Moses: "I've done everything I could to fulfill my mission. I just didn't tell folks."[27]

Meredith didn't try to desegregate Ole Miss on instructions from the National Association for the Advancement of Colored People (NAACP), CORE, or the Student Nonviolent Coordinating Committee (SNCC). He just did it, although he did obtain legal support from the NAACP. After the civil rights era ended, he went on, like Bevel, to take a rightward turn. He endorsed former Ku Klux Klan leader David Duke in 1991 in a Louisiana state election. He became a domestic policy advisor from 1989 to 1991 to the segregationist Senator Jesse Helms.[28]

As King and others knew, Meredith took orders from no one.

James Bevel

To appreciate both the benefits and the risks of psychological maladjustment, a better case example than James Bevel cannot be found.

As described throughout this book, Bevel was very close to King and was a central leader in many major civil rights successes. His closest friend in the movement probably was Dr. Bernard Lafayette, a friend from their Nashville days and the founding of SNCC, later coming over to the Southern Christian Leadership Conference (SCLC) together as aides to King. Lafayette describes Bevel as "a master strategist" and "highly competitive." Lafayette calls Bevel "the creative genius" on King's staff: "For the most part, Dr. King didn't start movements . . . he'd come in at a strategic point to bring the attention of the nation."[29] King himself called Bevel a "genius."[30] Ralph Abernathy added that "the civil rights movement would not have been as successful as it was, and Dr. King could not have done the things that he did unless he had a James Bevel."[31]

As noted previously, Bevel was a key planner of the most successful mass direct action SCLC campaigns: Birmingham, the March on Washington, Selma, Chicago. This resume is stellar in the world of civil rights activism.

In the midst of all this activism, Bevel married Diane Nash, a SNCC leader; together they had a number of children. They later divorced, and Bevel eventually fathered 17 children with six women. Impatient with King's initial reticence about Vietnam, Bevel left SCLC to join the anti-Vietnam movement, organizing the 1967 March on the Pentagon. After King's death, Bevel, like many of the movement leaders, drifted away from national activity. He was hospitalized psychiatrically in 1970, the same year he left SCLC. He wrote an open letter to Andrew Young accusing him of tricking him into psychiatric hospitalization. He then moved around to various cities and performed a variety of activities: running a farm cooperative near Nashville, starting a mental health clinic in Philadelphia, working briefly as an associate pastor in Brooklyn before being fired for dressing up in a devil's costume and marching around the neighborhood, and running human sexuality clinics in Baltimore and Chicago in which he asked group members to take off their clothes. Eventually, he returned to Chicago, where in 1984 he ran for Congress as a Republican and supported Ronald Reagan for president (as had Ralph Abernathy).[32] He then became a public supporter of the Rev. Sun Myung Moon's Unification Church; ran for vice president on the ticket of Lyndon LaRouche; and was viewed by his critics as a proto-fascist who believed the world was ruled by an oligarchy of elites, including Jews.

In some ways, Bevel had changed his thinking, no longer attacking most or all Whites as sick. "It's time Negroes stopped blaming White folks for what's going on in our community," he said. He had become an opponent of affirmative action and quotas, which he said "make Blacks lazy"; he opposed busing for integration. He stated, "If you live according to the Constitution and the Bible, the White folks will leave you alone." It was clear, by then, that Bevel's psychiatric condition had worsened. A 1984 newspaper profile described how Bevel shocked an audience of teenagers with a graphic description of anal sex, while jumping up and down to a blackboard to diagram his answers to a journalist's questions. The journalist noted that "Bevel—his colleagues say—may have lost his mind." At that point, he had fathered 14 children, 4 of whom lived with him. He lived off welfare, receiving $304 monthly. The journalist finally confronted him directly that some people say he's crazy. Bevel replied, smiling, "The standards that they use to measure sanity and insanity—teach them to me . . . so that I can learn."[33]

In 1995, Bevel became a central organizer of the Million Man March on Washington, DC, led by Louis Farrakhan's Nation of Islam. A few years later, one of his adult daughters accused him of sexually abusing her and other daughters throughout their childhood; taped confessions were produced in a Virginia court, which led to his 2008 conviction at age 72 years and imprisonment with a 15-year term. After serving 7 months, while free on bail during appeal, he died of cancer. His conviction was posthumously upheld by the Supreme Court of Virginia.

Bevel clearly was a sick, and unusually gifted, man.

How can one make sense of a man who did so much for the public good for so long; who would later go in different political directions; and who was, in private, apparently so evil? The story of Bevel is one that, in its denouement, civil rights leaders don't like to discuss publicly. But they don't deny his likely mental illness, nor his amazing political and intellectual talents.[34]

Even during the height of the movement's successes, with Bevel organizing its central activities, he was psychiatrically unstable. Lafayette describes how, at one point, SCLC staff decided that Bevel needed to enter a psychiatric hospital. They knew he wouldn't agree, so they decided to tell him that one of the staff needed psychiatric hospitalization, and he was asked to join Lafayette and two others to visit a local Atlanta psychiatric hospital to determine what they could arrange.

Lafayette recalls,

> Four of us went up to the hospital. When we got there, we told him he was the staff person. He said to me: "You're my friend. If you think I need mental health care, I will go." But then, as soon as he was inside, Bevel organized the patients against some of the staff people. They then asked him to leave.[35]

Lafayette recalls one other psychiatric hospitalization besides this one, with a similar outcome: short-term admission with no long-term treatment.

After King was killed, Bevel grew less influential and was dismissed from the SCLC a year later. He grew increasingly unhappy, and he began to express his views in interviews with historians with more venom than he would have used during the height of the movement's successes. In the most extensive interview with him, conducted in 1968, he clearly expressed his psychiatric diagnosis of White America at the time. It suffered from the mental illness of racism:

> Dr. King . . . still had some notion that maybe there were some decent White men in the White House and in Wall Street. I know these guys are insane. . . . These cats are sick . . . you have to see them as immature, overgrown, White kids who are spoiled. . . . Dr. King wasn't about to take that kind of position. I maintain that you cannot solve the problem, or the dilemma of this world, until you empathically tell the truth about who the American White people are. They are the most savage, bestial,

corrupt murderous people on earth; and they engage in war games, killing, scheming, tricking all the time. They can't help that. It's not because they are mean. It's because they are mentally ill."

The presumably shocked interviewer asked, "This is why you call it social psychiatry?" Bevel responded, "Yes. Political psychiatry."[36]

Dr. William Anderson

In 1961, a new leader emerged in Albany, Georgia: the first and highest ranking Black physician in the civil rights leadership, Dr. William Anderson. Tall, thin, usually dressed in suits, and sporting a narrow dark mustache, Anderson was a suave figure. A young osteopathic physician, he was one of few Black doctors in the region, widely respected in the community.

He began to urge something that hadn't been done before: to turn the rising tension in Albany against not just certain types of segregation but against all segregation anywhere in the city. Said Anderson later, "The facets of segregation seemed to be equally important, and I attacked them all."[37]

This was novel, radical, audacious—and fated to fail.[38]

Anderson knew King from their adolescence together in Atlanta, when Anderson had been a visitor to the King household. Anderson's brother-in-law, James Madison Dixon, had been a close childhood friend of King. The physician called on King for help. King arrived on December 15, 1961, about a month after the start of the movement, and the protests received national attention. Soon King and Anderson were both arrested, along with Ralph Abernathy and other SCLC leaders. King vowed to stay in jail until Christmas, if needed, to force White Albany to compromise and loosen segregation laws.

Then something completely unexpected happened.

As King and Anderson shared a jail cell, with Abernathy and Bernard Lee in the cell next door, Anderson began to see visions. He reportedly began to believe that King was Jesus and that he and the other civil rights leaders were King's chosen disciples. "You are Jesus" he told King, "and we are the saints." King became concerned, as did Abernathy and Lee in the next cell. Anderson was jumping up and down in the cell, not sleeping, describing visions. The next morning, King told reporters he wouldn't accept bond. But Anderson worsened, now having hallucinations about extraterrestrial matters. Lee and Abernathy proposed to Anderson that he leave jail under bail, but the doctor refused, not wanting to betray his master.[39]

King realized that they all needed to leave. "Andy's not going to make it," he told a visiting aide, Wyatt Walker, in reference to Anderson. King and the other leaders were worried that their critics would use Anderson's state of mind as a means to attack the movement. See, the movement's leaders really are crazy, they could say. Walker had planned to carry on tough negotiations in Albany, with King's jailing as the pressure. But now, if King was to leave jail soon, Walker was forced to compromise. King agreed to leave jail and accepted mere verbal assurances of further negotiations from the leaders of Albany's White community, rather than real changes. After he left, the White Albany leadership reneged.

At the time, King and his circle kept the reality of Anderson's likely manic episode quiet, out of fear "that it would be disastrous for the movement if the white jailer discovered and informed the world that one of the key local black leaders was mentally ill."[40]

The stigma against mental illness was so strong that King would accept the failure of the Albany campaign rather than be open about what happened. He was attacked by many of his own allies for reneging on his promise to stay in jail until the campaign succeeded; he accepted the attacks and hid the reality.

The stigma against mental illness was stronger than the fight against racism. Albany would have to be a lost battle in the war on segregation.

The secret to Albany is Anderson; he was an audacious and committed political leader, but at the time of highest crisis, he reached his mental limit. As he recounted decades later,

> There was a point in which I was overwhelmed; I felt like the weight of the world was on me; my wife recognized that I was on the brink of a nervous breakdown. Many of us were going on nervous energy, I didn't sleep for days on end, lost 20–30 pounds. My wife took me to the Tuskegee Veterans Hospital and I was checked out by a psychiatrist for a few days, got some mild sedatives, and they told me there was nothing physically wrong. Then I went to Silacauga, Alabama, the home of my wife's grandparent. I went there for my mental health. The advice he would give me would strengthen me mentally. After a week away, I went back and picked up where I left off. I never experienced anything like that any other time, not even during wartime on a ship to the Philippine Islands.[41]

When Anderson returned, the Albany movement had lost its momentum. Two years later, Anderson left Albany, moving to Detroit, where he practiced medicine actively for five decades, being elected the first president of the American Osteopathic Association in 1994. He continued his civil rights activities, maintaining his old friendship with King, including a role as one of King's physicians.

What happened to Anderson? Corroborated interviews with those in jail with him suggest that he had lost touch with reality, had experienced delusions.

Delusions usually happen in two conditions: schizophrenia (which he clearly did not have because this condition involves chronic delusions, meaning present at all times in one's life) and manic depression. The second likelihood is further confirmed by his usual temperament. As Anderson's adult son said in a speech in his father's honor,

> He seems to have more energy than any person I've ever met. At office at 7:30 a.m., on the golf course 2–3 times per week, on airplanes 2–3 times per week. . . . Growing up in our house, it was hard to get a word in edgewise; he's a very gifted talker.[42]

These are manic symptoms, and if mild and constantly present, they represent hyperthymic temperament.

Apparently, under extreme stress, Anderson's constant mild manic temperament gave way to severe mania with delusions, as can happen in such severe states. It quickly resolved within weeks, however, as typically happens in such conditions. This weakness was the flipside of the benefits of his hyperthymia, however: his energy and commitment and creativity, which made him the first audacious leader to attack segregation in an entire city all at once, rather than piecemeal.

Dr. Arthur Logan

King had multiple physicians on whom he called for care, but perhaps the one who consistently and most formally performed the role of his personal physician was Dr. Arthur Logan, a prominent man in the medical world of Harlem (Figure 18.1).

As described previously, Logan was partly White in his background, very light-skinned, with blue eyes. With a shock of White hair brushed straight back, he could have "passed" easily for White. But he never did. He was faithful to the memory of his parents, close associates of the leading African American activist of the late 19th century, Booker T. Washington. Growing up as a boy in Tuskegee, Alabama, where Washington had built his famous institute to educate freed Blacks, young Arthur Logan was raised to be an activist.

His mother Adella Hunt had been born in Georgia to a White father, graduated Atlanta University in 1881, and married Arthur C. Logan Sr. in 1888. The elder Logan had been born a slave, and he later became a close friend of Booker T. Washington. Half a century later, as he diagnosed his most famous patient with a psychiatric condition, Dr. Logan may have thought back to his

Figure 18.1 Dr. Arthur Logan.

Reproduced with permission of the Journal of the National Medical Association. 1974 May;66(3):272–3. PMCID: PMC2609167.

mother's final years—to her hospitalization for depression in 1915 and then, that same year, her despair when Washington died. A month later, she jumped to her death from the top floor of one of the Tuskegee Institute buildings.

After his early schooling, Logan went North to attend Williams College in Massachusetts in 1930, and he later completed medical school at prestigious Columbia University in 1934, one of the first African Americans to do so. He became a surgeon and worked the rest of his years in Harlem, serving the local community at Harlem Hospital and as part of a prominent medical group practice. In addition to serving the poor in his hospital work, he was the personal physician to the Black elite.

For all his accomplishments, he was a quiet, gentle, unassuming man, ceding the public limelight to his wife Marian Bruce, a former cabaret singer who was a prominent donor to SCLC and close friend to King.

After King's death in 1968, Logan continued his medical work in New York. He was close to the mayor and governor, was appointed to multiple city commissions, and was on the guest list for White House events. He was elected to the prestigious Institute of Medicine in 1971.

Logan had become involved in plans for expansion of the Knickerbocker Hospital, a 100-year-old Harlem institution whose purpose was to serve the poor. Three days after Thanksgiving, on November 25, 1973, the 64-year-old Logan left home early in the morning and told Marian that he was going to inspect a future construction site for the hospital. He went up approximately 90 feet to a viaduct, which had a 3-foot railing. He straddled the railing, looked over, and fell—or jumped. No one really knows. As multiple obituaries wrote, when he was found dead on the future construction site, suicide made no sense; he had everything going for him. An article in *Jet* magazine, a prominent media outlet for the Black community, speculated he might have been seeking a better view of the site below. But there was no real reason for him to lean over the railing to see anything. The *Jet* article speculated that he had an inner ear condition that might have explained losing his balance.[43]

Another possibility is that he jumped, like his mother had done. Early news coverage made that claim though Logan's family and supporters were skeptical.

On his body were his keys, identification cards, and his wallet with $84 in it. There were no signs of foul play.

A local neighborhood advocacy group eulogized him best: "He was one of those rarities in our society—a doctor who had time for the people, a man who believed in the dignity of man, and practiced that belief."[44]

Benjamin Van Clark

As a 16-year-old high school student in Savannah, Georgia, in the early 1960s, Ben Clark (Figure 18.2) organized fellow students to support a principal who was fired for trying to create a Reserve Officers' Training Corps group for Black students. By the year of his graduation in 1963, Clark was marching for voting rights, soon becoming youth chairman of the Chatham County Crusade for Voters, founded by Hosea Williams, a local NAACP leader. From June to December 1963, Williams and Clark led an all-out campaign to desegregate Savannah. Williams spent more than 2 months in jail. Clark was arrested approximately 25 times. Clark organized sit-ins, a "wade-in" at a local beach, boycotts of White businesses, and "kneel-ins" at churches. Short of stature at 5 feet 2 inches, Clark became known as the "Little Hosea Williams." Others called him "Little General" for the community-organizing skills he showed even in high school. The two were so successful that by the time SCLC sent King to the city at the end of the year, he declared that Savannah was "the most desegregated city below the Mason–Dixon line." King brought Williams back to Atlanta to work for SCLC; a year later, in Selma, Williams was in the first line, next to John Lewis, crossing the bridge that led to full voting rights. Ben Clark also came to Atlanta, working as a SCLC field organizer.[45]

Figure 18.2 Benjamin Van Clark, leading a march in Savannah, Georgia.

Clark's future life is shrouded in some mystery. Nothing is written about it. By 1982, however, he appears to have descended into serious mental illness. He was psychiatrically hospitalized for an extended period of time, and his friends sought to raise funds for his medical care. The only document available from that era is a fund-raising proposal. In it, Clark is identified as "the loneliest minority of all," a Black man, who fought against a racist society and descended into insanity.[46]

When historian David Garrow visited him in Savannah for an interview just after Christmas 1983, Clark was working as a custodian in a local Catholic church.[47] Benjamin Van Clark died by suicide in 1984. No public obituaries are accessible. In the year of his death, Savannah renamed a section of the city after him.

A. D. King

As discussed in more detail in Chapter 3, King Jr.'s younger brother, Alfred Daniel Williams King, was a troubled man. He couldn't hold a position as pastor in a church for an extended period of time. He was reported to drink alcohol excessively and also to be sexually impulsive. Approximately a year after his brother's death, A.D. was found dead in the swimming pool behind his house. He was last seen by family sitting in his chair, watching television. He had been drinking. His autopsy showed an elevated blood alcohol level of 0.27 but was reported normal otherwise, and the death was deemed accidental.

Another possibility is that his death was the effect of severe depression with suicidal ideation, augmented by the impulsive effects of alcohol. He was known to have expressed suicidal thoughts repeatedly. He had been diagnosed by his psychiatrist with bipolar disorder.

Henry Arrington

An attorney in Miami who kept a low profile, Henry Arrington was a good friend of King. He served on the board of SCLC from its founding in 1957. He was a former assistant state attorney and municipal court judge. He coordinated many of the legal affairs of SCLC and was known partly for helping King get away to quiet vacations in south Florida.[48] In 1969, at age 45 years, he died by suicide, shooting himself at the home of his friend Dr. Edwin Shirley. Financial concerns were cited as a reason, although the amounts involved, such as an Internal Revenue Service tax lien, were not large ($325 or approximately $2,500 inflation-adjusted today).[49]

John Wilson

John Wilson was a rising star among the student leaders in SNCC, quickly rising to became national vice chair. Raised in Maryland, he moved to Washington, DC, in 1969 and became engaged in political activity there, eventually becoming a long-standing city council chairman. Widely expected to become mayor eventually, Wilson suffered from bipolar illness, which was diagnosed formally by psychiatrists and for which he was treated with various medications. In the months before his death, he had overdosed and was taken by ambulance to the hospital, where he recovered but did try to hang himself. A long *Washington Post* magazine article detailed these facts after his death. He was treated in the early 1990s by psychiatrist Jacob Katzow, who tried to convince Wilson to be hospitalized. Concerned about the impact of the stigma of mental illness on his political career, Wilson refused.

Wilson was highly sociable and had a large circle of friends—and enemies. He was famous for having an incredible sense of humor. Malcolm X reportedly said he was "one of the funniest guys in the movement."[50]

Alcohol, sexual indiscretion, and high spending had been part of his life.

In 1993, soon after refusing hospitalization, he hung himself in his basement. He didn't leave a note.[51]

Walter Fauntroy

Born in Washington, DC, Walter Fauntroy attended Virginia Union University and then graduated from Yale Divinity School in 1958, a university that had rejected a young King Jr. a few years earlier. Fauntroy had met the 22-year-old King in 1951, and they formed a lifelong friendship. When the SCLC was formed in 1957, Fauntroy became its DC representative. He was King's main collaborator in the nation's capital, helping organize the 1963 March on Washington, and heavily involved in coordinating King's lobbying activities. He also became pastor of his home church, New Bethel Baptist. He was close to the Johnson administration, which appointed him vice chair of the DC city council in 1967. In 1971, he won election as the first delegate to Congress from DC; his campaign manager was a charismatic young former SNCC leader, John Wilson. Fauntroy served in that role for two decades. After returning to his pastorate in the 1990s, he was out of the public limelight until he disappeared in 2012, leaving the United States after he was charged with check fraud. His wife filed for bankruptcy and reported she didn't know his exact location, although he occasionally telephoned from Dubai. He returned to the United States in 2016 and was arrested.

This change in behavior stood out to his friends. "I'm a lawyer, not a mental-health professional," his attorney, Johnny Barnes, told *The Washington Post*. "But he doesn't seem to be himself." The *Post* reported that when he went to the United Arab Emirates, he hoped for help from a local prince. But he ended up in a hostel, homeless for a time, and living with a family for whom he agreed to babysit. A friend reported that Fauntroy believed he had been followed by many spies, which is why he left the country, and that a Jewish conspiracy was running the world, including paying off U.S. presidents. He sent emails attacking the "1% cabal" who rule the world and were responsible for the assassinations of King, Malcolm X, John F. Kennedy, and Abraham Lincoln.[52]

Whether Fauntroy had any aspect of a mood temperament, such as hyperthymia, with mild manic traits, is difficult to discern from publicly available information. There is evidence that he had some traits that are consistent with hyperthymia: He was highly energetic, talkative, charismatic, and tended to spend money somewhat excessively. One possibility is that he had a mood temperament all his life, which was beneficial to his charismatic and energetic leadership, but that as he aged, he developed a full manic episode, which led to his impulsive traveling, excessive spending, and possible paranoid delusions.

Whether such a diagnosis is correct cannot be known solely based on publicly available information, but it is a possibility.

Stokely Carmichael

Born in Trinidad, Stokely Carmichael's family moved to New York, eventually settling into a mostly White section of Bronx. As a teen, after hearing Bayard Rustin give a speech, a young Stokely told a friend that's what he wanted to be as an adult: a political activist. He attended Howard University in Washington, DC, and immediately joined the first Freedom Rides of 1961. He was beaten and arrested numerous times. Back at Howard, as a leader of the Nonviolent Advocacy Group, he organized a 1962 debate between his two heroes, Bayard Rustin and Malcolm X. Later, he would say that his nonviolent beliefs were challenged by sitting in the front row and watching Malcolm X completely decimate Rustin, in his opinion. Carmichael graduated with a degree in philosophy and went South to join the SNCC. He spent much of 1964–1966 organizing in Mississippi and Alabama. By 1966, he had risen to prominence and defeated John Lewis to become chairman of the SNCC. He had become close to King, but his nonviolent views were weakening, and during the 1966 Meredith march, Carmichael broke with King and popularized the Black Power slogan. By 1968, he had joined the Black Panther Party, and the SNCC disbanded. A year later, he went into exile in Guinea and rejected the Black Panther Party as not radical enough. For the next 30 years, he lived in Guinea until his death at age 57 years in 1998 from prostate cancer. During that period, he became close to Kwame Nkrumah, former leader of Ghana, who was exiled to Guinea. Carmichael organized an international African party seeking to unify all Black peoples in a socialist anti-imperialist agenda. He befriended Fidel Castro.

Carmichael's journey from Rustin and King to Nkrumah and Castro is a fascinating story. But for the purposes of this chapter, some aspects of his personal psychology deserve mention, mostly to raise questions for future scholars, as well as to show analogies to some of the other leaders described.

Carmichael was very charismatic, a powerful natural orator, and also highly self-absorbed. He had very high self-esteem, was talkative, and had high physical energy levels. He also was impulsive. During the Meredith march, in its early days,

> with Carmichael linked arm-in-arm with the Rev. Martin Luther King Jr., a Mississippi lawman shoved King. Carmichael recounts what ensued: "I yanked free to go after him, got one arm free, but Dr. King had my right hand and was not letting go. I was fighting to get to that

> cracker. But Dr. King hung on to my arm shouting, 'Get Stokely, somebody, lay on him.' "[53]

After King was assassinated, many American cities exploded. Carmichael had moved to Washington, DC, and as *The Washington Post* reported,

> Carmichael "waved a gun over his head and shouted, 'Stay off the streets if you don't have a gun because there's going to be shooting.' . . . Cleveland Sellers, one of Carmichael's closest SNCC colleagues, explained that Carmichael "is volatile and tends to have had little control over his emotions when he is angry."[54]

In addition to this emotional volatility, Carmichael appears to have had at least brief periods of depression, during which he would be nonfunctional and drink multiple bottles of wine.[55] Based on current evidence, one cannot conclude that these depressive periods should be attributed solely to the stresses of his activist life, as a recent biographer does,[56] including the killing of some close friends in the Southern campaigns. It is reasonable also to consider a biologically based predisposition to a mood illness. Both are possibilities, but Carmichael's personality certainly seemed at the least emotionally reactive, and within the range of mood illnesses.

Vernon Johns

Then there was the John the Baptist of the civil rights movement. As mentioned previously, King Jr.'s first job was as successor to Vernon Johns as the pastor of Dexter Avenue Baptist Church in Montgomery, Alabama.

Johns had only been there about 5 years himself, having been hired partly through the influence of his wife, who was a professor at Alabama State University in Montgomery. Johns was from southern Virginia, near Petersburg, where his family owned a farm. He initially attended Virginia Theological Seminary and College, but he was expelled. In 1915, he was accepted at Oberlin College in Ohio, which was racially integrated and where he was a classmate with and friend of the future prominent president of the University of Chicago, Robert Hutchins. He excelled academically there and was selected to give the senior oration at his 1918 graduation, after which he studied for a year at the University of Chicago. Johns' academic background thus was stellar in an era in which options were limited for Black Americans. Accomplished in Greek, Latin, Hebrew, and German, and a generation older than King Jr., three of Johns' grandparents had been slaves. This legacy of slavery, contrasting with his intellectual accomplishments, remained alive in Johns' mind throughout his life.

Johns next took a pastoral job in Virginia, and in 1929 he became president at the same Virginia Theological Seminary and College that had expelled him previously. Four years later, he lost his presidency because the students couldn't stand him and went on strike until he was dismissed. In a formal complaint, the student leaders wrote,

> We want a president whose presence on the campus will be a source of joy and not intense displeasure. We want a president who will not regard students and trustees as enemies of the school simply because they oppose or object to certain of his policies or actions. We want a president who will not convert classrooms into coal bins and chicken houses. . . . We want a president whose remarks to students in chapel services will be advisory and not adverse criticism or lambaste. We want a president who will not stoop to the use of profanity and vulgarity in addressing the students in chapel services and in the presence of young women on the campus.[57]

He developed a pattern of not keeping any job for an extended period of time. He was pastor to a church in Charleston, West Virginia, for 3 years, and supplemented his income by catching and selling fish. Then he became a pastor in Lynchburg, Virginia, but was removed 2 years later by the congregation. In 1947, Johns received his most prestigious job at Dexter Avenue Baptist Church in Alabama.

In his first experience living and working in the deep South, Johns immediately became a rebel. He refused to sit in the back of a bus years before Rosa Parks. He tried to integrate a lunch counter. He organized a cooperative supermarket run by the Black community and grew vegetables in his garden and sold them from his church, along with other things such as clothes (including female undergarments), as he tried to encourage the Black community to become more economically self-sufficient.

He appears to have been a highly energetic man. He slept very little, often going to the house of a Dexter congregant to drink Scotch and talk all night.[58] He was very talkative and highly distractible; as Abernathy later related: 'Sometimes he would park the car in Atlanta and get to telling stories and go on to Montgomery and pop his finger three or four days later and remember that he had left the car in Atlanta."[59]

He was somewhat impulsive. In his car, he carried a loaded double-barrel shotgun in case he was harassed by police or others. When he once asked a friend to ride with him through the South, the friend worried for his own life because he knew that if Johns was challenged, the likelihood of using that shotgun was high.[60]

Johns was temperamental. His sermons were fiery and often not intended to please his audience but, rather, to provoke them. The effect could be more haranguing than inspiring, and the middle-class members of Dexter became disillusioned with their minister. He often offered his resignation to get his congregation in line.

When a member of the Dexter church was murdered by police, Johns had enough, and he preached an incendiary sermon called "It Is Safe to Kill Negroes." A young Ralph Abernathy sat in the congregation as Johns attacked his audience for its indifference and acquiescence in this injustice to one of their own.[61] As King wrote of Johns a few years later, "One of his basic theses was that any individual who submitted willingly to injustice did not really deserve more justice."[62] Years later, King often used a phrase that reflected exactly what Johns repeatedly preached—that segregation would end when Blacks stood up, because a man can't ride your back if it isn't bent over.

The Dexter leadership accepted Johns' resignation. Their pastor was shocked; he didn't think they would let him go. He changed his mind, and although his wife moved back to Virginia and took a faculty job there, Johns refused to go quietly. He wouldn't leave the parsonage, and so the Dexter leaders cut off the electricity and gas. Johns turned to burning the multiple newspapers he read daily (including *The New York Times* and *The Washington Post*) in the fireplace for warmth. He spent most nights at Abernathy's home, where he ate his only meal of the day. When winter came and he no longer could tolerate living off burning newspapers, he finally left and went home to Petersburg, Virginia, in 1952. For the next 2 years, the Dexter congregation considered different possible new pastors, without settling on anyone.

In 1954, when Johns heard that the Dexter congregation had invited the young King Jr. to give a trial sermon as his possible replacement, he asked Abernathy to invite him to give a guest sermon at the rival First Baptist Church (where Abernathy was pastor) in Montgomery on the same day. Unaware of the stratagem, Abernathy agreed. Johns hitchhiked from Petersburg to Atlanta and then called his friend Mike King Sr. from the bus station. He asked if King Jr. could give him a ride to Montgomery.

The two men rode together in King's car, the older rejected radical and his young moderate successor. They went to Abernathy's home, where he and his wife were expecting their old friend Johns. It was one of the first times Abernathy met his future best friend; they had met socially in Atlanta previously when Abernathy's date had canceled and he saw her later that night with King. Thus, except for that brief earlier social interaction, Johns is the man who introduced King to Abernathy; he brought the two prominent leaders together.

Abernathy's wife had been preparing Johns' favorite meal of sirloin steak and hot rolls and other fixings, and she rushed out and hugged the older man. The Abernathys invited King to stay for dinner, but he demurred repeatedly until he saw the spread. Johns convinced King to give up his other dinner invitation from one of the Dexter deacons ("You will get white people's food: a little cheese and crackers and a salad"), and the men stayed up late talking about religion and politics. King said he wanted to implement the social Gospel, and after the 1954 U.S. Supreme Court decision against school segregation, he hoped that Black churches could lead the fight for freedom from segregation. Johns and Abernathy were pleased; the new man was thinking as they did.[63] Johns also gave King some advice on the Dexter congregation.

In retrospect, it's interesting to note that the main competitor for King's position was his old best friend, Walter McCall, who now was destined to be replaced by Abernathy. McCall already had preached, and had some support among Dexter leaders, but King's sermon on "Three Dimensions of a Complete Life" so impressed the Dexter deacons that they asked McCall to come back and give another sermon as a comparison. McCall apparently made up a sermon called "Four Dimensions of a Complete Life," which didn't impress. Within a few weeks, the deacon leadership hired King. Abernathy was very pleased: "The Lord had sent me a friend to replace Vernon Johns."[64] Johns left after his sermon that Sunday afternoon. He never returned to Montgomery.

Throughout the years, as King rose in prominence, Johns wasn't in King's circle, and the "Father of the civil rights movement" didn't participate centrally in the movement he had helped spark. Johns moved back to the Virginia family farm and bought 100 more acres to raise livestock through an economic cooperative (it went bankrupt 5 years later). He also met and befriended Wyatt Tee Walker, a young preacher in Petersburg, who would later become King's chief of staff at SCLC.

Johns would travel for months on end away from his family, hitchhiking when possible to save money, preaching at any church that would have him for a sermon, and then move on. He described himself as a "dreamer and prophet, leaving the more practical affairs to those who have more time and love for details."[65]

Such was his lot.

Johns never again would have a prominent position. He was hurt that his old friends King and Abernathy didn't invite him to speak at the March on Washington. He never engaged in any civil rights direct action movement. But he kept preaching when he could, and he kept farming. He became more interested in economic independence than legal desegregation, and King also would move closer to a focus on economics later in his life.

A few years before Johns' death in 1965, King apparently heard that Johns had fallen on hard times and had not been living with his family for years. He sent

Chauncey Eskridge, a key SCLC lawyer, to Petersburg. Eskridge found Johns living in an abandoned gas station, tending a vegetable stand, with no laces on his shoes and no socks. Apparently he was homeless. He had no belongings except a round trailer, meant to be attached to a car, though he had no car. For some time, Johns apparently had opened a convenience store and used to preach to "winos" from there.[66]

A friend, Samuel L. Gandy, who had become president of Howard University, offered Johns a low-stress faculty job there, teaching only one course per semester. Johns moved to Washington, DC, and upon arriving in 1965 gave what would be his last sermon, in Rankin Memorial Chapel on the Howard campus: "The Romance of Death." Ten days later, after being hospitalized, he died of a reported heart attack.

Wyatt Walker and Samuel Gandy were pallbearers at his funeral. Johns was buried on his family farm, on a spot he had picked out years earlier, between two cedar trees.[67]

He had been no minor firebrand. He had proven himself in decades of scholarship and ministry. His sermons were reported to be incredibly powerful; Abernathy had called him "the greatest mind the Black community has ever produced."[68] In this judgment, Abernathy was putting Johns above his best friend, King Jr.: "Dr. Johns did not possess the oratorical ability of a Martin Luther King, but he was so profound. . . . MLK admired everything about Dr. Johns."[69]

Johns also demonstrated multiple manic traits consistent with cyclothymia or hyperthymia: He changed residence frequently, traveled constantly, talked much, slept little, was high energy, and was impulsive. Perhaps his main weakness is that he had an irritable bent of mind, unlike King, who was much more pleasant. Manic states can include either happy or irritable moods, as is well-known;[70] King went in one direction, Johns in the other.

Johns was indeed John the Baptist, not Moses: He harangued his people to stand up and refuse their oppression; he pointed the way to the Promised Land, but he couldn't lead them there.

William Lewis Moore

In 1963, as the events in Birmingham, Alabama, captured the nation's attention, a young White postman in Baltimore had long been thinking about how he could contribute to the civil rights struggle. He finally decided to act boldly and to make the impact on human history that he had hoped to make his entire life.

In April 1963, William Lewis Moore (Figure 18.3) had been liberated from the state mental hospital for almost a decade. Now 35 years old, he had married, and was working at a stable job as a postal carrier in Baltimore. His original

Figure 18.3 William Lewis Moore.

goal of bringing about world peace was now connected in his mind to the new struggle for civil rights for Blacks. He collected up his vacation time, put some belongings on a pushcart, and walked approximately 40 miles from Baltimore to Washington, DC. He approached the White House gate with a letter for President Kennedy, stating that he would soon walk from Chattanooga, Tennessee, to Jackson, Mississippi, to support civil rights. He would deliver a letter at his destination to the governor of that state, urging support for desegregation. "If I may deliver any letters from you to those on my line of travel, I would be most happy to do so," he added. The guards refused to pass the letter along.

Moore turned around and began to picket on the sidewalk, wearing two signs: "Equal rights for all" and "Mississippi or bust." He handwrote a PS to the letter to the president ("Keep up your fight against the Cuban war hawks! And read over your Senate speeches on Vietnam!") and placed the letter in a mailbox.

Moore was a member of CORE and had written to the organization of his planned march. He received no response and began his trek alone. Approximately 70 miles beyond the Alabama border from Tennessee, a local reporter caught up with him, and upon hearing his plans, the reporter became concerned for his safety. The reporter offered to set him up in a motel. Moore declined.

As he walked, he might have been thinking about what he had written in the 1955 memoir he wrote about his psychiatric hospitalization, *The Mind in Chains: Autobiography of a Schizophrenic*. If schizophrenia was defined as not being adjusted to reality, as was the standard psychiatric definition in the mid-20th century, then Moore rejected the idea. Speaking of the liberal principles he had been taught, he wrote,

> The difference between me and other people is that others literally believe the things they were taught in childhood, but subconsciously they rationalize most of it away; in practice they compromise their beliefs in order to adjust to reality. But I did not compromise. I took my teachings literally, and where the world was not like the ideal, I believed that the world was wrong and so did not adjust my behavior to reality.[71]

In the 1950s and for decades thereafter, it was common for American psychiatrists to misdiagnose manic–depressive illness as schizophrenia.[72] In both cases, psychosis (meaning delusions or hallucinations) could occur, except in manic depression, those symptoms were temporary, happening during manic or depressive episodes, whereas in schizophrenia the delusions were constant and never-ending. People with schizophrenia rarely married, nor could they hold full employment and be self-sufficient. People with manic depression usually recovered and often could function normally outside of severe mood episodes.

It's obvious in retrospect that Moore had manic depression, not schizophrenia, as he recovered after approximately a year of hospitalization (which was typical in that era) and was able to work full-time, get married, and be self-sufficient. It is clear from Moore's memoir that when he was hospitalized, he demonstrated classic symptoms of a manic episode, not schizophrenia.[73]

During his hospitalization, however, he had a delusion that an old teacher of his who had died was still alive and able to influence world affairs. He believed that his teacher, Gus Youngstrom, was pulling strings so that Moore could reach President Dwight D. Eisenhower and change the world. This delusion was "knocked out of his head," as his doctor told him, after a year of electroshock and insulin coma treatments. But he still had his doubts: Maybe Youngstrom was still alive. As he walked, Moore might have thought about his doctor, as he had written in his memoir,

> He got me in a position where I either had to be right and prove it, or I was crazy. That seems hardly fair. Apply that reasoning to the rest of the world and you would have to put every man on earth in the insane asylum.[74]

As Moore walked the byways of Tennessee alone, he wrote in his diary that some boys had tossed rocks at him; others yelled "nigger lover." He pushed his little cart with his belongings as he walked. His feet became swollen and blistered. A little dog followed him a while. By all accounts, he was cheerful, even when a local White man argued with him.

About an hour after the reporter left Moore, a passing motorist noticed a body on the side of the road. Moore had been shot twice in the head at close range. No one was ever arrested or charged with his death, although years later the White man who had hassled him admitted to the deed.

On his body, people discovered Moore's letter to the governor of Mississippi. "The White man cannot be truly free himself until all men have their rights," he had written. "Be gracious," he advised the governor, "and give more than is immediately demanded of you."

Such rational thoughts from a mentally ill man.

President Kennedy heard about the event from an aide, who had unearthed the poor postman's original letter to the president. At a press conference the day after the killing, no reporter mentioned Moore, but the president decided to do so. When asked generally about civil rights, Kennedy commented,

> We had an outrageous crime, from all accounts, in the state of Alabama in the shooting of the postman who was attempting, in a very traditional way, to dramatize the plight of some of our citizens. We have offered to the state of Alabama the services of the FBI.[75]

Kennedy's direct and forceful comment embarrassed not only Governor Wallace of Alabama, in whose state the murder occurred, but also civil rights organizations, which had ignored all of Moore's lone efforts. John Lewis led SNCC activists on a march in Moore's memory in Nashville. James Bevel and Andrew Young organized a mass meeting in Birmingham in which tributes were given to Moore. CORE, which had denied Moore's request to sponsor his march, issued public denunciations of his killing.

In an editorial 2 days after Moore's death, The *New York Post* wrote, "He spent his life tugging at the world's coat sleeve. When at last it began to listen, William Moore was gone."

Conclusion

The purpose of this chapter is not to imply that all or even most civil rights leaders had some kind of psychiatric illness. It is presented rather starkly, with a list of figures, about half of whom committed suicide.

Yet there presumably were many mentally healthy civil rights leaders, such as Andrew Young, Vincent Harding, A. Philip Randolph, and Roy Wilkins, all well-known to be quite moderate and calm persons. King spoke of "maladjustment" to society's evils. It seems that these highly sane, stable persons should have adjusted themselves to society as it was and become dentists (as in Young's family) or otherwise mainstream figures. But they didn't. Why?

The perspective proposed in this book is that many of those who were maladjusted to society's evils were able to do so because they were not adjusted in general, in a psychological way, to the world around them. They were not psychiatrically normal, which is a compliment to them. But how can normal, adjusted, psychiatrically middle-of-the-curve persons become maladjusted to society's evils? Why would they risk their lives to change the world, rather than adjust themselves to the world around them, which is one way we define mental health?

Perhaps you can become voluntarily maladjusted, by consciously deciding to be so, by not accepting your culture's norms just because they are norms and rationally trying to determine if they deserve to be followed. Those who have mood illnesses are born to be maladjusted; it comes to them naturally; they are even maladjusted if they don't need to be. But if the times and their natures meet—if terrible social evils cry out for great leadership—maladjusted leaders with mood illnesses rise to the occasion, whereas healthier souls pause and ponder, and maybe follow soon thereafter.

The claim here is not that you have to have a mood illness to be maladjusted but, rather, that among the maladjusted, there are more persons with mood illnesses than among the adjusted. In addition to the leaders mentioned here, it is likely that others may have had psychiatric conditions that have been kept private. It is difficult to obtain publicly available information about such conditions because of the wish for privacy, partly driven by stigma against mental illness. Suicide is an extreme and uncommon outcome of psychiatric illness; many less severe conditions can be present but hidden. In addition to those mentioned here, a number of other activists in the civil rights movement, unknown to history, may have committed suicide in the 1970s and 1980s.[76]

The resistance to accepting the common occurrence of mood illnesses among civil rights activists has to do with stigma against mental illness. And this stigma comes from those who often are not mentally ill and who fear mental illness.

William Moore struggled with this problem, and he clarifies that the problem is not with mental illness; it's with mental health.

He wrote, "Who declares the insane insane? Answer—the sane. Then who declares the sane sane? Answer—the sane. So what right of appeal do I have? I am judged from the beginning by those not of my own kind."[77]

And toward the end of his memoir, he concludes,

> Now I think I have resolved it as well as it ever will be resolved. My answer is, "Yes, I was crazy. And I still am. Just like everyone else in this world of us." Daddy quotes the doctors as saying I believe I have a message to give to the world. . . . Now I think I do know that message. It is a terribly depressing one, but its intentions are good and its object is to make all people more tolerant and more understanding of the shortcomings of others. It strives to make people less certain of their own prejudices. For my message, if I have one, can best be summed up in the words, "All the world are schizophrenics."[78]

And finally,

> If men are rational and sane, if the world is not made up of schizophrenics, then let the Christians and the Moslems and the adherents to all other faiths discuss religion logically until the Truth becomes established among them; let Republicans and Democrats reconcile their differences among themselves by sheer force of thought and understanding. In the meantime, let no one be dogmatic in his prejudices. . . . No one is sane. All the world are schizophrenics.[79]

Unfortunately, all the world are not schizophrenics. They are mentally healthy, which means they are limited in their empathy and realism and creativity. They are mentally healthy and therefore are adjusted to an unjust world. It's the mentally ill—not the schizophrenics, in fact, but those with manic-depressive illness—who are maladjusted to the world as it is. It is they who have the empathy and realism and creativity to lead the masses of sane humanity to a better world.

Maladjustment to society's evils is good for society, which can be improved by those who take upon themselves the difficult task of changing society for the better. But those activists often pay a high personal price for their courageous unwillingness to adjust to an unjust world.

As one of Ben Clark's friends said of him, reciting lines from Jimmie Hendrix, these leaders truly are the loneliest minority of all:

> The morning is dead and the day seems to be through,
> There is nothing up here to lead or lead me but the velvet moon.
> All my loneliness I have felt today,
> It's a little more than enough to make a man throw himself away.
> But I continue to burn the midnight lamp . . . alone.[80]

Notes

1. David Gallen, *Malcolm X: As They Knew Him* (New York: Carroll & Graf, 1992), p. 169.
2. Malcolm X, *The Autobiography of Malcolm X: As Told to Alex Haley* (New York: Ballantine, 2015).
3. Gallen, *Malcolm X: As They Knew Him*, p. 37.
4. Ibid., p. 175.
5. Ibid., pp. 29–30.
6. Manning Marable, *Malcolm X: A Life of Reinvention* (New York: Penguin, 2011).
7. Karim states,

   > Just before dawn Malcolm would again be up so that he could say his first prayer at sunrise. Like Einstein and Edison, Malcolm did not need but fours of sleep each night. Still he never lacked energy for his work.

   Benjamin Karim, *Remembering Malcolm* (New York: Carroll & Graf, 1992), p. 166.

   Notice how Karim, like King's allies, tends to attribute decreased need for sleep to some kind of superhuman or creative power, whereas it's simply and solely a manic symptom. It occurs in no other condition, disease, or human phenomenon.
8. These recollections are from his close friend and last assistant, Benjamin Karim. Karim, *Remembering Malcolm*, pp. 171–172.
9. Biographers have papered over this incident. Manning Marable, who has written the most extensive recent biography on Malcolm X, attributed the psychosis to nutmeg poisoning! Nowhere in 539 pages does he raise the possibility of any psychiatric condition, despite the strong family genetics for mental illness in his mother and brother. Marable, *Malcolm X: A Life of Reinvention*.
10. Malcolm X, *The Autobiography of Malcolm X*.
11. https://en.wikipedia.org/wiki/Malcolm_Shabazz.
12. Malcolm X, *The Autobiography of Malcolm X*.
13. https://en.wikipedia.org/wiki/Malcolm_Shabazz.
14. https://www.themilitant.com/2015/7906/790650.html.
15. John D'Emilio, *Lost Prophet: The Life and Times of Bayard Rustin* (Chicago: University of Chicago Press, 2004); Michael Long, ed., *I Must Resist: Bayard Rustin's Life in Letters* (San Francisco: City Lights, 2012).
16. Interview with Michael Long, November 3, 2013.
17. http://hometown-pasadena.com/history/a-civil-rights-leader%E2%80%99s-pasadena-ordeal/33364.
18. Interviews with Michael Long (November 3, 2013) and Walter Neagle (January 6, 2014). These observations are based in part on interviews with Michael Long, an academic expert on Rustin, and with Walter Neagle, Rustin's last long-term partner. In the interview with Neagle, his partner discussed Rustin's drinking in the following manner:

    > Some doctors would say he was an alcoholic. But he could stop alcohol and smoking whenever he wanted. He liked to drink and he drank. When he was young, he could

drink a lot. Sometimes he would drink too much: His speech might slur and he'd be a little unsteady in his gait. But he wouldn't binge.

Regarding Rustin's sexual energy, Neagle said, "We were committed to each other and happy with each other but neither of us was completely monogamous. We weren't promiscuous. It wasn't an ongoing or every day thing, but instead very infrequent."

In the interview with Long, he discussed different claims regarding Rustin's sexual orientation and the allegations of his relationship with King. Long said that Rustin admitted that "he was reckless" in some of his sexual behavior. When imprisoned during World War II, he was close to succeeding in an attempt to desegregate the dining rooms. He was caught engaging in homosexual sex with other White prisoners and was transferred away. He ended up apologizing.

In the California incident, David McReynolds picked up Rustin from prison right after he was arrested in public. McReynolds recalled that Rustin had a clear sense of psychological state, that he was being "reckless at that point." Rustin was arrested several other times, including once in New York City. Muste had warned him that he would lose his job if it happened again. Long's view was that Rustin had a desire to be publicly risky. His lovers tended to be young, White educated men from upper-class strata. His sexual behavior was not beyond his control, because he went to psychological counseling in the 1950s. His psychologist was open-minded and didn't view Rustin's sexuality as an illness, contrary to mainstream psychiatry at the time. Rather, his psychiatrist suggested that Rustin go about his sexual life "a little quieter than you usually do." He took that advice and did well with it in the years to follow.

When asked about the rumor that Rustin and King had a sexual relationship, Long replied, "Please, Dr. King was not Rustin's type. On the other hand, Rustin had a lot of types throughout his life. Clarence Jones denies it very strongly. I wouldn't be shocked, but I would be surprised."

Regarding FBI tapes that seem to include homosexual banter between King and others, including Abernathy, Long said that Clarence Jones viewed it as locker room banter: "We talked like that in the army when we were in the showers."

After 1960, King wrote a letter to Rustin in which he sounded apologetic about having had to distance himself due to Rustin's homosexuality. "He loved Rustin's fierce intelligence and his ability to get the job done."

King's views were expressed in a 1957 *Ebony* column, in which King accepted the limited views of the psychiatry of his day on some matters, such as homosexuality. A boy wrote to him about having the problem of feeling about other boys the way he ought to feel about girls. King replied,

> Your problem is not at all an uncommon one. However, it does require the most careful attention. The type of feeling that you have toward boys is probably not an innate tendency but something that has been culturally acquired. Your reasons for adopting this habit have now been either consciously suppressed or unconsciously repressed. Therefore, it is necessary to deal with this problem by getting back to some of the experiences and circumstances that lead to the habit. In order to do this I would suggest that you see a good psychiatrist who can assist you in bringing to the forefront of conscience all of those experiences and circumstances that lead to the habit. You are already on the right road toward a solution, since you honestly recognize the problem and have a desire to solve it.

King Center Archives, Box 87, *Ebony* column, October 21, 1957.

19. http://archive.pov.org/brotheroutsider/ask-the-filmmaker:

> Toward the end of his life, Rustin introduced Dr. Robert Ascher, his former psychiatrist, to Jervis Anderson, who was writing the first Rustin biography. He undoubtedly wanted to set the record straight about what happened, and wanted to be clear with Dr. Ascher (who has himself since passed away) that he would like to waive the

normal rules of confidentiality in the interest of allowing traditionally off-limits material to be shared with biographers.

20. John D'Emilio, *Lost Prophet*, p. 47.
21. https://en.wikipedia.org/wiki/Bayard_Rustin_Sings_a_Program_of_Spirituals.
22. https://www.villagevoice.com/2020/10/28/malcolm-x-vs-bayard-rustin-black-on-black.
23. https://kinginstitute.stanford.edu/king-papers/documents/debate-james-j-kilpatrick-nation-s-future.
24. http://archive.pov.org/brotheroutsider/ask-the-filmmaker.
25. http://www.jacksonfreepress.com/news/2008/sep/24/a-soldiers-story-the-jfp-interview-with-james.
26. Ibid.
27. Ibid.
28. https://www.thedailybeast.com/james-meredith-is-not-nearly-as-dead-as-some-people-think.
29. Interview with Bernard Lafayette, January 15, 2013.
30. Interview with Bernard Lafayette by James Findlay, session 7, p. 27, https://www.loc.gov/folklife/civilrights/survey/view_collection.php?coll_id=949.
31. Randall Kryn, "James L. Bevel: The Strategist of the 1960s Civil Rights Movement," in David Garrow, ed., *We Shall Overcome: The Civil Rights Movement in the US in the 1950s and 1960s* (Brooklyn, NY: Carlson Publishing, 1989), Vol. 2, p. 535.
32. Ben Joravsky, "James Bevel Turns to the Right: 20 Years Ago He Was One of Martin Luther King's Most Trusted Advisers. Now He's on Ronald Reagan's Side. Is He a Leader, or Is He Lost?" *Reader: Chicago's Free Weekly*, July 20, 1984, Vol. 13, no. 24.
33. Ibid.
34. Randy Kryn, "Movement Revision Research Summary Regarding James Bevel," http://cfm40.middlebury.edu/node/287. The extent of his importance to the movement has been underappreciated. Journalist Randy Kryn, who knew Bevel for years in his later life, interviewed Bevel extensively in the 1980s, as well as many others who knew and worked with him. Activist James Orange told Kryn, "I'd say 98% of the plans and activities in Selma were Bevel's. The Selma movement was Bevel's baby." Andrew Young said, "I don't think we would have had a movement without [Bevel]. . . . He played a very important role, and that role was translated into a successful movement." In an August 1967 *Ebony* magazine interview, Jesse Jackson said he was inspired by "Jesus, Malcolm X, James Bevel, and Dr. King." Jackson later wrote that "Bevel was the real creative genius of that period." All cited in Kryn, above.
35. Interview with Bernard Lafayette, January 15, 2013.
36. Interview with Reverend James Bevel by Katherine Shannon, July 6, 1968, The Civil Rights Documentation Project, transcript p. 15, in David Garrow papers, Pittsburgh, PA, Manuscript Collection 832, pp. 4–5. This material still is inaccessible to researchers, for unknown reasons, at the Ralph Bunche archives at Howard University, where the original document is located.
37. William Anderson, *Eyes on the Prize* interview, November 7, 1985, http://repository.wustl.edu/concern/videos/1j92g932w.
38. Most historians now think that the mistakes of Albany made possible the successes of Birmingham and, later, Selma. The usual view is that Anderson and his colleagues in Albany were faced with a police chief, Laurie Pritchett, who wasn't mean enough. Unlike Bull Connor, who was the most rabid kind of racist, Pritchett was a more typical Southern racist: a gentlemanly, polite, friendly supporter of segregation. To Northern journalists, Pritchett seemed too nice to be evil. Anderson knew his adversary was formidable; Anderson later would say, "Laurie Pritchett was a sensitive man. He did his job in a professional manner, using as little brutal force as necessary." Pritchett himself spoke of practicing "nonviolent law enforcement." James Bevel later commented that Pritchett seemed prepared to handle King's group. "You set up the situation, and you wait for a mistake," Bevel said. But in Albany, there was no mistake on the part of the city's White leaders.
39. Taylor Branch, *Parting the Waters* (New York: Simon and Schuster, 1988), pp. 550–552.
40. Louis Lomax, King's friend, is quoted here by John A. Williams. In John A. Williams, *The King God Didn't Save* (New York: Pocket Books, 1971), pp. 142–143. Without identifying Anderson, Williams writes, "One of the local black leaders jailed with King became mentally

ill while in jail, and King accepted bond in order to take the man out with him so he could receive treatment."

41. Interview with William Anderson, April 17, 2013.
42. https://vimeo.com/10900633.
43. "Famed Harlem Doctor Falls to His Death Near Hospital Site," *Jet*, December 19, 1973, pp. 16–17.
44. Obituary, "Dr. Arthur Courtney Logan," *Journal of the National Medical Association* 66 (1974): 272–273.
45. https://aspace-aafa.galileo.usg.edu/repositories/2/archival_objects/49738; https://www.crmvet.org/info/savanah1.htm; Caprice L. Roberts, "Remedies, Race, and Civil Rights in the Old South," *Savannah Law Review* 2 (2015): 73–117.
46. Written by a friend, J. Ervin "Rock" Gardner, the essay states the following:

    > Today, this little giant continues to struggle. Unfortunately the struggle is a movement within himself, and it seems to suggest an indescribable experience constituted by an interaction of mental entrapment. One can only surmise that Ben's delicate young mind, having been subjected to too much brutality and other physical acts of violence, and excessive incidents of intimidation related to his participation in the movement of the sixties, are the reasons he experiences this as his greatest hardship. There are a few scenes in this life more tragic than that protracted combat with death. The little giant's decline from his former level of intellectual capacity has forged Ben Clark into being the loneliest minority of all. SCLC records, Pittsburgh, PA, Box 413, Folder 18, "The Loneliest Minority of All," J. Ervin Gardner.

47. Email from David Garrow, December 20, 2021. Also, David Garrow, *Bearing the Cross* (New York: HarperCollins, 2004 [1986]), p. 751; interviews with Clark on August 16, 1981, and December 27, 1983.
48. https://www.sun-sentinel.com/news/fl-xpm-2006-01-15-0601140418-story.html.
49. "Says Money Woes Caused Judge's Suicide," *Jet*, October 16, 1969, p. 10; SCLC records, Pittsburgh, PA, Box 413, Folder 18, "The Loneliest Minority of All," J. Ervin Gardner.
50. https://www.washingtonpost.com/archive/lifestyle/magazine/1993/11/14/a-bridge-he-could-not-cross/ec8fcd0b-9c5c-4b58-8326-be3335d6a61e.
51. Ibid.
52. https://www.washingtonpost.com/local/a-renowned-civil-rights-leaders-descent-into-debt-and-delusion/2016/05/05/74bd5c34-0d57-11e6-bfa1-4efa856caf2a_story.html.
53. https://www.latimes.com/archives/la-xpm-2004-jan-25-bk-garrow25-story.html.
54. Ibid.
55. Peniel Joseph, *Stokely: A Life* (New York: Hachette, 2014).
56. Ibid.
57. https://historynewsnetwork.org/article/171536.
58. Ralph Abernathy tells an amazing story about a member of the Dexter congregation, Dr. Roman T. Adair, who murdered his wife while she was in the company of her boyfriend. "Vernon would go to his home every night and have scotch and talk all night long." The Adairs divorced and the court had given their house to Mrs. Adair. Dr. Adair was upset, so he waited outside the house one day, and when she exited with her younger boyfriend, he shot and killed her with his pistol and then went to the sheriff's office, where he turned himself in. He wasn't jailed. That Sunday, at Dexter services, Johns bellowed,

    > There's a murderer in this house! God said, "Thou shalt not kill." This is my domain, and you must not invade my domain. . . . Dr. Adair, you have committed a sin, and I pray that God have mercy on your soul.

    At the end of the services,

    > Dr. Adair stood in line and waited to congratulate the pastor. And said I want to thank you for having the courage to tell me what saith the Lord, but [whispers] be sure to come by tonight, because I got some good Scotch.

    Interview with Ralph David Abernathy by Taylor Branch, March 5, 1984, University of North Carolina at Chapel Hill, transcript pp. 6–7.

Dr. Adair later was acquitted of murder. One of his shots hit the neck of Jesse Dawson, who had been with his wife. Dawson later sued Dr. Adair for $2,000 in civil damages. "Alabama Doctor Sued for $200 in Shooting," *Jet*, September 24, 1953, p. 21.

59. Interview with Ralph David Abernathy by Taylor Branch, March 5, 1984, University of North Carolina at Chapel Hill, transcript p. 3.
60. Cooney and Powell wrote,

> After Johns rejoined his wife in Petersburg, he continued to go back and forth to his farm in Darlington Heights. One day Vernon came to Henry Powell . . . and asked him to drive with him down to Montgomery to pick up Altona's grand piano that had been left behind. At that time Powell was afraid to drive with Vernon through the deep south. Given Vernon's temperament, wrote Henry, any situation could develop into a life threatening predicament. Johns carried a loaded double-barreled shotgun with him whenever he drove. At this time he drove a white Mercury. Johns was not afraid of anything. He once said "We must not fear dying. There's a lot of things worse than dying, and one of them is being alive when you should be dead!" Luckily perhaps for Henry, he did not have to make that trip.
>
> Patrick L. Cooney and Henry W. Powell, *The Life and Times of the Prophet Vernon Johns: Father of the Civil Rights Movement* (1998), accessed at https://web.archive.org/web/20030407035111/http://www.vernonjohns.org/tcal001/vjtofc.html

61. Interview with Ralph David Abernathy by Taylor Branch, March 5, 1984, University of North Carolina at Chapel Hill, transcript p. 4.
62. Martin Luther King Jr., *Stride Toward Freedom* (New York: Harper & Row, 1964 [1958]), p. 42.
63. Ralph David Abernathy, *And the Walls Came Tumbling Down* (New York: Harper, 1989), pp. 124–128.
64. Ibid., p. 128.
65. Letter to Prof. G. W. Fiske, Oberlin College, August 9, 1920, https://www2.oberlin.edu/external/EOG/BlackHistoryMonth/Vernon%20Johns/LetterToFiske.html.
66. Cooney and Powell, *The Life and Times of the Prophet Vernon Johns*, Chapter 27. Accessed at https://web.archive.org/web/20030407035111/http://www.vernonjohns.org/tcal001/vjtofc.html.
67. Ibid.
68. Interview with Ralph David Abernathy by Taylor Branch, March 5, 1984, University of North Carolina at Chapel Hill, transcript p. 1.
69. Ibid., p. 4.
70. The psychiatrist Hagop Akiskal has done extensive research on this topic and has shown that an irritable subscale to mood temperaments is secondary and orthogonal to the primary mood temperaments of dysthymia, hyperthymia, and cyclothymia. Thus, one can be cyclothymic, for instance, and low or high on irritability. If irritability is low, Akiskal calls it "sunny" cyclothymia; if irritability is high, he calls it "dark" cyclothymia. Hagop S. Akiskal, Elie G. Hantouche, and Jean F. Allilaire, "Bipolar II with and Without Cyclothymic Temperament: 'Dark' and 'Sunny' Expressions of Soft Bipolarity," *Journal of Affective Disorders* 73, nos. 1–2 (2003): 49–57.
71. William L. Moore, *The Mind in Chains: Autobiography of a Schizophrenic* (New York, Exposition Press, 1955), p. 59.
72. H. G. Pope and J. F. Lipinski, "Diagnosis in Schizophrenia and Manic–Depressive Illness: A Reassessment of the Specificity of Schizophrenic Symptoms in the Light of Current Research," *Archives of General Psychiatry* 35, no. 7 (1978): 811–828.
73. Moore had classic manic grandiosity:

> Why, my mind was never more keen! I was never happier. Never before had I been able to figure out the world's problems so beautifully and finally come with answers which were real and true. . . . I am living a captivating experience, so why not just enjoy this venture into another world? . . . And the inevitably wonderful future—this would follows as the night the day.

Moore, *The Mind in Chains*, pp. 8–9.

74. Moore, *The Mind in Chains*, p. 184.
75. President John F. Kennedy, News Conference 54, April 24, 1963, https://www.jfklibrary.org/archives/other-resources/john-f-kennedy-press-conferences/news-conference-54.
76. Interview with Tom Houck, July 2, 2015.
77. Moore, *The Mind in Chains*, p. 14.
78. Ibid., p. 238.
79. Ibid., p. 242.
80. SCLC records, Pittsburgh, PA, Box 413, Folder 18, "The Loneliest Minority of All," J. Ervin Gardner.

19

Coda

His funeral procession wended 4 miles through the streets of downtown Atlanta, the body carried on a simple farm cart pulled by two mules, perhaps reminding all how Jesus had entered Jerusalem on a donkey (Figure 19.1). No horses, no pageantry; a king had not died, but rather a servant of the dispossessed.[1]

Beside the carriage walked those who would be recognizable now: Jesse Jackson to the right, Andrew Young straight behind; and those in the process of being lost to history—James Bevel next to the casket on its left, Hosea Williams directly in front of the mules, Bernard Lee to the side, Ralph Abernathy at the front of the crowd, near Coretta. James Orange, whose 6 foot 3 inch frame had sought to protect King from snipers, walked behind, his head tilted in sorrow.

The carriage worked its way to the campus of Morehouse College. There, the final eulogy was given to Martin Luther King Jr. by his old college president Dr. Benjamin Mays, the man who had inspired the young college student. Mays spoke at length, and with a sense of personal loss: "It was my desire that if I predeceased Dr. King, he would pay tribute to me on my final day. It was his wish that if he predeceased me, I would deliver the homily at his funeral." Fate decreed that the 70-year-old teacher should eulogize the 39-year-old student.

So it had been a century earlier, when a 44-year-old man died in Concord, Massachusetts, eulogized by his mentor. Unlike King, Henry David Thoreau was unknown at the time, but like King, his fame would grow. In college, a young King would read and reread Thoreau, learning for the first time about nonviolent resistance.[2] Thoreau's mentor, Ralph Waldo Emerson, almost 60 years old, was America's most famous living philosopher.

In front of a small local crowd, toward the end of a tender, long eulogy, the older man looked down on the grave of his disciple (who had experienced clinical depression and probably manic states)[3] and commented, "The country knows not yet, or in the least part, how great a son it has lost."[4]

In his eulogy, Mays was overcome by the injustice of the tragedy. He blamed the climate of racism for King's murder, his many enemies, the nation's resistance

Soul on Fire. Nassir Ghaemi, Oxford University Press. © Oxford University Press 2026.
DOI: 10.1093/9780197657614.003.0021

Figure 19.1 Martin Luther King Jr.'s funeral procession.

to end violence, and hatred toward Blacks. He called for his audience to take up King's cause.

But a dozen years earlier, in happier times, Mays had given King's real eulogy. In 1957, at the peak of the success of the Montgomery bus boycott, when the young man had bolted to prominence, Morehouse had given its newest celebrity an honorary degree. Mays read the citation, as he handed the degree to his greatest student:

> Because you did not seek fame, it has come to you. It must have been a person like you that Emerson had in mind when he said, "See how the masses of men worry themselves into nameless graves when here and there a great, unselfish soul forgets himself into immortality."[5]

Notes

1. https://specials.myajc.com/mlk-funeral/.
2. King stated,

   > When I went to Morehouse as a freshman in 1944, my concern for racial and economic justice was already substantial. During my student days, I read Henry David Thoreau's essay "On Civil Disobedience" for the first time. Here, in this courageous New Englander's refusal to pay taxes and his choice of jail rather than support a war that would spread slavery's territory into Mexico, I made my first contact with the theory of nonviolent resistance. . . . I was so deeply moved that I reread the work several times. . . . No other person has been more eloquent and more passionate in getting this idea across than Henry David Thoreau. As a result of his writings and personal witness, we are the heirs of a legacy of creative protest.

   The Autobiography of Martin Luther King Jr., ed. Clayborne Carson (New York: Grand Central Publishing, 1998), p. 14.
3. Thoreau clearly had mood states alternating between euphoria and sadness with the accompanying traits that would describe manic and depressive states. These aspects of his psychology have been explored by the psychiatrist Michael Sperber, who connects them to a rationale for probably bipolar illness. Michael Sperber, *Henry David Thoreau: Cycles and Psyche* (Higganum, CT: Higganum Hill Books, 2004).

   For instance, here is a key description from Thoreau's journals:

   > All existence, all satisfaction and dissatisfaction, all event was symbolized in this way. Now I seemed to be lying and tossing, perchance, on a horrible, a fatal rough surface, which must soon, indeed, put an end to my existence, though even in the dream I knew it to be the symbol merely of my misery; and then again, suddenly, I was lying on a delicious smooth surface, as of a summer sea, as of gossamer or down or softest plush, and life was such a luxury to live. My waking experience always has been and is such an alternate Rough and Smooth. In other words, it is Insanity and Sanity.

   Quoted in Sperber, *Henry David Thoreau: Cycles and Psyche*, pp. 27–28.

   Harmon Smith notes that at the start of the 1850s, Thoreau began to experience in his mid 30s "less and less of the ecstatic states he had experienced in his youth." Of these mystical experiences, Thoreau had written, "There comes to into my mind or soul such an indescribable infinite all-absorbing heavenly pleasure, a sense of elevation and expansion—and [I] have nought to do with it. I perceive that I am dealt with by superior powers." Smith adds, "The diminishing frequency of these moments of epiphany came as a severe blow to him. Where he had previously felt himself to be 'part and parcel of Nature,' he now seemed to be merely observant of her." Harmon Smith, *My Friend, My Friend* (Amherst: University of Massachusetts Press, 1999), p. 161.

4. And more that connects the two young dead men: Emerson said of Thoreau,

> He was a speaker and actor of the truth—born such—and was ever running into dramatic situations from this cause. . . . No opposition or ridicule had any weight with him. . . . It was of no consequence, if every one present held the opposite opinion. . . . No truer American existed than Thoreau. . . . Thoreau was sincerity itself. . . . [He had] such dangerous frankness. . . . The country knows not yet, or in the least part, how great a son it has lost. . . . He had in a short life exhausted the capabilities of this world; wherever there is knowledge, wherever there is virtue, wherever there is beauty, he will find a home.

Ralph Waldo Emerson, "Thoreau," *The Atlantic*, August 1862, https://www.theatlantic.com/magazine/archive/1862/08/thoreau/306418.

5. Benjamin Mays, "Citations to Recipients of Honorary Degrees: Martin Luther King, Jr.," *Morehouse College Bulletin*, July 1957.

Appendix 1

A PSYCHIATRIC PRIMER ON DEPRESSION AND MANIA

Although depression and mania have been defined in the text, along with diagnostic terms such as hyperthymia and manic depression, some further detail is provided here for interested readers and to clarify potential misinterpretations that are expectable given the current state of psychiatric discourse.

These concepts are described in much more detail elsewhere,[1] but this appendix is intended to provide enough basic psychiatric knowledge so as to help readers interpret the text without common misconceptions that have to do with either lack of information or cultural discrimination against psychiatric conditions.

Manic–depressive illness (MDI), as the name implies, has two parts. The depressive side is better appreciated by most people. Clinical depression, as opposed to normal sadness, involves a severe feeling of sadness that lasts a long time (2 weeks or more in the official definition), along with an overall physical and mental slowing: You talk slower, move slower, think slower; sleep and eat poorly (either too little or too much); lose most of your interests; enjoy things less; and you might even wish you were dead or think of killing yourself. Approximately 5–10% of persons with clinical depression eventually commit suicide. These periods of depression are "episodes" that come and go; they last weeks to months, usually, and then are followed by months or years of being yourself again, whatever your usual personality is. Then, after some months or even years, another depressive episode happens, lasting weeks or months, and the cycle is repeated.

The manic side is less appreciated by most people. The word "manic" is mistakenly interpreted to be similar to a "maniac," which implies being out of control, angry, violent, crazy, loony. This scary linguistic distortion is behind some of the discrimination against using the word manic or the diagnosis of manic depression (as opposed to "depression," which is less stigmatized these days).

But manic symptoms, like depressive symptoms, are just variations on normal moods. Mania means being happy, just more so than the normal state of happiness, just as depression involves more than a normal amount of sadness. Manic symptoms also involve the opposite of depressive states: a speeding up (not slowing down) of mental and bodily function. You talk more quickly; think fast; sleep much less but have increased energy (unlike depression); move quickly; and become much more active at work or at home, cleaning and cooking and working and having sex increasingly more often. Because everything is sped up, when mania is more severe, you can get impulsive, having sexual affairs, spending money excessively, and driving recklessly. It is these severe states that many will recognize as mania, but the milder states of manic symptoms are common as well, and more difficult to appreciate, because our society values having high energy and being productive and fast in what one does. Typically, manic symptoms, when milder, are also associated with an excellent sense of humor, being very extroverted and sociable, and being charismatic: a life-of-the-party type of character.

Depression and mania are mood states; they are not diagnoses. They are clinical experiences, like fever. Fever isn't a diagnosis; it's a clinical experience that the clinician needs to assess, and combining it with other clinical features, the clinician may or may not identify a diagnosis that explains the fever.

Depression is part of human experience, but it doesn't mean just feeling sad. In fact, the feeling of sadness isn't central to the experience of depression. Rather, the core of depression is being slowed down in your thinking, movement, and feeling—called psychomotor retardation. One can be slowed down and not be sad in one's mood at all. The whole constellation of the depressive syndrome technically involves having four or more of eight standard criteria for 2 weeks or longer: sad mood, low interest or energy or concentration, suicidal thinking, and changes in sleep and appetite (either more or less of each). Usually, the syndrome is present more months or longer. This clinical depression is quite different than feeling sad for a few days or so.

A period of such clinical depression for a few weeks or more is called an "episode." By definition, the term *episode* implies a beginning and an end. Thus, depressive episodes come and go; they end naturally. They don't last forever. To say someone has had clinical depression could mean that in 80 years of living, the person had 3 months of depression. That's not a whole life of depression.

* * *

The repetition of episodes is central to defining depression as a disease. The disease of depression involves repeated episodes that come and go, over and over again in one's life. This disease has been carefully studied for two centuries or longer. It is the case that it begins usually in one's 20s (sometimes earlier and sometimes slightly later), that an episode tends to last 6–12 months, and that episodes tend to recur once every 3 or 4 years. These are averages. There are plenty of people with longer or shorter episodes, and with more or less frequent recurrences. But these averages are derived from large statistical samples.

This recurrent depressive episode disease has been called "unipolar" depression to contrast it with the other setting of recurrent depressive episodes in which manic episodes also have occurred in the past, called "bipolar" depression.

Mania, like depression, is a clinical experience of a constellation of symptoms, and it is not the same thing as being happy. Again, the feeling of sadness isn't central to the experience of depression. Rather, the core of mania is being sped up in one's thinking, movement, and feeling—called psychomotor excitation. One can be sped up and not be happy in one's mood at all. The whole constellation of the manic syndrome technically involves having three or four or more of seven standard criteria for 1 week or longer: happy or angry mood (euphoric or irritable), high interest or energy (reflected in increased activities), distractibility, rapid or racing thoughts, high self-esteem, impulsive behavior, and decreased need for sleep. Usually, the syndrome is present weeks or longer, but for a shorter time than depressive episodes. This clinical mania is quite different than feeling happy for a few days or so. Mild versions of manic episodes are called "hypomanic" episodes, and they share the same characteristics except they can be shorter (officially, though without scientific evidence, 4 days or longer) and impulsive behavior does not occur or is not harmful in its consequences.

Again, such a period of clinical mania or hypomania for a few weeks or a month is called an episode, which implies a beginning and an end. Thus, manic and hypomanic episodes come and go; they end naturally. They don't last forever. To say someone has had mania could mean that in 80 years of living, the person had 3 weeks of mania.

* * *

These are the basic definitions of the diseases of unipolar depression and bipolar illness, and how they differ from "normal" sadness and happiness. A few other key points are needed here.

First, the reader will note that this book tends to use the phrase manic–depressive illness, as opposed to unipolar or bipolar illness. Many believe that manic depression is an "outdated" phrase. This viewpoint is not based on scientific evidence, and it ignores the meaning of the term. This is not unusual because many clinicians have not been educated in the history of these terms.

"Manic–depressive illness" was coined in the late 1890s (originally called "manic–depressive insanity" by Emil Kraepelin, a late 19th-century German psychiatric leader). It meant what we today call *both* unipolar depression and bipolar illness. In other words, it meant recurrent mood episodes *of any kind*. It didn't matter if those episodes were only depressive (unipolar) or both depressive and manic (bipolar). The type of episode didn't matter to Kraepelin; what mattered was the fact that they were repetitive. An analogy would be to ice cream, which can be of different varieties, such as chocolate and vanilla. Those flavors are different, but they are the same thing: ice cream. So too vanilla unipolar depression may differ from chocolate bipolar illness, but they are the same disease: MDI.

In summary, MDI is not just an outdated term that is synonymous to bipolar illness. It is a different way of thinking about mood illness, and it is much more than bipolar illness; it includes also unipolar depression.

So why is it not used as much anymore?

* * *

In fact, MDI was used widely in psychiatry for almost a century, from the mid-1890s until 1980. In contrast, the term bipolar illness was not used officially until 1980, when it was included in the American Psychiatric Association's (APA) official diagnostic manual (*Diagnostic and Statistical Manual,* third edition [DSM-III]). The term "manic–depressive" was removed. The term "unipolar" also was not included and was replaced with "major depressive disorder" (MDD). The scientific claim for making these changes was that Kraepelin was wrong and that bipolar illness and unipolar depression were two different diseases. This claim was made primarily on two grounds: that they differed in genetics and in their course of illness. These other factors, called diagnostic validators, are independent lines of evidence that a set of symptoms reflect the same versus different diseases. If you have a cough and fever, in one case it could be pneumonia and in another case it could be lung cancer. The symptoms are the same, the diseases are different. In psychiatry, the claim was made that if the mood symptoms occur with different genetics and different courses of illness (different age of onset, duration of episodes, and frequency of episodes), then they are different illnesses. In 1980, the APA leaders of the DSM-III committee referred to a few contemporary studies that found different family genetics and different course of illness for patients with bipolar illness versus unipolar depression. Hence, MDI was split up into those two categories.

In the intervening four decades, much more genetic research has been conducted that shows major overlap between patients diagnosed with "major depressive disorder" and bipolar illness, thus contradicting the whole claim of the 1980 division and supporting the original view that these syndromes are part of one disease: manic–depressive illness. Furthermore, studies on the course of illness have found notable overlap between unipolar depression and bipolar illness in age of onset and duration of episodes. There is a notable scientific literature to support the view that MDI may be a legitimate way of understanding mood illnesses, and that it is different from and more valid than more common terms such as bipolar illness.

A final rationale for a preference for the MDI terminology is that it allows for the common occurrence of clinical states that are ignored by the DSM system of diagnosis, such as mood temperaments. As described in this book, manic and depressive symptoms also can occur as part of one's personality, called dysthymia (mild depression), hyperthymia (mild mania), and cyclothymia (mild manic traits alternating with mild depressive traits). These traits are not symptoms that come and go in episodes, as in unipolar depression or bipolar illness. They are mood traits that are present all the time as part of one's personality. Thus, a patient can have depressive episodes, and in between those episodes, the patient could have cyclothymic temperament (meaning mild manic traits alternating with depressive traits or brief depressive episodes). This clinical picture is consistent with what has been reported about Martin Luther King Jr., as documented in this book. The DSM system ignores manic traits as part of personality. Hyperthymia is not included at all as a diagnosis, and cyclothymia is labeled as a "disorder" equal to "bipolar disorder" or "major depressive disorder." In other words, you can't be diagnosed with MDD and cyclothymia at the same time; they are mutually exclusive. This false judgment ignores the fact that many patients have mood temperaments in between mood episodes. The MDI concept accepts this idea and explains it by the fact that the type of mood symptom doesn't matter. All that matters is if they are severe and episodic (as in the disease forms of unipolar depression or bipolar illness) or whether they are mild and constant (as in the temperament forms of dysthymia, hyperthymia, and cyclothymia).

If someone has cyclothymic temperament with recurrent clinical depressive episodes, as King may have had, the DSM system would diagnose "major depressive disorder" and ignore the hyperthymia. A more sound scientific analysis would not ignore manic symptoms and would diagnose this clinical presentation as one of the many classic presentations of MDI.

For these reasons, this book uses the phrase manic–depressive illness rather than bipolar illness to describe these clinical phenomena.

* * *

A final comment has to do with the attribution of a disease construct to these mood states. Again, the claim will be made that this is "just" depression and not a disease. As noted previously, one response is that recurrent depressive episodes are a disease, and it appears that King had repeated hospitalizations and other states of "exhaustion" that are consistent with depressive episodes, as documented for the first time in this book. A second response is to turn to the other diagnostic validators, especially genetics and course of illness. If a recurrent depressive disease (which is the same thing as saying "manic–depressive illness") is present, it is well-known to be notably genetic. Thus, others in the extended family also should have some variant of the mood illness (in the whole range of MDI, ranging from mild mood temperaments of any variety to full mood episodes of any variety). This aspect has been described as well to some extent in this book, consistent with the available information for family members. Furthermore, the course of illness should match the known pattern (adolescent onset, episodes every year or two, and duration of a few months or longer). The course of possible depressive episodes in King's life would be consistent with this pattern as well.

King seems to have had periods of depression, usually lasting a few weeks, during which he became exhausted, with very low energy, slept a lot, ate more, felt less able to be interested in or enjoy things, couldn't function, felt guilty and blamed himself excessively, and was very sad in his mood. His wife and friends called these periods "depression" in a colloquial sense, without realizing that they were, quite likely, clinical depressive episodes. Typically, he would be hospitalized once yearly for these episodes, although the hospitalizations were in medical, not psychiatric, wards. Near the end of King's life, his personal physician recommended that he get a psychiatric evaluation.

As noted previously, King could be seen as having manic traits as part of his usual personality, which alternated with frequent but brief depressive periods (on the order of a few days), and thus approximates "cyclothymic" temperament. In between his yearly longer depressive episodes, which could last a week to a few weeks, he was a very high-energy man, sleeping approximately 4 hours nightly (which is approximately half the biological norm), very talkative, very active, with a high sexual libido, an incredible sense of humor, and a very highly sociable and extroverted personality. This was the King most people knew, and much of his charisma grew out of his cyclothymic personality, making the contrast with his depressive episodes all the greater.

* * *

There are aspects of manic and depressive symptoms that can help a person be a more successful leader, especially in crises. Mania is associated with being more creative and being more resilient to traumatic experiences. One of the key features many people appreciated in King was his courage—his ability to stand up to repeated attacks, threats, and criticism and continue to move forward steadfastly in his nonviolent resistance program. Resilience was a hallmark of his personality. He was also creative, taking a stubbornly nonviolent political path that most Black leaders and activists found difficult to accept, and extending it from domestic racism to foreign militarism (in his anti-Vietnam War stance), despite opposition from most of his civil rights allies, Black and White.

In making this claim, there is no way to prove causality with a psychological smoking gun. Causality is, as the philosopher David Hume described so well, about the constant conjunction of events. It is correlation that is repeated and cannot be otherwise explained. If B follows A over and over again, then we say A caused B. If we can study it scientifically, we might look into physical mechanisms by which A might cause B. In the world of history, which is always interpreted as past observations, not future experiments, causation cannot be definitively proven. But Hume's constant conjunction of events can be claimed. It can be shown that King had behaviors and traits consistent with manic symptoms and depressive episodes, that scientific research shows benefits of manic creativity and depressive empathy, and that those leadership traits are seen in King's life. These correlations are the best any historian can do, and they are at least as good, if not better, than traditional interpretations of King and other leaders, which are based simply on common-sense psychology.

Some will see the view that King may have had a variety of MDI (which is not the same thing as saying he had bipolar disorder, as described previously) as a criticism. It is not. It would be ironic to refuse to discriminate against mental illness in discussion of a great leader against discrimination.

There is bigotry behind the stigma of being "crazy," just as there is behind homophobia, racism, and sexism. There is a deep need in human nature to view ourselves as superior to others. This is part of the unnaturalness of radical empathy: We are better than foreigners, or Blacks, or women, or gays, or those crazy people with mental illnesses. They are bad, we are good. Mental illness is bad; so to say King had a psychiatric condition is to say something bad about him. There is another approach. It is a species of praise to assert that King had mood states that are different than those of the average normal mentally healthy person. His depressive and manic states and traits can perhaps then be appreciated as something positive, in many ways, in his life. And then we can better appreciate that there are positive aspects to MDI and psychiatric conditions in general.

Bigotry is not based solely on feelings; it is also based on beliefs, opinions, and mistaken statements of fact. Racists justified discriminating against Blacks based on the belief that Blacks were intellectually inferior to Whites; sexists similarly justified discrimination against the "weaker sex"; so too homosexuals were viewed by psychiatrists as suffering from a medical "perversion." These are all factually false statements, disprovable scientifically.

Bigotry is based on ignorance, more than malevolence. To break these bigoted beliefs, it is not enough to appeal to morality, to altruistic acceptance of these poor inferior "others." Bigotry is defeated only if the falsity of false beliefs is proven. (This is not to say that these false beliefs have now been dropped in relation to racism, but it could be claimed that they are less utilized to justify racism than they were in the 1950s and earlier).

Medical ignorance doesn't imply lack of education. In fact, some of the most educated individuals, often self-identified as "liberal," hold very stigmatizing attitudes toward describing psychiatric illness in any revered public figure. Such "liberal" persons are only liberal toward the humanities; they are quite willing to attribute literary and personal gifts to great leaders. They are illiberal with regard to science and biology.

Stigma against psychiatric illness will end only when the public learns that there are benefits to psychiatric illnesses—that they are not purely harmful and bad and dangerous but, rather, beneficial in many ways. One benefit of getting to know the real Martin Luther King Jr. is that he will teach us not only to reject racism but also to see how we are bigoted against psychiatric illness, too, and to reject this stigmatizing ignorance.

Note

1. Frederick K. Goodwin and Kay R. Jamison, *Manic–Depressive Illness*, 2nd ed. (New York: Oxford University Press, 2007); S. Nassir Ghaemi, *Clinical Psychopharmacology* (New York: Oxford University Press, 2019).

Appendix 2

ON PSYCHOLOGICAL HISTORY

In *A First-Rate Madness,*[1] I diagnosed depression or bipolar illness—or their temperaments—in historical leaders. A common question raised with that work, and with this one, is how one can legitimately make such diagnoses historically. How can one document such diagnoses?

This legitimate question can be answered on a number of grounds.

First, I rely almost entirely on primary source material: direct observations of family or friends, contemporary newspaper accounts, personal letters, or medical records, including original scholarship for this book. For instance, in *First-Rate Madness*, I was the first psychiatrist to analyze and document John F. Kennedy's medical records; those records are not allowed to be copied, and I hand wrote and then typed many important medical documents into the endnotes. In this book, I am the first psychiatrist to interview Martin Luther King Jr.'s close friends, and the first person to learn that King's doctor recommended that he consult a psychiatrist near the end of his life.

Second, in my experience in the field of writing psychological history, I have come to conclude that there is a 50 Year Rule. In the 5 years of research that went into *A First-Rate Madness*, and the decade of research that went into this work, I found that sufficient historical documentation tended to become available to be able to make psychiatric diagnoses approximately 50 years after a leader's lifetime. Because of stigma against mental illness, public figures hide psychiatric symptoms or diagnosis or treatment, if present, and so do their families and friends. It takes a few generations for the truth to come out. Kennedy's medical records, for instance, weren't released until four decades after his death, and, even now, few physician–scholars have studied them. This is why most of the leaders I studied were active 50 years ago or earlier, and it is also the reason why women were not represented—a reflection of those years. When I discussed recent leaders—such as George W. Bush or Tony Blair or Richard Nixon—I did not diagnose them with psychiatric illness but, rather, with normality, always with the awareness that psychiatric assessments of current or recent leaders are more provisional than those of older leaders.

The same holds for King. He has been dead now for just over 50 years, and more material is emerging. The classic and definitive work on King was David Garrow's 1986 *Bearing the Cross*. This work was immensely important because it was the outcome of about a decade of research by Garrow in the late 1970s and early 1980s. Garrow's effort was irreplaceable because he did his work within a decade or two of King's death. In that time, almost all who knew him or had been close to him were alive and available for oral history interview. Garrow tracked down almost everyone of any relevance to the civil rights movement. He conducted hundreds of original oral history interviews, which he has preserved in written transcripts or on cassette tapes. I accessed his written transcripts directly through him. His cassette tapes were made available also as needed. Vincent Harding, a friend from the very first Montgomery days, would write in the 1980s that each generation needed to re-evaluate King's meaning, and even he, as King's close friend, found Garrow's research as indispensable to that effort.[2] In short, Garrow got to know King better than many of his closest friends did, maybe even better than King did. This is not unusual.

Contrary to popular belief, human beings don't know themselves very well. Psychiatrists know this fact as a matter of course in their daily practice. We don't know ourselves well; it shouldn't surprise us that others who investigate us well, whether psychiatrists or historians, might get to know us in ways beyond our self-awareness. The German philosopher of history Wilhelm Dilthey called this concept "Besser verstehen" or "Better understanding."[3] With a larger awareness of history after them and with broader social scientific understanding of their eras, we can better understand why Hitler and Napoleon made certain decisions than they themselves comprehended.

On top of Garrow's primary material obtained in the lifetimes of most participants, new material has begun to be released in the past few decades that allows for further factual knowledge. Garrow himself has begun to revise some of his judgments as this new material has been produced.[4] Much of it has been re-evaluated now in a biography by Jonathan Eig, who has completed the remaining oral history interview work that can be added to the foundation laid by Garrow. With the work of these researchers, among others,[5] the oral history material on King is becoming more and more complete. Last, the Federal Bureau of Investigation files on King have been gradually released. Garrow revealed much in his 1980s work,[6] but more has come out in the past decade, and the final records are due to be released in 2027. At that point, the documentary record will be complete, and more definitive judgments can be made. The 50-year period will have passed, and the picture of King will be even more clear.

Third, the approach taken in *A First-Rate Madness* and here is not Freudian. Many people think of "psychohistory" as a psychiatrist speculating about the childhood unconscious fantasies of a historical leader. This image is not relevant to my work. It is understandable, however, because Freud took that approach himself in his book on President Woodrow Wilson, whom he despised.[7] Or perhaps psychohistory would be understood more broadly, as emphasizing the social context of an individual leader, so that the "psychosocial" interpretation is broader than early childhood, and extends into young adulthood. This is the approach famously taken by the most prominent exponent of psychohistory, Erik Erikson, in his work on Martin Luther and on Gandhi.[8] It has been applied even to King once, in the work of Frederick Downing.[9]

That work can be seen as complementary to my approach, although, I would suggest, it is still more speculative than my method. Downing, for instance, tries to apply Erikson's stages of development to King, emphasizing identity issues. He also pays a lot of attention to King's family structure and to the impact of his culture, especially the Southern Black church. These influences are very important, no doubt, in understanding King. But they are not sufficient. They leave out his physical body.

King himself, in a talk given at Purdue University titled "What Is Man?" said that man is, first of all, "a biological being with a physical body."[10] If you don't start there, you misunderstand humankind. You can't ignore the economic needs and social conditions of people, King argued at Purdue. Well, the same holds for understanding any human being, including King. You can't ignore our physical bodies; they influence us too. We all are biological beings. Why should we ignore biology in understanding any person?

I do not claim that the approach taken here is sufficient either. Manic–depressive illness, if present in Dr. King, is a necessary condition for understanding who he was, but it is not sufficient by itself. His social and cultural and familial influences also are important. My only claim is that we shouldn't admit the latter and exclude the former.

* * *

This book is a species of psychohistory, but it's not the kind of psychohistory of the past. The Eriksonian psychosocial approach was popular in the 1960s through the 1980s, but like much Freudian thinking, it has not survived the skepticism of time.[11] Erikson was perhaps the best of that school, but other clinicians tend to be simplistic in their psychological interpretations. They apply psychoanalytic concepts, such as narcissism or one's relationship to one's mother or "projection," to the biographies of individual leaders. At their best, those psychohistorians emphasize historical and cultural context in trying to explain the behavior of great leaders. At their worst, as is common in psychiatric evaluations, for instance, of Nixon or Saddam Hussein or Adolf Hitler, this approach uses psychiatric clichés to pejoratively criticize those we don't like. The weakness of this approach is that it is purely speculative and requires, like a Marxist approach to economics, the acceptance of a whole ideology about psychology—the Freudian theories about how unconscious childhood experiences affect adult personality. The problem with the Freudian approach is, on the one hand, you can't prove it, and on the other hand, you can't disprove it. You can't prove it because unconscious mental experience is, by definition, not clearly at hand; it can't be shown, quantified, and proven in statistical studies. You can't disprove it because if you think some Freudian idea is not relevant, one could always claim that the person in question had those ideas unconsciously. If you can't prove or disprove an idea, then it's not a scientific idea. You can call everyone in the world narcissistic and antisocial, but it's unscientific. Historians, rightly, have veered away from this Freudian psychohistory.

My approach to psychohistory is much more simple. I apply definitions of psychiatric diagnoses based on long-standing syndromes that have been described for about two centuries in Western psychiatry. In modern medicine, this is a rather good consensus. I'm not discussing psychiatric categories that are debatable social constructs, such as "drapetomania" (the psychiatric illness in which slaves wanted to escape from masters) or even more modern terms such as attention-deficit/hyperactivity disorder. The classic mental illnesses, described clearly for 200 years, and even relatively well for 2,000 years, are mood illnesses and psychotic conditions. Mood illnesses are called depression or manic depression, and the remaining psychotic conditions when severe are generally termed schizophrenia. These definitions are simply and clearly applicable, and we can say whether or not someone has those syndromes.

The approach I take isn't Freudian at all. I make no judgments about childhood experiences with one's parents, or any unconscious wishes or emotions. Instead, this work might be called *Kraepelinian psychohistory*. Emil Kraepelin is a late 19th-century German psychiatrist, and contemporary of Freud, who is much less known to the general public because he is much more scientific than Freud. Science tends to be dry, and most scientific work is not interesting enough to be of general interest. In modern psychiatry, it is a mainstream view that much of Kraepelin's thinking has stood up well a century later. His approach was to view some severe mental illnesses as mostly biological in origin. He further is famous for organizing the varied presentations of severe insanity into two major groups: schizophrenia (which he called dementia praecox) and manic–depressive illness.[12]

The approach to diagnosis in *A First-Rate Madness* and in this book is not just based on symptoms. It would not be good psychiatry to diagnose solely based on symptoms; it's not good psychohistory either. It's simply poor medicine to focus on symptoms alone. You can have chest pain and have a heart attack, or you can have chest pain and have nothing important at all. You can have nausea from gastritis or from a heart attack. Your shortness of breath could be pneumonia or it could be a heart attack. The same symptom occurs in different illness. Different symptoms occur in the same illness. A good physician knows that symptoms aren't the main or sole basis of diagnosis.

The lay public often make that assumption, and they will complain that you can't diagnose leader X with the illness of depression just because he had the symptoms of depression. That's not what is being done here. In medicine, the relevance of symptoms is sorted out by pathology; doctors get the organ and they look at it under a microscope to see what's wrong. In psychiatry, we can't get pathology of the brain, usually, so that option is not available; or it turns out that brain pathology isn't clearly abnormal. Kraepelin was faced with that problem, and he held, again in the tradition of classical medicine, that the *course of illness* could be the best external validator of diagnosis. The course of the illness could help differentiate whether symptoms represented disease X versus disease Y. He also noted that heredity could be a predictor of illness, and later research has confirmed that manic–depressive illness and schizophrenia are highly genetic. Furthermore, later researchers identified treatment as a way to validate a diagnosis, to say that it is real and independent of other conditions. If someone is sick enough to get medical treatment, the likelihood of a medical illness is higher than if someone never gets treated. Of course, this last validator is weaker than the other two, but no validator is definitive by itself. None is like organ pathology. But all together, if the validators point in the same direction, the probability of a valid illness is increased. This approach is not my opinion; it is the widely accepted mainstream approach to diagnosis in scientific psychiatry for the past half century.[13]

That's the approach taken in this book and in *First-Rate Madness*. We can verify syndromes based on independent criteria, of genetics, course, and treatment. So, with each leader, we look for mood illness in their family members, a predictable course of illness consistent with these conditions, and symptoms severe enough to warrant treatment. The more of this evidence along all four lines we have, the higher the probability of illness. This evidence has been presented in this book for Martin Luther King Jr.

Notes

1. Nassir Ghaemi, *A First-Rate Madness* (New York: Penguin, 2011).
2. Vincent Harding, *Martin Luther King: The Inconvenient Hero* (Maryknoll, NY: Orbis Books, 2008 [1996]).

3. Michael Ermarth, *The Critique of Historical Reason* (Chicago: University of Chicago Press, 1978).
4. David Garrow, "The Troubling Legacy of Martin Luther King," *Standpoint*, June 2019, pp. 30–37.
5. Such as Patrick Parr. Patrick Parr, *The Seminarian: Martin Luther King Comes of Age* (Chicago: Lawrence Hill Books, 2018).
6. David Garrow, *The FBI and Martin Luther King Jr.* (New York: Norton, 1981).
7. Sigmund Freud and William C. Bullitt, *Thomas Woodrow Wilson: A Psychological Study* (Boston: Houghton-Mifflin, 1966).
8. Erik Erikson, *Gandhi's Truth: The Origins of Militant Nonviolence* (New York: Norton, 1993 [1969]); Erik Erikson, *Young Man Luther: A Study in Psychoanalysis and History* (New York: Norton, 1993 [1958]), https://en.wikipedia.org/wiki/Young_Man_Luther.
9. Frederick L. Downing, *To See the Promised Land: The Faith Pilgrimage of Martin Luther King Jr.* (Macon, GA: Mercer University Press, 1986).
10. William Robert Miller, "The Broadening Horizons: Montgomery, America, the World," in *Martin Luther King Jr.: A Profile*, ed. C. Eric Lincoln (New York: Hill & Wang, 1984 [1970]), p. 52.
11. https://en.wikipedia.org/wiki/Psychohistory; https://www.sciencedirect.com/topics/social-sciences/psychohistory.
12. Paul Hoff, "The Kraepelinian Tradition," *Dialogues in Clinical Neuroscience* 17, no. 1 (2015): 31–41.
13. Carol S. North and Sean H. Yutzy, *Goodwin and Guze's Psychiatric Diagnosis*, 7th ed. (New York: Oxford University Press, 2018).

A NOTE TO THE READER

Racism is the original sin of America[1]—ever since the Pilgrims killed the Wampanoag Chief Metacom in 1678, when the Harvard University-educated son of Chief Massosoit rebelled against the Europeans;[2] and ever since the first African slaves arrived in chains in 1619.

The deep impact of racism on American culture has produced a range of cultural attitudes that continue to influence both racists and anti-racists. Combined with millennia of discrimination against mental illness, the impact of racial conflict in American culture will lead to a number of predictable misinterpretations of this book.

This note seeks to predict and preempt those misinterpretations.

An initial general statement is in order. As Ralph Abernathy noted in his memoir, those who get upset when the humanity of Martin Luther King Jr. is described tend to be concerned about preserving his legend. King has been made into an icon, an untouchable perfect man. And then we ask why there are no more Martin Luther Kings. Well, he wasn't that Martin Luther King either. If we appreciate his humanity, we can realize how there are more Martin Luther Kings, and there will be more, because many human beings can rise to be like him, although not like the false icon many believe him to be.

As Abernathy put it, the legend of Martin Luther King Jr. will live on because it is safe now in the national imagination. What is needed is not to exaggerate the legend even further; what is needed is "to give the legend flesh and blood," to make him human, to make him real. And truly "you don't fool history by withholding the truth."[3] Another friend, historian C. Eric Lincoln, wrote within 2 years of King's death: "It is imperative that we create *King, the Myth,* because we were unprepared to deal with *King, the Man* [italics in original]."[4]

Abernathy told the truth, and he died within weeks of writing the above words in a new introduction to his memoir a year after its original publication. His historical memory has grown, while those of his critics have suffered. It is likely that

King would have been more sympathetic to his friend Ralph Abernathy than to King's allies who wished to burnish a legend at all costs.

* * *

Misinterpretation 1: *See, King and all the civil rights leaders were crazy.* This perspective reflects that discrimination against mental illness which is the psychiatric equivalent of racism. It was the view held by King's enemies, such as J. Edgar Hoover and Lyndon Johnson. The usual phrase, "stigma," fails to capture the racist-like bias of this way of thinking. This psychiatric racism is as likely to be held by Blacks as by Whites. It is more generational than racial; those born in the 1990s and onward are much less discriminatory around psychiatric illness than those of my Generation X and earlier.

Misinterpretation 2: *King may have had depression, but that's not a mental illness.* Or its variant: King may have depression, but it's not manic depression or any kind of illness. It's an implicit variety of racist-like discrimination against psychiatric illness to accept the latter states but to try to normalize them. We see this subtle bias in the common current usage of the term "mental health" instead of "psychiatric," or "mental health problem" instead of mental illness or psychiatric disease. We don't say "physical health problem" for a medical illness.

Again, as this book seeks to show, something can be abnormal but good. Normality and abnormality are not value judgments but, rather, medical ones. Appendix 1 explains these clinical concepts in more detail for interested readers, as well as provides more scientific discussion of the clinical concepts in this book—that is, depression, mania, manic–depressive illness, bipolar illness, and cyclothymic temperament.

The cultural roots of these two misinterpretations are connected: As described very well in a classic book by Alexander Thomas and Samuel Sillen, *Racism and Psychiatry*, for many years, the White establishment, including the psychiatric profession, argued that Blacks were more prone to psychosis than Whites. Interestingly, studies claimed that Blacks were less likely to experience depression or suicide than Whites.[5] The resistance to diagnose King or other civil rights leaders with any psychiatric condition may have some roots in this long-standing racist approach to psychiatric diagnosis. It's interesting to note that the diagnosis of depression and observations regarding suicidality, which are being made regarding King and others, go against standard past racist psychiatric attitudes.

* * *

Misinterpretation 3: *King may have engaged in sexual infidelity, but any discussion of it reflects racism.* Many who value King will oppose a discussion of his sexual behavior, which, although it cannot be denied any longer, can be de-emphasized or normalized culturally. They often assert that White historians seem to take moralistic or puritanical tones on this subject, meant to undermine King's status.[6] The hypothesis presented here that such behavior could be explained by cyclothymic temperament could be rejected for the same reasons. This reaction of course would not explain why Black activists such as Abernathy, Georgia Davis Powers, James Bevel, or John A. Williams would describe King's sexual life openly, without seeing such behavior as diminishing his social leadership.

As Thomas and Sillen persuasively explain in *Racism and Psychiatry*, there was a "sexualization of racism" present in American culture.[7] Negative reactions to descriptions of King's sexual behavior likely have roots in the White establishment's racist perspectives on Black men as being hypersexual, which was viewed as a mark of their lower level of civilization. This attitude fed into the White fear of Black men as dangers to White women, which not only was the source of most lynchings but also was central to White racism in general. For instance, in pre-Civil War debates, many opponents of slavery believed that White Southerners liked slavery to a large extent because of their sexual freedom to rape Black women. Abolitionists such as Massachusetts Senator Charles Sumner gave anti-slavery speeches with often lurid sexual metaphors. After the Civil War, intermarriage was allowed for a time, but then it was outlawed again with segregation, which was justified partly on the claim that the hypersexuality of Black men needed to be controlled by racial separation.[8] Given this cultural legacy, it's understandable that attitudes about the sexual behavior of Black leaders will be influenced by this heritage.

The presentation given here is clinical and psychiatric, and it stands on its own. Sexual behavior is only one component, and not an essential one, to the assessment of manic states. But if correct factually, it can help analyze the matter with less impact of the distorting biases of current and past racism.

* * *

Misinterpretation 4: *This book is dangerous. How does it help current movements to fight racism?* This book is primarily a work of historical scholarship; it seeks to answer a factual question: Did King have depression, manic depression, or any related psychiatric illness? And if so, how did that condition help or hurt his leadership? These facts stand on their own, irrespective of how readers will interpret those facts in relation to contemporary racial conflict. Will a White racist interpret this work to devalue King? Possibly, though wrongly. Will others interpret this work to deny its factual evidence, so as to support a purist image of King? Possibly, though wrongly. The claim of this work is that King may have had a common psychiatric condition, mainly depression, which helps, not hurts, current and future efforts against racism, by better understanding the psychology of what it takes to be a successful nonviolent activist.

As discussed previously, current and future movements for racial progress will suffer if they are not led by an organized leadership. If nonviolence is the approach taken, it will succeed better as a philosophy of life than as a mere tactic. If so, activists would need to take seriously the task of learning how to be nonviolent as a way of life. The study of King's life, in its greatness and in its weakness, is a royal road to that goal.

More than half a century after King's death, we would do well to get to know him in reality. His friend, the fiery leader of the Birmingham Southern Christian Leadership Conference, Rev. Fred Shuttlesworth, predicted so more than three decades ago: "I don't think America has yet learned to appreciate the greatness of Martin Luther King Jr. I think that his life will be constantly revealing itself to us."[9] We might add that as with any human being, his greatness had limitations, and in fact his weaknesses were his strengths, and his strengths were his weaknesses.

Notes

1. Interview with Rev. Gil Caldwell, February 5, 2016. Caldwell refers to the work of Jim Wallis on this concept, which can be found in the following articles and book:

   Jim Wallis, "Racism: America's Original Sin," *Sojourners*, July 29, 2013, https://sojo.net/articles/remembering-trayvon/racism-americas-original-sin

   Jim Wallis, "America's Original Sin: The Legacy of White Racism," *CrossCurrents* 57, no. 2 (2007): 197-202

   Jim Wallis, *America's Original Sin: Racism, White Privilege, and the Bridge to a New America* (Ada, MI: Brazos Press, 2016)
2. https://en.wikipedia.org/wiki/King_Philip%27s_War.
3. Ralph David Abernathy, *And the Walls Came Tumbling Down* (New York: Harper, 1989), pp. xiv, xvi, paperback edition.
4. C. Eric Lincoln, "Introduction," in *Martin Luther King Jr.: A Profile*, ed. C. Eric Lincoln (New York: Hill & Wang, 1984 [1970]), p. viii.
5. Alexander Thomas and Samuel Sillen, *Racism and Psychiatry* (Secaucus, NJ: Citadel Press, 1972), pp. 122–134.
6. Lewis V. Baldwin, *Behind the Public Veil* (Minneapolis, MN: Fortress Press, 2016), pp. 95–100.
7. The near-fatal attack on Sumner by a Southern congressman in the Senate in 1857 was influenced by anger raised by the sexualized content of a specific speech by Sumner. Thomas and Sillen, *Racism and Psychiatry*, p. 103.
8. In his famous "Bleeding Kansas" speech, Sumner said, "Not in any common lust for power did this uncommon tragedy have its origin. It is the rape of a virgin Territory, compelling it to the hateful embrace of slavery; and it may be clearly traced to a depraved desire for a new Slave State, hideous offspring of such a crime, in the hope of adding to the power of slavery in the National Government." https://en.wikipedia.org/wiki/Caning_of_Charles_Sumner

   In his criticism of a Southern senator that led to the violent assault on Sumner in the Senate by a Southern congressman, he stated:

   "The senator from South Carolina has read many books of chivalry, and believes himself a chivalrous knight with sentiments of honor and courage. Of course he has chosen a mistress to whom he has made his vows, and who, though ugly to others, is always lovely to him; though polluted in the sight of the world, is chaste in his sight—I mean the harlot, Slavery. For her, his tongue is always profuse in words. Let her be impeached in character, or any proposition made to shut her out from the extension of her wantonness, and no extravagance of manner or hardihood of assertion is then too great for this senator. The frenzy of Don Quixote, in behalf of his wench, Dulcinea del Toboso, is all surpassed." https://en.wikipedia.org/wiki/Caning_of_Charles_Sumner

After the Civil War, intermarriage was allowed for a period during Reconstruction but then outlawed again. By the 1890s, part of the rise of segregation involved an emphasis on the hypersexuality of Black men, and thus a need to separate the races. James Kinney, "Miscegenation: The Long, Cruel History of Our Last Taboo," *The Washington Post*, February 23, 1986. https://www.washingtonpost.com/archive/opinions/1986/02/23/miscegenation-the-long-cruel-history-of-our-last-taboo. According to a scholar:

> "Abolitionists routinely accused slaveholders of maintaining slavery so that they could engage in forcible sexual relations with their slaves. In 1858, Wendell Phillips went so far as to call the South a gigantic brothel in a speech in Boston. . . . Southerners did not practice slavery because African-Americans were disgusting beasts, but because Southerners found them sexually appealing."

William James Hoffer, *The Caning of Charles Sumner* (Baltimore, MD: Johns Hopkins University Press, 2010), p. 62.

9. Flip Schulke and Penelope McPhee, *King Remembered* (New York: Pocket Books, 1986), p. 274.

ACKNOWLEDGMENTS AND A PLAYLIST

This book was more than a decade in the making. The concept grew out of my book, *A First-Rate Madness*, in which Dr. Martin Luther King Jr.'s depression, along with that of other leaders, was described. My experience was that readers from different countries reacted, often critically, depending on the leader: Englishmen reacted to my analysis of Winston Churchill, Germans to Adolf Hitler, Indians to Mahatma Gandhi. And, among the multiple American leaders I discussed, I received the strongest reaction from Americans about King. Given that he was a recent figure, and many of his friends and colleagues were still alive, I thought it could be useful to interview them and add to the historical record about King by getting more detail about his personal life, medical history, and psychological state from his still-living associates. The first person I interviewed was Dr. Vincent Harding; he consented to a second interview as well. He was kind and thoughtful and open; the experience encouraged me to continue the project and interview others who knew King. I realized there were many more than I had known—civil rights figures who are little known to the general public but who were actively connected to King and the movement in the 1950s and 1960s. In addition to Harding, these included others documented in the oral history section of this book: Dr. Bernard Lafayette (the next person I interviewed after Harding, with repeated follow-up), Dr. Michael Haynes, Dr. Alvin Poussaint, Dr. William Anderson, Tom Houck, Lonnie King, Warren Logan, Dr. Lonnie MacDonald, Rev. Gilbert Caldwell, and Dr. Mervyn Warren, among others. I thank them for their generosity in talking to me, whom they did not know, especially after having spent much of their lives patiently responding to many interviewers throughout the decades. It was a privilege to speak to them.

I also experienced sympathetic and supportive guidance from established scholars with expertise on King. Clayborne Carson, who oversaw the King Institute at Stanford and has archived the King papers there, was the first scholar I met. Over breakfast, he gave encouragement to a younger man who was new to the subject, and encouraged me to do what had not yet been done: to describe King, not from the outside, but from within. Carson later assisted me in some of my research interview requests.

The project took much longer than I expected, and King's generation continued to leave us gradually, as the work wore on. In the process, Dr. Vincent Harding, Dr. Lonnie MacDonald, Rev. Michael Haynes, Lonnie King, and Rev. Gil Caldwell all passed away. With each person, I felt greater urgency to complete this mission of talking to those who walked and talked with King, or even those who may have only known him briefly. I especially regretted not being able to show some results to those who expressed strong interest in the work, such as Rev. Caldwell. The process was difficult. I faced rejections from some who didn't, or more commonly, a simple failure to respond. This was understandable. Even those who agreed to be interviewed, though, would at times be reticent. My training as a psychiatrist was useful, I think, to be able to talk with others, but there were still limits. Being a psychiatrist itself might have raised more defenses than it could lower. "Over time human memory remembers happy things and unremembers unhappy things," concluded Garrow, who had interviewed many more people than I had. Sometimes, though, it's useful to investigate the unhappy experiences so as to better appreciate the happy ones.

I am extremely grateful to Oxford University Press and my editor there, Peter Stevenson, for taking the risk to publish this book after multiple other publishers declined.

In the long process of learning about King's nonviolent worldview from his friends, I felt that I was receiving an invaluable education. Whatever happened to the finished book, I realized that the process of researching it had helped me grow as a person, as I better understood King's philosophy of nonviolence. For that experience, I am thankful that I undertook this project.

In the course of writing this book, I often listened to King's sermons in the collection *A Knock at Midnight.* I recommend those sermons, such as "Three Dimensions of a Complete Life," "Loving Your Enemies," and "Unfulfilled Dreams"—not his famous public speeches—as a resource for readers to augment their understanding of King's nonviolent worldview and his basic philosophy of life. Harding's introduction to "Unfulfilled Dreams" is insightful about King's personality, and it was an inspiration to this project.

After the bulk of my research was concluded, I was able to add important aspects to it by benefitting from the work of Tavis Smiley in his 2014 biography of King's final year of life and also from the magisterial 2023 biography of King by Jonathan Eig, who did extensive new research and carefully revisited past documentation. Jon helped me get new information from his oral interviews with many more people than I had interviewed, and he generously shared his findings with me.

Both Jon and I were extensively supported by David Garrow, the dean of King scholarship. He had interviewed almost everyone connected to King when most of them were still alive in the 1980s, and his archives are an irreplaceable source of oral history information, along with his award-winning book, *Bearing the Cross* (1986), the first extensive biography of King. As a scholar, perhaps no one knows as much detail about King as Garrow. Dave met with me repeatedly and helped extensively in connecting me to others who were studying King. He encouraged my project throughout its many phases, including when it seemed it might not get to print. He was extremely generous in the best academic spirit of wanting to advance knowledge. His continued work on expanding our knowledge of King, even if sometimes uncomfortable, reflects an intellectual honesty that is often professed but infrequently applied.

I thank my wife Heather who suggested this book as a follow-up to A First-Rate Madness, which she also had encouraged. And I appreciate the support of my children, Valentine and Zane, who, as preteens, tolerated Dr. King's sermons on their drives to school, and who, into young adulthood, engaged in dinner table discussions about his life.

A final comment, inspired by my son Zane Ghaemi, and encouraged by my friend Tavis Smiley, who asked me during an interview for my walk-on song for this book (which we decided was the first on the list below). While writing, I listened to a playlist of songs that put me in the mood of different aspects of the book. I am providing that playlist here for readers who may want to read or re-read the book in the same mood. The relevance of these songs to King's life and experiences may become apparent as readers listen and read at the same time.

A Playlist for *Soul on Fire*

"Soul's on Fire," Anthony Hamilton
"Jesus Is Love," The Commodores
"Happy Birthday," Stevie Wonder
"Nobody Knows," Pastor T. L. Barrett
"Otherside," Red Hot Chili Peppers
"This is Why We Fight," The Decemberists
"Luz de Dia," Los Enanitos Verdes
"Why Are Sundays So Depressing," The Strokes
"Ode to the Mets," The Strokes
"Praying Right," Jeezy
"I Always Knew I Had It in Me," George Benson
"Amazon," Earl Klugh
"Crazy (Live from the Basement)," Gnarls Barkley
Life Goes On, 2Pac
I'll Be Missing You, Diddy
New Orleans Instrumental No. 1, REM

SOURCES AND REFERENCES

Readers interested in more detail and explanation than provided in the main text are encouraged to read the chapter endnotes, in which further analysis is provided of the content in the main text, along with documentation.

This book is based on available sources, including published books and prior published or unpublished oral histories, as well as original research. The two main archives that contain the most primary source material on King are the Martin Luther King Collection, Howard Gotlieb Archival Research Center, Boston University (cited hereafter as MLK BU Archives); and King Library and Archives, at the Martin Luther King Jr. Center for Nonviolent Social Change, Atlanta (cited hereafter as King Center Archives). Supplementary material exists in many archives on the civil rights movement. Those consulted most in this book are the archives of David Garrow in Pittsburgh, Pennsylvania; the Ralph Bunche oral history collection, Moorland–Spingarn Research Center, Howard University, Washington, DC; and the archives of the John F. Kennedy Presidential Library in Boston.

Original Oral History Interviews

Original oral history interviews were conducted with the following individuals:

Rev. Vincent Harding—a close associate who knew King since the 1950s, now deceased, by telephone from Denver, December 28, 2012

Dr. Bernard Lafayette—a close Southern Christian Leadership Conference aide to King, by telephone from Atlanta, January 15, 2013

Rev. Michael Haynes—a Boston friend of King from the 1950s, now deceased, in person, Boston, April 15, 2013

Dr. Alvin Poussaint—a psychiatrist and associate of King in his last campaigns, in person, Boston, May 15, 2013

Mubarak Awad—Palestinian leader of the nonviolent movement of the First Intifada, in person, Silver Spring, MD, March 15, 2013

Dr. William Anderson—a childhood acquaintance and ally in the Albany campaign, by telephone from Detroit, August 17, 2013

Lynn Cothren—Coretta Scott King's longtime personal assistant, by telephone from Nashville, March 1, 2013

Tom Houck—who left high school in Cambridge, MA, to join the Selma movement, and became King's personal driver and family friend, in person, Atlanta, July 2, 2015

Wilhelmina Harris—a child during the Montgomery boycott who was personal friends with the King family, in person, Concord, MA, July 19, 2015

Lonnie King—leader of the Atlanta sit-ins and a King family acquaintance, now deceased, by telephone from Atlanta, August 13, 2013

Dr. Melyvn Warren—a minister who interviewed and studied with King for a 1966 PhD thesis on King's preaching, by telephone from Alabama, September 16, 2015

Warren "Chip" Logan—son of Dr. Arthur Logan, King's personal physician, in person, New York City, May 20, 2013

Dr. Clarence Jones—King's personal lawyer and close confidante, via email from San Francisco, March 13, 2013, and May 21, 2013

Dorothy Foster—parishioner at Ebenezer Baptist Church in the mid-1960s, August 21, 2013

Dr. Lonnie MacDonald—a psychiatrist and personal friend of Coretta Scott King, from college, later also close with King and his family, in person, New York City, August 19, 2016

Susannah Heschel—daughter of Rabbi Abraham Heschel, King's close ally, in person, Newton, MA, May 15, 2013

Walter Neagle—Bayard Rustin's last partner, by telephone from New York City, July 15, 2013

Rev. Gilbert Caldwell—a Boston University colleague of King, by telephone from New Brunswick, NJ, February 5, 2016

Rev. James Lawson—one of King's earliest activist friends, by telephone from Los Angeles, January 25, 2021

Rev. Joel L. King Jr.—King's paternal first cousin, by telephone from Columbus, OH, January 24, 2022

Dr. William Beal—A. D. King's son-in-law, by video from Atlanta, February 21, 2023

The following scholars who specialize in Dr. King or the civil rights movement were interviewed:

Dr. Clayborne Carson—Stanford University Professor of History, expert on King and the civil rights movement, in person, Boston, November 20, 2012

Dr. David Garrow—University of Pittsburgh Professor of History and Law, expert on King and the civil rights movement, in person, Pittsburgh, PA, February 25, 2012

Dr. Michael G. Long—Elizabethtown University, expert on Bayard Rustin, by telephone, November 3, 2013

Dr. Keith Miller—Arizona State University Professor of English, expert on the origins of King's sermons and theology, in person, Tucson, AZ, April 27, 2014

Dr. Charles E. Collyer—University of Rhode Island Professor Emeritus of Psychology, expert on King's nonviolence, by telephone, Providence RI, September 25, 2015

Previously unpublished material from oral histories was obtained in archival sources of the following associates of King (most of whom are now deceased): James Bevel, Bayard Rustin, Bernard Lee, Robert Kennedy, Burke Marshall, Ralph Abernathy, Amiri Baraka, Harry Belafonte, Diane Nash, James Forman, A. J. Muste, Glenn Smiley, James Meredith, and James Lawson.

INDEX

For the benefit of digital users, indexed terms that span two pages (e.g., 52–53) may, on occasion, appear on only one of those pages.

Figures are indicated by an italic *f* following the page number.

www.ingramcontent.com/pod-product-compliance
Ingram Content Group UK Ltd.
Pitfield, Milton Keynes, MK11 3LW, UK
UKHW022019150926
475595UK00014B/310

9 780197 657584